Observations

Observations

Hector Mackenzie

The Pentland Press
Edinburgh – Cambridge – Durham – USA

© H.C.B. Mackenzie, 1997

First published in 1997 by
The Pentland Press Ltd
1 Hutton Close
South Church
Bishop Auckland
Durham

Typeset by Carnegie Publishing, 18 Maynard St, Preston
Printed and bound by Bookcraft Ltd, Bath

One of the characters in this book, now in his eighties, was recently diagnosed as having a threatening cancer. I 'phoned him to commiserate, having been similarly afflicted. "Isn't old age a sod?" I said. 'Yes,' he replied, 'but think of the joys we've had these fifty years which were denied to all those chums who were taken out in their mid-twenties.' How right he is and I dedicate this book to the memory of those chums.

Acknowledgements

Tʜɪs ʙᴏᴏᴋ is really entirely due to my daughter, Katharine Coleman. She pressed me to make a memoir for the family and then, when those who read it suggested publication, she set about the word processing and editing. She collated the pictures from which the illustrations have been selected. All the time she gave was taken from her glass engraving profession at a critical time for that. The author only did the easy bit!

My thanks also go to the Editorial and Publication Departments of Pentland Press. Their friendly but very professional talents have worked the miracle of converting a crude script into what appears to be an acceptable book. To acheive this without bullying the author in any way demands his gratitude!

Preface

THIS ACCOUNT was written in the mid-1980s, and subsequently edited in small parts by Hector Mackenzie as an explanation to his daughter, and his family in general, of his time spent as a young sailor in the Navy at War.

It was inspired by a request from his daughter (Katharine Coleman), who was at the time struggling to research her maternal grandfather's Boer War record. She felt it would be enormously helpful to have an account from her father while he was still alive to answer vital questions.

The original brief was to answer the question: 'What was it like to be a schoolboy and young naval rating/officer?' rather than 'What heroic feats did you accomplish during the dreadful years of 1939–45?'. This he achieved, with great care and surprisingly vivid recollection, with only a few photographs and his flight record to help his memory.

Names occurring in the text include:

Granny: The author's mother

Your Mother: Frances Evelyn Mackenzie (née Purkis)

Sandy: Alexander Gavin Mackenzie, his elder brother

Kenneth: Kenneth Bruce Mackenzie, his younger brother

Ian: Ian D. Mountain Mackenzie, his youngest brother

Colin: his first child.

London, September 1996

Contents

Illustrations

Chapter 1

Before Joining Up

T HE STORY should perhaps begin in the lovely summer weather of 1940, when I was still at boarding school at Eastbourne. The news was coming through of the disaster in France, with the Allied armies in total defeat.

My main friend at the time was Richard Smith. We had arrived at Eastbourne College the same term and gone through five years together. We were both in the 1st XV (first school rugby team) and we had always been travelling partners to away matches. My mother lived sufficiently near to our school to attend matches assiduously. After these matches she would take me and my brothers out, often taking Richard out with us as well. Sometimes Richard's mother performed the honours; sometimes we all went together. The two mothers got on well together – both were widows.

In summer, we saw less of each other in the afternoons. Richard was a successful member of the school cricket team, while I was Captain of Boats. When we could, therefore, we would take a walk along the Front between tea and 'Prep'. One day we had heard the news that everyone who had a boat should take it to Ramsgate or Dover – the collation of the rescue force for the Army which was preparing to evacuate Dunkirk. Smarting from being mere schoolboys at such a momentous time, we decided during our walk to 'nick' a fishing boat that night and set out for Dover. After dark, we escaped from school, only to find that there was not a boat to be found on the beach with cross-Channel potential. So back to school, tails between legs, and the first opportunity of 'active service' was lost.

It was a bitter disappointment. Somehow it had never occurred to us that navigating the boat, finding money for the necessary fuel, avoiding being picked up, and not least persuading the authorities to take on two patently inexperienced eighteen-year-olds, were each problems we could never have overcome. However, as it turned out, 'active service' was not too far from our grasp.

Only a few days later, Anthony Eden (Home Secretary at that time) appealed on the radio for volunteers with a modicum of military training to join a new force called 'The Local Defence Volunteers', who were to sustain patrols, particularly at night, to counter the expected fairly immediate landing of German Paratroops as a prelude to invasion. Local Army Command telephoned the Headmaster of our school asking for patrols to be made up from boys over eighteen years old who were in the OTC (Officers Training Corps). He agreed, subject to parental permission. This was quickly available on the phone for Richard and me, as our mothers lived not far away.

The OTC had been started around the time of the Boer War, and existed to provide officers who with very little further training could take commissions in the Territorial Army during an emergency. To qualify, cadets had to exercise half a day a week during termtime, do ten days' summer camp with the Army and achieve Cert A – an exam set by the Army, which most of us passed. We only had infantry in OTCs, but otherwise they were very like the Combined Cadet Corps in boys' schools today. I believe that in the 1914/18 War, holders of Cert A did far less training than others before being sent to France as officers. By 1939/46, Cert A made no difference. Infantry fighting had got a lot more technical and what we did for Cert A was very out of date, so it was pretty useless. Also there were no longer 'short-cuts' to commissions. In all three services (Navy, Army and Air Force) everyone had to start in the ranks and earn his commission. Except when operating as LDV (later Home Guard), OTCs had zero military status. OTC training was recognised by the services to the extent that it made one volunteer more acceptable than another, but he suffered the disadvantage that known ex-OTCs were expected to do better than the rest of the recruits at such things as arms and squad drill.

It was the first great moment of the War for us to parade at dusk in our 1914/18 style full kit, complete with Lee-Enfield rifle and five rounds of live ammunition. How long we could have kept regular paratroops at bay is a moot point! No patrol marched out of Eastbourne on to our designated pitch of the South Downs with greater swing and pride – you might think we were off to relieve Mafeking. As a point of fact, though, since we were on patrol within hours of Eden's call, we must have been about the very first Home Guard, as it subsequently was called. We did night patrols from then on two or three times a week. After the first excitement it became a rather cold and very exhausting occupation on top of normal school work and play. However, it was only to last a few weeks, because the order came that all boarding schools near the south coast were to evacuate inland away from the immediate invasion threat.

Looking back on it, I never would have believed that schoolmasters could organise such an upheaval so well. Within forty-eight hours of the order, they found somewhere for us to go (Radley), got the entire school, staff and considerable domestic staff of those days packed, all the equipment loaded and everyone aboard a special train which took us direct to Radley station. When we arrived, there was a bed of some sort for every one of us, some in Radley College, the juniors across the river in the stately home of Newnham Courtney. Within twenty-four hours of arrival, classes and or-ganised games began again by dint of Radley making considerable changes in their arrangements. I do not think we boys were all that impressed at the time. It was by no means comfortable. Those of us from School House were billeted in Radley's enormous, brand new gymnasium on camp beds, living out of suitcases.

Richard and I, together with several prefects who were in their last term at school, had done our Oxbridge exams the previous Christmas term, and so were let off classes whenever there was anything useful to be done. For a week or two, this was the case – unpacking Eastbourne equipment, rigging classrooms out of spare corners and that sort of thing. When this work dried up we pointed out to an understanding Headmaster that there was little point in attending classes which were short of space when we intended to join up as soon as we were free of school. He thus found us a wider range of things we could do in school hours with partial conviction that they were relevant to the war effort.

For a week or so, I dug over the whole of the Headmaster's cottage garden for growing food (Dig for Victory was the popular slogan). His wife gave me a present in gratitude – Masefield's *Reynard the Fox*, which I still have and still have to read! This was followed by something more akin to penal servitude for several of us: we cycled over daily to a concrete factory in Abingdon where, armed with heavy sledgehammers, we spent the day breaking up scrapped jobs to recover the steel reinforcing bars. Richard got such heavy callouses he was unable to bowl properly in the house matches.

At night, 'active service' continued in the Home Guard, where we alternated with Radley OTC. While we were further from 'The Front', which the Sussex coast had seemed, it was more interesting in that there was more opportunity to 'be soldiers'. At that time, authority was preoccu-pied with the fear that not only might paratroops drop anywhere but that small groups of 'Fifth Columnists' would probably precede them. These might be in British uniforms or might even be disguised as nuns – a cover to which the Germans were thought to be particularly addicted. Thus we had to set up a road block on the main Abingdon/Oxford road, stop all vehicles and insist on seeing everyone's identity papers. (In no way was the enemy reckoned fly enough to forge these simple documents!)

At the outbreak of War, everyone was given an identity card. It was used for this sort of purpose – establishing one's *bona fides* – and also for such administrative purposes as the issue of ration books. We had no difficulty in establishing our authority. Although dated, our uniform was still recognisable as standard military and our ages were in the same ball-park as the new army conscripts. The traffic was mainly military (mostly RAF), petrol rationing having cut back civilian traffic. All seemed to accept without question (thank goodness) our right to stop them and verify identities.

We did have one or two laughs and frights. The worst was at about two o'clock one morning, when the master (Corps Officer) in charge came through on the field phone from his headquarters four miles back at the College, to say that the national paratroop landing alarm had been given. A force was thought to be making its way up our road. Only one of us was to continue checking identities, the rest to dig in on the Oxford side of the roadblock facing Abingdon, spread either side of the road. This at last was real business – so real, it seemed, that it was no longer any fun at all. One suddenly realised that a schoolboy on the upstream end of a World War I rifle with five rounds in it was going to have a hard job to give a good account of himself.

Because of the national alarm, I suppose, our pretty steady traffic stream dried up and the night became eerily still. It started to rain; besides getting wet and cold, one could now hear the enemy creeping up on one from all directions. I had already had a preference for joining the Navy if I could; I was now determined that at all costs I would resist being swept into the Army. Three hours later, when told in the dawn we could stand down, I felt positively light-headed in a way I have only experienced in war and then only rarely. At breakfast, we heard that down in Hertfordshire (I think it was) some old fool had accidentally pulled the rope of a church bell, which was the arranged national alarm signal. Church bells did not ring again until once in celebration of the El Alamein victory. After that, they were only rung regularly after VE Day.

Another night, in my absent-minded way, I forgot to draw the LDV arm bands we had to wear on patrol. When we got to our patrol point, I rang the dear old Corps master (another relic of World War I) on the field phone and confessed. He seemed very concerned but said (I thought) that he would come out with them right away. We were to forget about stopping traffic and take cover at the roadside until he came. An hour went by, then two hours. As he had only four miles to cover and a bicycle which he could just ride, one could only assume that he had come to grief on it, doubling the offence I had committed. Just as I was deciding to search for him and administer first aid, there was a stirring in the undergrowth and much laboured breathing. Then followed the following exchange in a loud whisper:

'Mackenzie – is that you?'

'Yes!' (overcoming the temptation to say, '*Nein, es ist Hermann!*')

'Where are they?'

'Who?'

'The enemy.'

'I hope they are at home in bed.'

'This is no time to be flippant, I have crawled all the way to be sure of getting through to help you out. What's happened to the people attacking you?'

'No-one has attacked us.'

'Why then do you ring me saying that you are being attacked by an armed band?'

'Well, you see, sir . . .'

We managed to control our giggles, but heard that there was much less control when it got round the Masters' Common Room.

And so term drew to an end with, owing to the circumstances, a feeling of unrealism in taking leave of school for the last time. Little did I realise that our casual farewell was actually the last I would ever see of Richard. On 15 June, not long after arrival at Radley, we had cycled into Oxford; he went to the RAF recruiting office, I to the RN one. He was going to be delayed a bit in joining because they were so busy with conscripts, so volunteers had to wait. Whilst I had no yen to fly, I opted for the Fleet Air Arm because they had fairly immediate vacancies for volunteers. It was explained that the Fleet Air Arm were desperate for aircrew and most particularly Observers. If, like me, you had 'A' Level Maths, or Higher Certificate as it was then, you would be forced to be an Observer rather than a pilot because pilots didn't need to be that clever! There is a photograph of Richard (Plate 15) on a later page in this account.

A curiosity of this period was the difficulty volunteers for the forces had in getting themselves accepted. The explanation is that the regular forces were at full stretch 'holding the line' and training the enormous number of conscripts coming in. Conscription had only just begun. There was just no spare capacity to train volunteers as well as all these conscripts. It was 'deemed expedient' that conscripts should all come forward on their due date. To take volunteers and defer an equivalent number of conscripts seemed too complicated. Authority did not prefer conscripts: on the whole, quite the reverse. You knew all volunteers wanted to be in and that quite a lot of conscripts did not!

By now the family home was a large, comfortable flat on the seventh floor (top) of a block in Princes' Gate (London). Here, somewhat restless, I enjoyed London and the family awaiting the Admiralty signal which would get me off to Portsmouth. War had already brought significant changes to civilian life. The biggest initial difference was the universal nocturnal blackout – no street lighting, no light allowed to emerge from anyone's windows or doors. Food was rationed; at that early stage not enough to make you hungry, but things like overseas fruits totally disappeared. Unless lines were damaged in raids, electricity, water and postal services ran as normal. The last was about a thousand per cent more efficient than today's!

Long distance rail travel was awful. Abbreviated timetables, to make way for military traffic, caused crowded trains. 'Express' trains had many more stops. Air-raids caused interruptions. Railway maintenance suffered from loss of manpower to the services and over-commitment of rolling stock. By the end of the War, the railways were totally run down. This made the excuse for nationalisation from which they never recovered. Similarly the telephone system became overloaded and under-maintained. It was all operator controlled; a strict limit was put on 'trunk' calls. Operators cut the line after three minutes or when (listening in) they thought the conversation non-essential.

Rationing had started, as said, and considerably complicated a house-wife's planning of menus but the skilful could still feed the family perfectly adequately. Eggs were very scarce and substituted by a disgusting dried egg powder. The difficulties progressed steadily during the War and beyond. The worst was after the War, when for the first time the two staples, bread and potatoes, which had never been rationed, were very tightly rationed in order to feed our starving conquered adversaries – and little credit did we get from them. The post-War generation believe there was a widespread black market, but British discipline through the War was such that, unique in Europe, there was at no stage a black market of significance in rationed commodities. Things that were unrationed – for example Scotch – were usually kept by retailers for favoured customers. If you knew a farmer, he might let you have the occasional egg illegally when you met him – but not at a profiteer's price. We tended to refer to all such deals as 'black market'.

We could telephone local friends as much as we wanted with no restrictions. Activities in London were much the same for youngsters as at any time except that nocturnally the blackout and shortage of taxis made getting about a bit more time consuming. I suppose girls just expected that you would either volunteer or be conscripted – don't forget that just the same applied for them. More girls would engage in sex, particularly the WAAF and ATS, than had been the case. I believe, however, that post-War novelists and journalists have grossly exaggerated the increase of sexual licence.

There was no contempt for the Reserved Occupations as a whole. Everyone was directed as regards occupation and many were stuck as 'civvies' however much they wanted to go to war. My elder brother Sandy, as a medical student, was one – he had to stay at his studies until qualified when he went straight into the RAMC. There were a few string-pullers to be 'Reserved' and I suppose we despised them. Sandy was in his last year at Clare before his three years at the Middlesex Hospital. I saw him in vacations and when on leave. Granny (the family's name for my mother) worried at my joining up, but accepted the inevitable philosophically and with some jingoistic pride. I honestly do not recall any wish to be absolved from what most others had to face – it was something we all had to do for the benefit of the community to which we belonged. Without wishing to sound too plummy, it was general in those days for people to think first about their obligations and last about their individual rights. What I bitterly resented after the War, when going into industry, was finding myself six years behind my contemporaries in experience when they had got themselves classified 'Reserve Occupation' (i.e. not to be conscripted) as engineers in manufacturing.

One lovely afternoon (7 September) the air-raid sirens went. Up till then this had been a not infrequent occurrence, but little had ever happened – one might just hear the odd AA (anti-aircraft) gun loose off. Thus Kenneth, my younger brother, and I went up on to the roof of the block to see what there was to see. He was in summer holidays from school before his last year as Head Prefect. It was astonishing; all across the clear blue sky at what seemed incredible height, the sky was covered with the loops of vapour trails of aircraft in combat. High flying aircraft were such a rarity in those days, I doubt that anyone had seen any vapour trail over London before. Few planes came as far west as Knightsbridge, but one could hear the zooming of engines, the fall of bombs to the east, and occasionally a plane spiralling to earth. It was totally unreal; we wondered whether combat would be broken off when the vast thunderstorm creeping in from the east reached the scene of battle. Then it dawned on us that it was no storm; we were seeing the piling smoke of what must be the whole of the East End on fire. As dusk fell, this was confirmed by the massive red glow in the sky. Only now after nearly a year of official war did one realise that it was going to be a terribly sordid affair.

Heavy raids came more and more frequently after that and the sight of aerial battles become more commonplace. I recall the thrill of seeing, on a cloudy day, a twin engined bomber, with no tail and much of its wings gone, appear through the cloud base in a vertical dive. It seemed very close but the explosion of its impact gave the impression that it had come down in fact somewhere near Victoria. The raids got heavier and much more nocturnal. A cellar shelter was rigged (seats only; no sleeping bunks!) for 7 Princes Gate's residents. My main recollection was of the noise – besides the bombs, we had a heavy AA Battery just across Kensington Road in the Park.

A diversion was the needle which existed between Granny and her co-occupant of the top storey, Lady Hope Morley, widow of the knitwear magnate. Each regarded the other snobbishly; on the one hand, a parvenu from 'Trade', on the other, someone obviously not really rich enough to inhabit 7 Princes Gate. Through all the noise – and it could be intimidating – there was great competition in keeping British upper lips stiff. Granny won this hands down, bless her, the night a land-mine demolished the Horse Guards' Barracks (across the road and a hundred yards east of us). There was a peculiar whirring, followed by a colossal bang and an earthquake shuddering. Granny remarked calmly, 'That must have been close.' Lady Hope, I believe, had to make a call for a laundry collection in the morning.

London was to have a long hard go of this treatment, but I escaped in a week or two. I cannot remember the exact wording but a telegram arrived saying approximately as follows:

'REPORT HMS ST VINCENT GOSPORT 18.00 HRS SEPT 23. JOINING INSTRUC-TIONS AND TRAVEL WARRANT FOLLOW BY POST. NA2SL ADMTY.'

The joining instructions probably said bring no civilian clothing beyond what you wear and only your toilet items. It may have explained how to get there – Portsmouth Harbour Station, Harbour Ferry and then walk the odd one and a half miles to St Vincent or catch the No.? bus. The travel warrant was a flimsy piece of official paper which the railway accepted as a ticket. NA2SL was 'Naval Assistant to the 2nd Sea Lord' – the Admiralty Department dealing with personnel matters. Records show that I actually was taken on on 25 September so I suppose the word came a few days before that.

Chapter 2

Learning to be a Sailor

O<small>N</small> 23 <small>SEPTEMBER</small> 1940, I left home after rather emotional farewells, because none of us knew when any leave would be given or when I could get home again. The strain was reduced for my mother because her friend, Charles Wakeling, something in the City and everything of a know-all, had had it on the highest authority that the Navy avoided exposing personnel under twenty to operational service. Little did he know that throughout the War, boy seamen served in capital ships (battleships, battle-cruisers and aircraft carriers) as part of their training. I suppose their ages ranged from fourteen to seventeen!

I suppose the main sensation on the Portsmouth train was excitement, more perhaps at now being more a man than everlastingly a schoolboy. After all the packing up which preceded each school term it seemed odd to be setting off for what might be years with no more than a sponge-bag and the clothes one stood up in, in accordance with instructions. In fact, those clothes had to be sent home as soon as uniform had been issued. Uniform was obligatory wear for the rest of the War – although I found later that this was considerably relaxed when at sea. For the next six years, I had to get used to a message arriving which could send me at a moment's notice to any point of the globe which was not enemy-held.

In no way was one venturing forth with the patriotic fervour of a Boer (or even Great) War volunteer. It was just a matter that Hitler must be stopped from overwhelming Europe and we must prevent a successful invasion of Britain following the Dunkirk disaster, and at that time this looked very difficult indeed. We were well aware of the situation. I read the news about as much as I do today. *Telegraph*, *Picture Post*, *Illustrated London News*, *Daily Mirror* (for Jane cartoon strip). We all thought Chamberlain a disaster after Munich and were glad to have the coalition under Churchill and Atlee.

Basically, as we then had a National Government, we believed that the best national first team had been picked and tended to accept them. The military disasters were blamed more on Chamberlain not getting us prepared in time rather than on the generals. In the Navy, we thought the Army a pretty hopeless lot, trying hard but usually losing, but better than the RAF, who seemed only to fight when they had a good chance of winning. In those days the BBC confined itself to factual news, albeit clothed in propagandist terminology, and enjoyed a worldwide reputation of total objectivity. We recognised that news was censored. Like the Germans and French, we always felt we could believe the BBC. Yes, of course we listened to Haw-Haw, but not that much because there was more tediousness than amusement. 'King & Country' debates were *de rigueur* for school debating societies as well as the Oxford Union, but more before the War. After the start, the results of such debates were too predictable.

Already, I think, one realised that it was going to be a long, hard, grind and subconsciously I believe one recognised that the Fleet Air Arm was not an especially safe occupation and that chances of personal survival were not great. I believe this gave the one antidote which carries people through war – a quick adaptation to the philosophy of savouring the present minute and not bothering about the future. That brings, incidentally, a terrific mental crunch for the survivors at the war's end – the sudden recognition that there is a life to live and that one must look at the future and plan for it. In the Navy the Fleet Air Arm was known as 'the Branch', formally the Air Branch, because the term Fleet Air Arm was no longer a term used by the Admiralty. In eight weeks we had to learn all the arts which would qualify one to be an Ordinary Seaman: square-bashing, ropework and knots, boat-pulling (you never 'row' in the Navy, it's always 'pulling'), flag and morse signalling and, not least, going aloft.

Arrival at Portsmouth left one feeling an outsider in civilian clothes. Never had one imagined that places existed where nearly everyone would be in uniform and that there were so many sailors in one port. Crossing the harbour ferry to Gosport was a disappointment; none of the major units of the Navy were in harbour. (They had, of course, withdrawn further from the Luftwaffe to places like Scapa Flow.)

HMS *Vincent* was easy to find – a large Georgian style red brick barracks a mile and a half up the main street. Until recently it had been Portsmouth Command's Boy Seamen training establishment. It was situated in western Gosport, with the rear fringes of the site reaching down to the shore of the western side of Portsmouth harbour. The entrance and Guardroom had a fine archway which still stands, but now what was the parade ground is covered with the bungaloid array of a brave new world comprehensive school.

In our day, inside the arch was a large parade ground. It was backed by four barrack blocks of well proportioned Georgian architecture: red brick with white stone facings and arched cloistering at ground floor level. Centrally in front of them stood the very tall flagstaff. Being equipped for the training of boy-seamen, with beds (albeit boards and palliasses), it was rather more comfortable for ratings (non-commissioned ranks of the Navy) than the main seaman barracks (e.g. *Victory*). We each had a bed, like an Army barracks, but spread our hammocks on the beds instead of conventional bedmaking. Hammocks were issued before the first night's kip. I handed mine back when I was made an officer.

Naval hammocks and their usage are well described, for those who may be interested, in the *Admiralty Seamanship Manual* of those days. There were good sized ablutions areas and we fed in a large messhall on ample if not thrilling food.

St Vincent had been turned over to the Fleet Air Arm for initial seamanship training of their massive intake of Pilot and Observer trainees. A Pilot's duties are obvious from the title. The Observer had to (a) captain the aircraft, (b) do the navigation, (c) code and cypher signals, (d) sometimes operate the radio in Morse code, (e) aim bombs for high-level bombing, also fire rockets, (f) be rear gunner sometimes, (g) report movements of enemy ships when in contact, (h) spot the fall of our shot in gunnery engagements of the Fleet, (i) take aerial photographs, (j) drop leaflets to civilians, (k) report on weather conditions.

Our course shared *St Vincent* with two pilots' courses. Each course had about 250 people. Plate 2 is a picture of myself, taken on my first leave at Christmas, in rating's uniform. We lived about twenty-five to a dormitory ('messdeck'), under the pretty kindly eye of a recalled pensioner 'Killick' (Leading Seaman).

These chaps were far too old for operational service, but the Royal Navy called them back off pension (some were in their fifties and sixties) and put them to extremely good use right through the War 'nannying' the newly recruited through their onshore training. We were kindly greeted by ours at the Main Gate on arrival and put to bed for the first night. It was not unlike school, as we were all from higher secondary education or early years at university.

Early in the morning we awoke to the traditional call which was to dog our lives for the rest of the War, with local variations. First the Drummer (actually a bugler, but the RN seem weak on identification of musical instruments) blew Reveille – the same as the infantry's call in the Army. Then the Bosun's Mate shrilled his pipe over the tannoy and announced 'Call the Hands!' Before he was through, a very loud Petty Officer came through the messdeck shouting the traditional call with his own blasphemous or pornographic additions at the end: 'Wakey, Wakey, Wakey, Whoooa . . . Rise and Shine, you've had your time . . . Here we go, Lash up and Stow.' This referred to one's hammock: there was a 'Pusser' way it had to be done, blankets folded in the prescribed manner on the thin palliasse, tacks (the strings for holding the hammock ends in the sleeping mode) folded in at the ends, then the whole rolled into a sausage of regulation diameter and secured by the

1. Leading Airman HCBM on Christmas leave, 1940

lashing run in half-hitches, number prescribed, along its length. The half-hitch was learned the first morning. It took less time to pass muster of the messdeck Killick each subsequent day until one achieved a reasonable time; many people knew the basic knots – membership of the Boy Scouts was far more common then than now.

Another cry, 'Show a Leg . . .', we were told, came from Nelson's day when ships in harbour allowed the matelots to share their hammocks overnight with their girlfriends, which must have required a technique of its own which was not handed down to us. Ladies were allowed to lie in and could avoid being rolled out of the hammock by sticking a leg out for identification as feminine. I suppose this was when ladies started to shave their legs (and perhaps some chaps?!).

Interesting things, hammocks. You could always tell a sailor 'on draft' (travelling between postings) or going on leave; he had to carry his hammock on one shoulder, kitbag under the opposite arm and 'pussers' attaché case in his hand. As the packed kitbag was about eighteen inches diameter and 3ft 6ins long, it all took some controlling. The mile and a half to the harbour ferry was no fun. If you were marched as a group on draft it was better; kit bags and hammocks would then be trucked.

On rising, the first duty was to lash up the hammock (so that in no way could it get ventilated) and put it in the messdeck stowage – usually a rack of vertical pigeonholes in which hammocks stood on end. It was said that a properly lashed hammock would keep a man afloat for twenty-four hours. In Nelson's day, there would be plenty around a foundering ship, because at 'Action Stations' they were all packed in the nets, netting along the bulwarks of the ship where they reduced the impact of enemy ball and the flying of splinters. All in all, quite a useful piece of equipment; many swore they were far more comfortable than a bed, but I was not among them. A great advantage was on long overnight train journeys – in wartime, it took about thirty hours from Euston to getting aboard in Scapa Flow – whilst officers and other services slept in train seats or sitting in the corridors, Jolly Jack could sling in the luggage van, if he were in time to get a pitch.

After breakfast we were paraded for the first time under the Gunner's Mate who was the bane of our existence for the whole course. Having all been in OTCs we were quite good at drill for beginners, but never good enough for him. He seemed so vile at first and his vituperation so foul, we were all scared stiff by him. Only with time did one realise that it was all done, like all the Navy's (and, I believe, the Guards') drill discipline, with a strong underlying sense of humour. His is the only name I recall of all our instructors – CPO Wilmott; he was a legend throughout all wartime Fleet Air Arm recruits. Proceedings started with one sentence :

'In the Navy we have three speeds just like your kiddy bikes, quick-time which is 120 paces to the minute left right left right double march which is running at 160 paces and Rush. When I say rush you don't walk, you don't run, you don't fly, you get there quicker than Christ would let you. If I say "as you were", you return to where you were at the rush.'

'Squad! To the canteen . . . rush!'

'As you were.'

'My Christ, my Granny can shift quicker than you lot with her knickers round her ankles and her sodding great boobs untied, but she's in a naval family . . .'

'Stop that tittering there, you syphilitic row of schoolgirls. I WILL NOT have you standing there mocking me; God help the Navy if we're to fight a war with college kids who can't control their fucking selves. War's not fucking funny, the Navy's not fucking funny, and I'm going to learn you lot in the next few days that I'm not fucking funny at all. To the canteen . . . rush!'

'As you were,' etc., etc.

With regard to Fixing Bayonets:

'When I gives the order 'Fix!', yer don't fix; all that happens is that the right hand marker takes two paces forward, except on one occasion, at a Funeral Firing Party. For why? Well, because he'd fall in the bleeding great hole, wouldn't he? Mind you, if you lot was the Firing Party at my funeral, you'd have me knocking on me coffin lid and my poor fuckin' widow weeping along astern. '

'Fred, mean to say you trained this fuckin' heap? You ought to be bloody well ashamed of yourself.'

And so to the relative peace of drawing uniform and kit and parcelling up our civvies to send home. Each of us was issued with a wooden block for printing our names on each item of kit in black or white paint. The printing blocks were made on the spot by an OD (Ordinary Seaman) who could carve your name in relief on a bit of gash (scrap) wood in a flash just with a penknife. The main items of kit were : boots (2 pairs), shoes (1 pair), socks (3 pairs), vests (singlet) and underpants (3 each), flannels (2), pullover (1), jumpers (2), silk (1), bluejean collars (2), caps (2), lanyard and seaman's knife (1), greatcoat (1), belt (1), trousers (2 pairs), jumpers and trousers in white drill cotton (1 each), overalls (1), hammock and mattress (1), kit bag (1), suitcase (1), polishing brushes (2).

Uniform took quite a bit of know-how to get right. I am wearing it in Plate 1. The flannel was a cotton shirt with a square neckline bordered in blue which can be seen filling the vee in the jumper front in summertime wear; in winter, the plain blue pullover is seen instead. The jumper was an outer upper garment worn by sailors, with a wide vee neckline and square sailor's collar behind. The flannel (cotton drill shirt) and collar had to be pressed in a special way and were the very devil to wash. The silk was a black silk square, in mourning for Nelson, and had to be pressed, folded and refolded into a strip of precision width. The ends were then knotted in a reef, which went under the collar of the jumper at the back. The bottom end of the 'bight' (loop) thus made was held by the tapes, fixed at the bottom of the vee of the jumper. The tapes had to be tied in an especially 'tiddley' bow round the silk, to leave a set length of looped silk below and set lengths for the free ends of the tapes.

The collar had the traditional three white lines round the border of its outer facing. It had a sort of 'dickey front', which was inside the jumper, held in place by tapes around the torso. The collar was put on before the jumper and then the part which showed pulled out. The white lines always had to be very white, difficult because the blue in the material always ran with our washing material, a bar of red Lifebuoy and scrubbing brush. The lanyard had to be kept scrubbed dead white, and was worn like the silk, with the whistle or knife attached stowed in the bosom pocket of the jumper. Cap ribbons had to have an exceedingly tiddley bow in just the right place round the brim and in relation to the Ship's name. We were a little put out to have 'HMS *St Vincent*' cap ribbons, thus identifying us to all of Pompey (Portsmouth) as beginners. During the War, for security reasons, sea-going matelots did not bear their ship's name, the ribbon merely saying 'HMS'.

The trousers were a bit peculiar; at the top, two flaps came together with three buttons like normal flies; a front flap the full width of the trousers, droppable to below crutch level, was held in the 'decent' position by a horizontal line of four buttons about an inch below the trouser waist. The corner button (underneath the jumper) could be left undone to make pocket access easy – but in issue trousers, there was only a pocket on one side. Trousers (these were never called bell-bottoms in the Navy) had to be pressed inside out so that when worn the knife-edge creases went inwards. Overalls were like ordinary boiler suits except that they had a 'choker' neck fastening. The kit bag was a canvas cylinder about 18 inches diameter and 42 inches long. The suitcase was made of fibre (pre-War of leather) and was a case for minor lockable bits and pieces, about 12″ x 9″ x 6″ (very small!). Shortage of pockets was the only disadvantage of this very comfortable garb. One for the money in the belt, which never needed to be big, one in the trouser and one in the bosom of the jumper. Stowage had to be found for the issue knife which was on a white pipecord lanyard worn over the silk. Jolly good knives – still have mine – strong blade and marlin spike for splicing.

We were to learn just how many skills ran through the lower decks of the Navy. At sea, many had their own businesses as carpenters, cobblers, tailors etc. In a big ship there would be several rivals capable of running you up a complete beautifully cut uniform. In the Army and RAF uniform was issued on the basis that when something wore out it could be exchanged for new free, unless wantonly damaged. In 'The Andrew' (Navy) we were initially issued with a complete kit but thereafter had to keep it up ourselves out of a 'Kit Upkeep Allowance' – one or two pence a week – and could go to any supplier we wanted, so long as the result conformed to regulations. This, of course, kept the tailors (known as 'snippys') in business (others: 'snib' = cobbler, 'chippy'= carpenter). Another prized skill was dressing tobacco. Free tobacco was issued to ratings monthly – about enough to make five hundred cigarettes – either as leaves of tobacco or shredded for rolling into cigarettes (ticklers, so called as they were harsher than bought cigarettes) at the choice of the recipient.

In some shore bases like *St Vincent*, a pensioner had a concession to bring in a lorry with a cigarette machine on it at issue time, so you could opt to have your tobacco issued to him and receive it back as 'tailor made' ticklers with the 'ship's crest' printed on them in blue. Pipe-smokers usually took their issued leaves to a dresser who had secret formulae for treating it. It involved dunking it in potions such as rum, molasses and, some said, Condy's fluid. It was then sewn in a tight cylinder in sailcloth like an oversized cigar (or undersized hammock) shape and then whipped extremely tightly with spun yarn and left for weeks to mature. The result was a black, gorgeous smelling plug from which flakes were cut with a sharp knife for chewing or for rubbing out and pipe filling.

The caps had a convenient lining within, with a central hole with a drawstring, so this could be used as stowage for flat things like identity cards, Watch cards and (more usually) half-consumed cigarettes, extinguished at 'Out Pipes'. The parade ground was always covered with lost and treasured 'nub-ends' which had made their escape when the order 'Off Caps' was given. Morning parades – called Divisions – always included a bit by the Padre, preceded by 'Fall out the Roman Catholics', who were able to go and have a quick drag on their nub ends behind the barrack block.

So, now kitted up, we got down to learning. First, organisation: a ship's company is divided into four units, Port and Starboard Watches and first and second part of each Watch. You had a card (red or green) and in it your name and part were entered. When you went ashore (as even going out of a shore establishment was termed), you had to deposit your Watch-card in the Regulating Office in the Guardroom. If you came back 'adrift' (late), your card would no longer be there for collection; it was only recoverable by appearing on a charge in front of the Commander next morning. Punishments included so many days confined to ship, extra drills, cleaning parties or, for more serious misdemeanours, cells. Cells were fairly tough; they had to be more uncomfortable than a small ship's messdeck in rough conditions. The worst were cells with hard lying; for this you were in an unheated cell in cotton drill uniform, no bunk, only one blanket at night and a quarter of a loaf of bread and a quart of water per day.

Before serious air raids, only one Part was required 'aboard' each night, so three-quarters of us could go 'ashore' until an hour which made it the hell of a scramble back at pub-closing time. For our first week, whilst we learned and recovered from our injections, we were confined to barracks. Injections against everything under the sun were doled out in a single parade. The result was agonising and a majority were unable to get their rather tight jumpers off at night for several days.

At *St Vincent* (or correctly, I should say 'in'), the boy seamen tradition was continued for us, whereby shore leave was for the evening only. At about 5.30 the pipe was given, 'Liberty men muster at the Main Gate.' Having fallen in there, we were inspected. Any faults in dress and no liberty; if you passed muster (the origin of the phrase), you put your Watch card in the appropriate slot in the Guardroom box and off you went to the pubs, cinema or whatever.

Daytime was spent learning all the arts of seamanship and naval lore. Knots, splices, boat handling, flag signals, semaphore, morse, rifle and AA (machine gun) drill and above all plenty of square bashing to ensure that we could drill better than the Army. We had eight weeks of that. The few course failures usually went off to be ordinary seamen. Adequate speed at reading morse, semaphore and flag-hoists were the commonest difficulties. Memory says that our pay was 4s. 6d. per day and 5s. 6d. per day later, when we were flying. 4s. 6d. is about 23 pence in today's money, and was the standard pay for Airmen, 2nd Class, our official rating. Beer ashore cost about 4d. a pint and was rather stronger than today's; cigarettes cost 7d. for 20.

I suppose that the most enjoyable 'lessons' we did were boat handling.

This was, for us, limited to 'pulling' in cutters or whalers. On a full seaman's course, we would also have sailed these boats. The cutter is a heavy fourteen-oared, seven a side, boat, with thwarts wide enough to take four men abreast and thus the oars could be 'double-banked'. The boat was 32 feet long, the oars 15 feet long. The whaler was lighter, faster, 25 feet long with oars of 17 feet. Under the kindly eye of a recalled seaman pensioner, we rowed ponderously around Portsmouth Harbour, slowly acquiring the knack of rowing in time and then racing other boats. Perhaps because it was fun, we only had limited time at this activity and I cannot claim that we achieved the polish of peacetime seamen.

One other of the horrors of *St Vincent* which I nearly forgot: at the side of the parade ground was a huge mast complete with yards on which we had to learn to go aloft. The compulsory exercise was to climb to each yard in turn and walk to its extremity, from which the asphalt below looked very hard. Having done the Topgallant, you could come down or (volunteering for bravado – not me) do the 'Button Boy' (climb onto and stand on the cap on the topmast head). Jack Stamper, a gymnast as well as scrum-half, did the Button Boy on his head, which even impressed the regulars. From the end of each yard to a point higher up the mast is a stay which is in reach when you are at the outer (thinner) end of the yard, but experts can manage without it. In the days of sail at sea, you went out on the yards on footropes below them, hanging on to the yard itself, but then it was all moving about somewhat. Topgallant is the yard for the highest sail. Some could not make this item of training; they attracted much scorn from the Petty Officer in charge of it, but it wasn't a reason for being chucked out. (I think I would have remembered if anyone had fallen because they would have been pretty dead or at least badly bent.)

At this period we got some quite good rugger. Being mostly public and grammar school in origin with a smattering of undergraduates, we could muster one of the better sides in the Pompey area. I managed a place in it as hooker. In the middle of our course, one of the Pilots' courses moved on to Flying School and the rugger captaincy descended to a New Zealander in the next Pilot Course. He selected an all New Zealand side to represent *St Vincent*. We were particularly incensed because they had a rotten scrum-half whilst in the UK pilots we had Jack Stamper, with a very distinguished record in that position in first class rugger. We got permission to pick a side to play the NZ official HMS *St Vincent* XV. All went well for the first twenty minutes by which time we were about 12 points clear; then they pitched in, fists, boots at every opportunity. Jack and several others were badly injured and the referee had to call off the game. In those days this sort of play just wasn't on. Both teams were paraded next day before the Captain and harangued about conduct unbefitting gentlemen not being acceptable in rugger or in the Andrew. We were to play again and any man fouling would be thrown off his course.

This time, although depleted by casualties from the first encounter, we still won reasonably handsomely and regained our places in the official team. We finished at *St Vincent* at the end of November 1940.

So, after eight weeks we emerged as 'NA2s' (Airmen 2nd Class – the equivalent of OD, Ordinary Seaman), and, wonder of wonders, were given a long week-end leave. I returned from that late, but was pardoned thanks to the good organisational thinking of the Brigade of Guards. I returned to Waterloo for my train in a taxi at the height of an air-raid, thanks to a very game taxi driver. He got me to the main entrance, although the station roof at the far side was well ablaze. The Pompey train was just short of the burning bit and, filled with terror at arriving late from my first leave, I went to climb aboard but was directed to the shelters by a huge Guardsman with a very live-looking rifle.

Under Waterloo, not normally available to the public, is a huge system of tunnels and catacombs. They were packed solid with naval (Pompey) and Army (Aldershot) personnel returning from leave. There we sat until about 2 a.m. soaked with the fire brigade's water which percolated through. Then, under Guards NCOs, we were fallen in in a massive parade in the Waterloo Road. The officer in charge announced that overnight billets were available for everyone (some organisation!), but as transport was limited, all except the Senior Service would have to march to their beds. We sailors were loaded into Guards' trucks and taken to a local YMCA for a comfortable remainder of the night.

Come morning, our chauffeurs called again for us and back at Waterloo each of us was armed with a chit certifying that we had been prevented from punctual return by enemy action. This seemed miraculous organisation, impromptu on such a night. Maybe, whilst away from London, I had not realised that the raids had been frequent enough for the garrison (the Guards at that time) to have evolved a well-practised drill for returnees from leave.

The next phase of our training was at Whale Island (HMS *Excellent*), the Royal Naval Gunnery School. Many would call it the original home of bullshit, but I have always been fond of it as the best run of shore establishments. A duty of Observers in ship to ship action (or ship to shore) is to fly about over the scene and spot the fall of shot, signalling the corrections. For this, some knowledge of gunnery method and procedure is required. Also the Gunnery Department is the one responsible in the Navy for 'Field Training' – the Navy's name for square bashing of all kinds. It is Whale Island which trains the marvellously drilled squads who haul the Monarch and a few other notables by gun carriage at their funerals. So we were there too to be given a final smartening up on parade before escaping from Portsmouth.

When they dug out the mud to make Portsmouth Dockyard, it was dumped up-harbour where it formed an island about a mile long and a third of a mile wide. Here was founded the gunnery school. At the south end is a vast parade ground, with drill shed alongside – large enough to hold a couple of parading battalions. From the northern corners of this ground runs the peripheral road going right round the island. On the seaward side of this as we go round clockwise, there are the experimental gun butts (big enough to stop a 9-inch shell), the long West Battery, containing modern guns and mountings for drill and about a quarter mile long, then the North Battery similarly equipped, the pig farm (swill from the messdecks provided them in due course with *Excellent* – pardon pun – pork), next the Main Gate by the bridge to the mainland and back to the parade.

The north side of the Parade had a steep bank with imposing central steps, then a large flat playing field – the best rugger pitch in Pompey. North of this an imposing Wardroom (Officers' mess) block ran the length of a further bank. To the right was the Quarterdeck – a small parade ornamented with Nelsonian cannon, figureheads etc. Behind the Wardroom were the barrack and instruction blocks.

We lived in extra huts put up for the War, about thirty to the hut, with plenty of space. We had a kindly Killick to look after us, a Gunlayer, but he was by no means a slack disciplinarian and we had to keep our room accommodation very spick and span. A Gunlayer was a guncrew member seated on the left of the breech whose wheel 'lays' (elevates or depresses) the gun. He is the next senior to the captain of the gun's crew or is sometimes captain. Also the term is used (as in my context) for a man with a fairly senior rating's gunnery qualification; such a man's rank would usually be Killick (Leading Seaman, in official parlance) or Petty Officer. (It was the former in this instance.) In the gun crew, the man sitting on the right of the breech is the 'Trainer', next in the hierarchy and of similar qualification. His wheel 'trains' the gun leftwards or rightwards.

Sunday lunch was a real pleasure. At 'Cooks to the Galley', our Killick Gunlayer would despatch three of us to the galley nearby. They returned with a gorgeous great crackling-covered joint of roast pork and two veg. with plum duff to follow. The Killick took head of table, where he insisted on first saying Grace before carving for us all, just like Dad. Sometimes if he thought someone had been particularly helpful during the week he would reward him with 'Sippers' – a singular honour usually reserved only for special friends in the Navy (a sip from his rum tot for that day).

Rum issue was a complicated affair. All ratings were categorised as G, T, or U/A (G= Grog-drinking; T= Teetotal; U/A= Underage). If U/A, bad luck; the penalty for being under age (twenty) was that you got nothing; over twenty you could opt to be G or T – to receive the daily grog issue or to receive 2d. (nearly 1p), a day extra pay instead. Each day, at noon on the quarterdeck, under the 'Jaunty's' (Master-at-Arms) supervision, measures of rum to the exact number of G ratings fit for duty (another necessary qualification), were ladled into the shining brassbound grog tub. Petty Officers could draw their tots neat; this amounted to about a large pub 'double', but the strength was such that it could be diluted to twice its volume to come down to pub strength rum. They were usually allowed to take theirs away for later consumption. The rum in the tub would be diluted twice then (converting the contents to 'grog') and then 'Up Spirits!' would be piped. The G ratings then paraded before the tub to receive their tots, which had to be drunk on the spot. This was to prevent storing it up for one large orgy – as it was, each man was getting somewhere between two and three pub doubles per issue. Officers never got the issue, except on the rare Fleet Order 'Splice the Mainbrace' in celebration of a spectacular achievement or victory. Then only the U/As got left out; even Ts could 'splice' if they wanted. It was lovely dark Demerara rum with a bouquet of its own; you keep hearing of supplies of Real Navy Rum still these days, but I have yet to smell the genuine article outside the Navy. I suspect that anyway it would be uneconomic to market a rum at the strength of the grog. I recall savouring later its powerful smell – breathing it second hand in a walk through *Indomitable*'s hot messdecks in the tropics after 'Up Spirits!' was a huge pleasure – almost an inebriating one!

Ratings found all sorts of ruses to save up their tots rather than obey the regulation to consume at the issue. Tots were currency with which one could pay, say, Snib (the cobbler). There was small change offered between friends for favours, known as 'Sippers' or, for a very major favour, 'Gulpers' might be extended. I recall a very sad AFO I read much later in the War. (AFOs were printed Admiralty Fleet Orders dealing with the administration and discipline of the Navy, which came out by the bookful each week and had to be read by all officers.) This one was titled 'Rum Issue – Toxic Qualities'. It emphasised the need for the greatest vigilance over the consumption at the issue point. It related the case of identical twin brothers, who, with consideration unusual to the drafting authorities, had been allowed to serve in the same destroyer. At the celebration of their twenty-first birthday their whole messdeck had given them 'Gulpers' and covered for their next Watch whilst they turned in to sleep it off. Neither had ever awoken. Enough for rum!

At 'Whaley' we got spectacularly good at drill as well as learning some new tricks. It is for example a rule there that no-one proceeding independently across the parade could do it otherwise than at the double. Thus if you happened to be with a rifle at the slope, you had to master the unorthodox and awkward skill of doubling at the slope. Each day everyone started with the Divisions parade, but on Friday it was a special one with the RM Band and much marching past after – usually some senior notable took the salute. Our last Friday, this was the Commander in Chief Portsmouth, a full Admiral. After it was over our Gunner's Mate was told to parade us at the foot of the bank for an address by our Divisional Officer – a mere Lieutenant Commander. The address:

> 'The Captain has ordered me to pass to 44 Observer Course the C in C's compliments on an excellent march past. Before your heads swell too large, I would like to tell you that the C in C has not got perfect eyesight and he is not a Gunnery Officer. I have A1 sight and I am a Gunnery Officer; in my opinion, yours wasn't a march past, it was hardly a slouch; it was more in the nature of a peasants' revolt!'

No-one can win at Whaley!

We had a good, if brief, time there again allowed ashore three nights in four. My two cobbers and I (Alastair McLean and Bill Orwin) usually slept at 'Aggie Weston's', a renowned Pompey institution. Dame Agnes Weston had founded a sailors' home where you could get a super plain meal and a clean bed in your own cubicle, the latter for only 2d. if I remember rightly. There was only one really strict rule there – and it was quite a restriction

– no drink could be taken in and no sailor was admitted if there was evidence of him having drink inside him.

From the weekend leave at the end of the *Excellent* course, we returned to HMS *Victory*; not Nelson's thing in the dockyard but the vast seaman depot for Portsmouth Command and which also housed the Royal Navy Signals School which we were to attend for about six weeks. Not only vast, it was grossly overcrowded – a real slum. Our course of 250 hands had a messdeck 35 feet square in which to eat, sleep and live. Sleeping would have been physically impossible if it had not been the case here that for most of our stay, libertymen could stay ashore overnight and only one part of one Watch was required to be aboard.

Later, when air raids got heavy, a whole Watch was retained aboard and even though quite a section of them were on duty and not sleeping, those in the messdeck were spread on the deck as well as the 'early birds' who had taken the hammock slinging space above. (The entire barracks was based on slinging for sleep.) The called back pensioner Killick in charge of us was a real shit: all the worst of CPO Wilmott, without any of his sense of humour, a man soured by his naval career, furious at being called back in his late fifties for the War and now doomed to mess with a bunch of 'upper class' youths for whom he had a deeply ingrained loathing. Those left to sleep on the deck had to chose their pitch with care. Luckily, there was a sag in the ancient floor which aided judgement. Our messdeck was across the landing from the 'heads' (loo) for the entire block, which responded to the overload by blocking and flooding through our way regularly.

The whole messdeck stank – overcrowded humans and proximity to constantly overflowing heads. When TV programmes of today tell us about the enormities of conditions in our prisons, it amuses me to think what commentators would say about conditions in Royal Naval barracks this relatively short time ago. Infections such as 'flu and colds passed round quickly and widely but our basic fitness prevented any devastating outbreaks. It was perhaps a good thing that we had to follow ancient tradition by scrubbing and holystoning the 'deck' first thing every morning. One saving grace in the place was a NAAFI canteen, which we had not had at *Vincent*. In this great dirty gloomy hall, very good beer, fry-ups and snacks were available, extremely cheaply.

My two main friends and I got away from *Victory* a lot. In Southsea there was no longer any holiday trade, so rents had plummeted. Even on our meagre pay (about 12.5p per day) and small parental subsidies, we managed to take a grubby furnished flat on the top floor of an old house on Southsea front. We were all three in the same Part of the same Watch, so with possessions from home such as gramophones and radios, we were very comfortable for a week or two. The digs were in Clarence Parade, and we were fairly keen attenders at the dances on South Parade Pier, more for the female company than because of any terpsichorean enthusiasm.

The weather was cold whilst we inhabited our flat – cold enough to don greatcoats for the step across the green to South Parade Pier. The dances were crowded occasions but good fun – mainly naval personnel, both officers and ratings (of both sexes, naturally!). One night, at the end, I found to my horror that some sod had nicked my uniform greatcoat. Luckily, they had not yet become a requirement for *Victory's* Divisions parades, so my lack of greatcoat was not noticed immediately.

Shortly after, I had a weekend leave. Granny was most concerned at my going about greatcoatless in such weather and insisted on buying me one. It was no good pointing out that ratings' greatcoats could not be bought in London's West End.

'We'll get one in Harrods; you can get anything there.'

So off to Harrods we went. The only thing remotely the right style (but of course not with the regulation black crown-and-anchor naval buttons) which fitted was in what I'd call a rather dark shade of sky blue. I loyed its warmth (it had a grey sort of fur-fabric lining) and it was no good saying that no-one would allow me to wear it with uniform.

'Tell them yours was stolen and this was the best your mother could find you.'

No good saying that that might go down with matron at school (well, just, perhaps), but not with a Gunners Mate – so the purchase was made.

Orders for the Day covering the first Divisions after my return: 'No.2 Uniforms; greatcoats will be worn.' So I wore it, tucking myself in the rear rank behind some tall guys, much to the amusement of my colleagues.

Divisional Officer: 'Mr ??? (the Gunners Mate); who's that man in a sky blue coat? Bring him here.'

I was marched over and saluted smartly. Where had I got it? My mother had bought it because mine had been stolen. Unbutton it. My God! It's fur-lined. Get back in the ranks. Addressing the whole course: Never again let me see a man on Victory parade in a sky blue coat, even if his Mummy did buy it!

So – there was nothing for it – back to the dance to leave early nicking someone else's greatcoat!

A diversion on several occasions was visiting Chichester. Pat King-Smith, a very pretty girl who had been a spectator fan of my rugby on Eastbourne College Field, was encountered at a dance on South Parade Pier. She was now a VAD nurse at Chichester Hospital. She and her two colleagues suggested that Bill Orwin, Alastair McLean (my two flat mates) and I go up to Chichester for an evening: easy by train and the pubs were better. We had several such jolly evenings, just able to catch the last train to Pompey as the pubs shut.

Life was spoiled for us before long; increasing severity of air-raids on Pompey led to us having to stop aboard every other night and then tragedy struck and our little home from home got hit (on a duty night, thankfully) and we lost all our goodies. It was in fact over forty-eight hours after the event before we discovered this because *Victory* too had been hit and both Watches were kept aboard until all had been cleared up. There were no buses after this heavy raid and walking down to Southsea we got lost several times – the scene had been transformed by disappearance of whole streets into rubble.

I had had a bad night of duty, my post being firewatcher on the barrack roof. Stick after stick of bombs came over, straddling us but hitting other parts of the barracks and surroundings. It was all HE (high explosive), so no fires in my pitch to be put out. Eventually the roof further along from me was hit and demolished and shaken; with two hundred years' of roof space dust on me, I was withdrawn. I was unhurt but quite shaken. The barracks had several fatal casualties that night.

Next day was misery: water cut off and only some tanked-in sea water to wash in. One meal only of a terrible stew, reputedly horse casualties of the raid cooked in largely sea water!

The purpose of this sojourn in squalor was to achieve proficiency in radio signalling. We had to be able to operate the sets commonly used in aircraft and send and receive morse at speeds rather faster than we could write – writing speed was my main difficulty – and learn how to code and cypher signals. Also, of course, remembering Nelson, we had to become quick at reading flag hoist signals, semaphore and flash.

There our general naval training ended, so after another weekend at home, we had to report for the first time to the Fleet Air Arm at its main base, the airfield at Lee-on-Solent. There in fact we never saw the airfield.

First thing the first morning we went on an injection top-up and fitness check out. The latter consisted of the doctor asking if you felt OK; then he shone a hand torch round your mouth (searching for scurvy?), and ditto round the balls and that was all. In the afternoon we were issued with tropical uniforms and flying kit which was very exciting, the latter being of very high quality. One extraordinary item, dreamt up by the Admiralty to add to standard RAF flying kit, was a tropical flying helmet. This was a small solar topee with ear flaps to take helmet phones and chin buckle. Anyone wearing one in our open cockpits would have had his head jerked off as soon as it went into the slipstream!

Chapter 3

Going Foreign

A T THAT TIME, there were only two Observer flying training schools in the Navy: Worthy Down near Winchester and Piarco in Trinidad. Having been issued with tropical kit, we reckoned we had a shrewd idea, it being January, which we would be sent to – but you never know in the Navy. We were a little apprehensive about this, having discovered that our quick admission as volunteers had been due to the course before us being lost at sea on the way to Trinidad and the one before that on the way home. If only they could get courses there and back there was logic in using Trinidad, just as the RAF used Canada for flying training; there were no air-raids or bad weather to interrupt the flying schedules.

As we were drawing kit at Lee-on-Solent we were told to parade with all kit just after the evening meal. After passing muster, we were put into trucks which trundled us down to Fareham station. This seemed stupid, because no line goes anywhere known to man from Fareham. Still, of course, no-one had told us where we were bound, 'for security reasons'. We started to wonder whether, having been bombed, the Fleet Air Arm airfield at Ford, Sussex (now a postwar prison) had been converted for training for us.

But no; the few coaches into which we were crammed were destined to spend the night being shunted on to the back of first this train and then that and we had no idea where we were going in the blackout. In the early hours of the morning, one chap thought, taking a peep through the blind, that he had recognised Crewe. Eventually in a cold wet dawn we were unloaded on to a quay recognisably (we had all seen pictures of the Liver Building) in Liverpool. We were alongside a great liner painted naval grey – the biggest floating thing I had ever seen – and we were told to go aboard. There we learned that she was *Georgic*, the trans-atlantic liner, former pride of the White Star Line (forced into amalgamation with Cunard as a condition for Government loans for constructing the *Queens* a few years earlier).

Our quarters were storerooms down over the screws, cramped, damp and stuffy as hell. Anyway, just room for all of us to sling our hammocks at night. We learned that during the voyage we would be deployed as U-Boat lookouts and AA (Boer War Maxim guns!) Gunners on a Watch on, Watch off basis.

We were below decks receiving orders about this watch-keeping whilst she sailed and I recall that we were childishly annoyed at missing taking a farewell look at Scouse and England. Just before dark we met a large convoy coming out of the Clyde and took our place in the formation. A very impressive sight, a wartime convoy – thirty or more ships not far apart in four or five columns waddling along in seemingly perfect precision. After dark, our escort of a few destroyers and corvettes came out from Loch Ewe.

So we settled down to four hours freezing up top, four hours eating and sleeping, which lasted for about ten days. (It took a long time to cross the Atlantic; speed that of the slowest ship, continuous zig-zag steering – to make life difficult for U-Boats taking aim – and a devious route.) We soon recognised by the cold that we were doing the northerly route, close to Iceland and Greenland. We never saw either, but small icebergs were ten a penny around the sixth day.

Only later did we realise that we were put upon unnecessarily with our 'four on – four off' routine. This is only adopted normally for a few days in real emergencies in the Navy, because for prolonged periods it causes exhaustion. I suppose it was a Merchant Navy Captain making sure he got good use out of his RN passengers. All the other passengers were civilian, mostly wealthy Jews on the run from Europe. They not only clarified that they did not want to know Naval Ratings but complained to the Captain about us going through their (still luxury) parts of the ship, which we had to do to get to our stations, but he still paraded us and ordered that we get through passenger spaces as inconspicuously as possible! On night watches we liked to loiter on the boat decks, where in spite of the winter deck chairs for lounging still stood. The number of passengers using them for copulation was phenomenal; maybe they thought they must not miss a chance on what might be their last night! Maybe it was having spectators from the Navy which had caused the complaints.

Anyway, the food was good – better than naval shorebases. It was a pleasure to know that the roughest weather did not make one sick and we had some of that. The grandeur of a convoy labouring through a storm in the winter Atlantic stands out as one of the sights of a lifetime.

About two days after the weather turned from tolerable to positively balmy, we came into Glassy Bay, Bermuda. Glassy Bay was the Naval Base. Barely had we anchored than it was realised *Georgic* had only come into Bermuda to drop our lot before going on to New York. (We had left convoy about a day previously.) An extraordinary cross between a tug-boat and a sight-seeing launch for tourists came alongside. Thick black smoke poured from its disproportionably large stack. We were ordered to board her with kit. At first we assumed she was doing wartime duty as a transfer tender, but she headed for the open sea. All alone, she was going to take us to Trinidad! I only wish I could remember the name of this gallant geriatric of the maritime world. It turned out that she was a ferry steamer on the St Lawrence River in peacetime and her very pleasant crew were thrilled to bits to be riding the green sea. Only one of them do I remember with any clarity, and not his name. He was half-cast Red Indian/negro – gaunt, bushy eyebrows, sorrowful look, thin as a rake and the biggest hooked hooter in Christendom. Marvellous string of stories, none of which I recall, and the best repertoire of card tricks anyone ever saw. He could make four people make a hand of bridge, he sitting behind one and seeing no other cards. After bidding and playing one hand (with us neither bidding nor play was expert!) all cards were put face down on the table. He would then correctly identify every card on the table, and he had neither shuffled nor dealt. RIP. After dropping us at Port of Spain, she sailed on another journey to the Cape, and we later heard that she had sunk with all hands: not the enemy, just that her boilers fell through the bottom of the ship in the South Atlantic swell.

She rolled like the devil all the way through the glasslike Sargasso Sea, but was gorgeous after *Georgic*. No watches: 'Who's scared of submarines? they couldn't make a torpedo run shallow enough to touch us.' Hot steamy total idleness, with the best food in the world and, in spite of our lowly status in the nautical code, we were treated like first class passengers.

All good things come to an end and after plodding for an idyllic ten days, for that is what she took, we came through the Bocas, Venezuela to starboard, Trinidad to port, and dropped the hook in Port of Spain, there to return to naval discipline, with a Gunner's Mate ordering us into the lighter alongside. For all intents and purposes, we had come under the wing of HMS *Goshawk*, the Navy's name for the air station at Piarco, about twelve miles east of Port of Spain. Life there can start another chapter.

Chapter 4

Flying Training

AS WE DISEMBARKED from the lighter and unloaded our gear, we were met by a line of American built trucks with locally constructed timberwork bodies. These had open sides with rolled-up waterproof flaps to more or less keep out tropical rainstorms and lines of bench seats down the middle and both sides. They were to become our familiar means of getting to and from the airfield from camp and to Port of Spain from Piarco camp for our 'runs ashore'. The drivers were all West Indian civilians and vied with each other to see who could scare us most and who could hold the record time from Port of Spain Post Office to the camp gates. We, I suppose stupidly, encouraged this by keeping the times and always telling the drivers their standard of achievement. Such was their skill, never once during our months there was there an 'incident' involving a 'jitney' as we came to call the vehicle. The journey was along roads only partially asphalted, through crowded suburbs of Port of Spain, and one or two small towns. There was only just room for two cars to pass and the road was always well cluttered with people, donkeys, ox-carts and so on. I seem to recall that the record in our time represented something like 55 m.p.h.

HMS *Goshawk* consisted of well-built timber hutting with a big parade ground just inside the main gates with the flagstaff and Wardroom (Officers' mess) beyond the Guardroom on the left as you came in. A large canteen/messhall for ratings the opposite side of the parade and later a cinema/dance hall was also built there. Across the far side of the parade from the gate were the 'messdecks' for us. These consisted of open-sided huts (above waist level) covered in with fly-mesh, elevated on timber posts about two feet from the ground. At ground level at one end was a shower room/loo ('the heads') connected to the main hut by steps. They proved very cool and airy to live in; there is a continuous breeze in Trinidad which blew through the huts.

Our every-day uniform was the standard 'flannel' (blue bordered square necked drill shirt worn in all uniforms), white shorts and stockings, which between them left only a marginal view of the knees, and black boots or white shoes for formal parades. Being wartime, we were not issued with the best shore-going uniform – white drill sailor suit with integral blue jean collar and blue trim at wrist and waist. Instead we only had the tropical working uniform of peacetime – a white (had to be bleached a lot to achieve that) coarse duck jumper and trousers with which were worn the standard collar and silk used with our serge uniforms at home. Pride got the better of most of us however; luckily there was a 'snippy' at *Goshawk* (a rating who would do tailoring for a consideration) and in no time we all got ourselves the smarter uniform. This got formal recognition to the extent that we were required to wear it for Sunday Divisions (Church Parade).

The working day at *Goshawk* was a novelty to us, but not unusual for tropical shore stations. It began at 4 a.m. with a cup of 'kye', after which we did four hours' work before breakfast. (Kye was the Navy's greatest invention: crude chocolate blocks containing all the original fat in the beans which commercial manufacturers remove. Flakes were scraped off with a seaman's knife from which cocoa was made in the ordinary way. It was especially popular on night watches on the exposed bridges of small ships in winter seas for its warmth-giving properties. If it were felt that even more were needed, a tot of rum could always be added. But I digress, we are in the tropics . . .)

One real pleasure in the heat of Piarco was a boon handed down to us from Nelson's time. In his day, the bane of life at sea was scurvy and they found that the vitamin intake available from citrus fruits was an antidote. Thus, whilst we were not short of vitamins in our diet, the tradition persisted whereby a vast wooden tub of lime juice stood by the entrance door to the mess-hall and we were encouraged to dip our mugs as much as we wanted. There was always a large block of ice floating in it. It was very good at all times, but particularly so on the day 'after the night before'.

After breakfast, another four hours' work and that completed the day's work unless one were on duty (every fourth day). In the afternoon one could go 'ashore', if not on duty, or catch up on overdue sleep. The latter was quite often a necessity; if you had returned 'aboard' at midnight or after, 'tropical routine' could be a little telling. Life ashore seemed idyllic. The local rum was very good, if you like the dark and heavy stuff. I seem to remember that Myers' top grade was only a (Trinidad) dollar (25p) and bottles of the fiercer fuels were about half that. Neither clothing nor foods were rationed; it seemed like paradise. Being a small island, about forty miles by fifteen, it was the aim of most 'nice' girls to get married out of the island with which they had become bored, so we became targets. This we appreciated greatly, but they stuck grimly to the effective tactic of not granting the larger favours before being led to the altar. In a pre-Pill era there was no local sympathy for the fool who got left behind with a souvenir of her courtship.

The local society was a wonderful mixture of all the world's strata and races. On the European side there were some very upstage land and business families who had been there for generations. Most, even the non-British (e.g. German, French, Spanish) sent their young to the UK or Canada for secondary education in peacetime. There was a big Indian community, largely shopkeepers and peasant farmers, who mixed least with other communities. There were the original indigenous 'Indians', poor, hirsute with a dignified and fearful ugliness, rather despised by all. Most were of African origin, brought in as slaves generations ago, just as the Indians had come in later as contract labour on the plantations. They spanned all levels of the social strata from prominent lawyers and public servants down to our jitney drivers and down again to plantation workers and the drunken unemployed. One must not forget the significant Chinese population, also descendants of contract labourers: rich traders and the community who shared with the Indians the provision of the island's needs for technician work, mechanics, and so on. The bulk of the population were a result of intermarriage and other interbreeding across all the racial and social stratum boundaries; a wonderful human cocktail it was.

My particular friends, Bill Orwin and Alistair McLean, and I quickly made friends with two families of Port of Spain through their sons. Cecil Eckel, of the German strain of the community in Trinidad for three generations, was a cadet trainee for the RAF. The Trinidad Air Cadets learned how to fly and did basic training as 'day-boys' at our establishment. He had a pal, Harry Ross, who was in the local Sea Cadets. Cecil's family lived in an old-style colonial house in Port of Spain near the Queen's Park Savannah. He had wonderful, hospitable parents, strict Roman Catholics, and a very pretty sister, Elaine. Harry's parents were equally like fosters to us; they lived in a hill suburb above the town in a modern 'planter-style' bungalow. They had been in the Island for two generations, coming from Edinburgh ancestry, and were Church of England/lapsed Presbyterian. They had two daughters, Jean and Peggy, also pretty ornamental. Our life ashore revolved around these families – it reached the stage when umbrage was taken if it were heard that we had been into Port of Spain and had not called. Almost invariably, it was heard, too; the Port of Spain social circuit was like a small village's and little was secret. To us English of those days it was a surprise that the daughters of well-to-do families all worked. Elaine was in the Post Office, Peggy and Jean in the National Provincial Bank. Elaine had a friend who was a telephone operator, which could be embarrassing as well as an interesting source of local gossip, because she was a keen listener in – sometimes participator – in conversations she handled. I remember once phoning someone to make a date when in chipped Elaine's friend, who recognised all the voices, to say, 'But you can't do that tonight, because you're taking Elaine and me to the Country Club Dance'!

One of the sons of the Pereira family, whose Ball is mentioned later, was another of the Trinidad air cadets. We met his brother at the Ball and I was to meet him yet again in the late seventies when I visited Trinidad as part of Metal Box; he had become Chairman of Metal Box Trinidad Ltd.!

The Country Club was the upstage place to meet friends, rather like a poor man's Tollygunge in Calcutta, but catering for the elite. Once the Committee were made aware that we were going to be officers after our course, we were all given honorary membership. Our other 'club', when we wanted to be bachelors, was the 'Sailors' Rest' in Port of Spain. As there were few naval ships calling, we had it virtually to ourselves. No girls allowed in, just like the one in Portsmouth, but here the rum flowed like Niagara.

Bill, Mac and myself were by habit and inclination paired on our outings with Peggy, Elaine and Jean respectively. There was no great intensity in the three relationships, except perhaps between Elaine and Mac, and we generally hunted as a gang with their brothers and their girlfriends along as well. We danced at night to superb calypso bands and hired cars and went to the lovely beaches on the east coast by day, or up into the 'mountains' to picnic by and swim in the beautifully cool streams. We all lost touch after the War, but I got a little news of the Rosses in the mid-seventies, when I met Harry whilst I was in Trinidad for Metal Box. He was manager of a big transport firm (if such can exist on a small island!); the parents had died not long after the War; Peggy and Elaine had both married Americans and produced large families.

They both called on us when I was up at Cambridge after the War. On the boat over for a holiday they had seen a picture of me putting our toddler son, Colin, into an afternoon creche run once a week for undergraduates' children at the Round Church, the caption indicating that I was at Caius College. From the College they got our address and came hot-foot round. My wife was none too pleased when these glamorous bits of her husband's past turned up to catch her in working togs doing the house and took her for the servant!

Enough of the social scene – you will think we had no work to do, when in fact it was a very hard course. Before moving to that, though, a word about the calypso cult in those days. The British West Indies had not been discovered then by the USA tourist and everything, particularly the calypso, was very simple. No steel bands, they were yet to be invented, but simple beat music to which was sung the singer's own composition – usually a comment on current affairs in outrageously salacious terms. At Carnival time there was a competition between the masters for the best song in the Carnival processions. Each master would set up his own booth in town where all of society would sit in judgement – all very democratic; you could see the Governor perched alongside the road sweeper at such times. Great names the masters had – The Lion and The Growler, being two I remember.

Our first morning, we were taken down to the airfield, some ten minutes jitney ride from camp. It was odd to visit Trinidad some thirty-five years later and see that absolutely no trace of the camp remained – even our lovely cinema had sunk into jungle or vanished – whilst the airfield has developed out of recognition into an international airport handling jumbo-jets. Then it was an airstrip facing east-west with three little huts to the north grandly titled 'Pilots' Room', 'Radio Room' and 'Briefing Room'.

The aircraft were lined up between them and the runway. There was one Walrus and a Swordfish and dozens of Percival Proctors and Blackburn Sharks. Proctors were adapted pre-War private light planes for radio and navigation exercises. Sharks seemed more businesslike, being torpedo-bombers recently replaced in the Fleet by Swordfish and the coming Albacore. They were bi-planes and seemed very big to us; we did all our bombing training and longer range navigation, search and radio exercises in them.

The pilots were a funny lot; the Navy were so short of them that for unimportant work like training Observers and TAGs (Telegraphist Air Gunners), they recruited middle-aged men who could fly small planes, contracted for strictly non-operational service. Most were from the pre-War idle rich who had learned to fly and a nice comfortable war they had in Trinidad. (Laurence Olivier was incidentally one of this brigade, but served at Worthy Down, where Vivien Leigh his wife was very popular – pity I never met her!) The most eccentric we had was Lt. Malet, a Frenchman, who had claims to having been a French Air Force hero of World War I. He would never take off without first urinating on the rudder of his Shark. We used to get hung up on training schedules if he was involved in short exercises, taking up a series of pupils in succession, because he ran out of piss. We used to buy oranges and soft drinks for him from the motley vendors who crept through the primitive security wiring to serve us, in order to keep up Malet's necessary fluid balance. 'I no pee, I no fly!'

Another of the pilots who flew us around was every bit as much a character as Malet. He was at that time also a Lieutenant RNVR and was English. Generally he was known as 'The Mad Major' – he had achieved that rank and some distinction in the Royal Flying Corps in World War I. He had subsequently achieved greater notoriety and an appearance before the Beak by flying a light plane through the arches of all the Thames bridges in London. (This he repeated in his sixties after World War II, because 'I was bored'.) The name was Chris Draper. I was later to get to know him well at Donibristle where he had turned up as a pilot in the Communications Squadron. There he postured as a raging queer and none of us ever knew whether this was part of his considerable acting skill put to use to be different, or whether he was a genuine case.

The most popular plane was the Walrus, because it was the only Fleet Air Arm type in which smoking was permitted. It was an amphibian – the standard plane for battleships and cruisers – and the crew sat 'indoors' instead in ye olde open cockpits. It had one bad point. As with all planes of the time, the aerial wire was spooled and run out through an insulated tube in the aircraft's side once airborne – and woe betide he who forgot to wind up again before landing. Connection to the radio was made by a clamp screwed onto the wire after unreeling. In a Walrus, the top of the tube had to be fairly high to be above the waterline when she was floating; this put the clamp in a position which left a run of wire past the operator's left elbow. If you accidentally touched a naked elbow (easy in our tropical rig) on the wire whilst transmitting you got a nasty shock and burn.

The Fleet Air Arm had not heard of radio-telephony (i.e. speech), such as the RAF used, in those days; all was in morse code. Our sets were crude: no push-button frequency changes; we carried sets of coils in boxes for each frequency and those in the set had to be changed each time the order came to make the change. The set was in two boxes, the black-faced master oscillator and the brown-faced power amplifier. Both had to go through this surgery and then be coaxed back into communication with the ground by much twiddling of knobs and watching of ammeters. We carried a code book which abbreviated words, phrases and whole sentences (e.g. Request permission to land on) into groups of four letters. You got to remember the more common ones, but it was almost a whole new language and no-one I ever met was totally fluent in it; even Leading Telegraphist Tomkin, our tutor and the ground operator for our exercises, used the code book occasionally for the out-of-ordinary message.

One day Tomkin was crewed with Malet's plane. Before take-off, Tomkin asked Malet to hold the unspooled aerial wire and to hold it up off the ground over his head 'to test the radio'. He then jumped into the Walrus and pressed the transmitting key, Malet jumping three feet into the air . . .

'What the fucking hell are you doing, you fucker!'

The enemy were expected to know the codes, so any message of high security had also to be cyphered and we had to learn that too. A quaint machine was used in which was inserted the card of the day containing a mass of figures and letters; the man the other end had (hopefully) the same card. Moving sliders with letters and numbers over the card in accordance with the composed message revealed card letters or numbers which were used instead for transmission. By this means, the letter 'X' for example, would not always have the same replacement as it recurred in the message but a different one, depending where it occurred.

Our radio exercises consisted of contacting base in code, then perhaps going over to conversing with Tomkin in cypher, which he preferred so he could quiz us about last night ashore and such things without the supervising officers being aware. They only inspected our radio pads (what we had actually taken down) for accuracy. Tomkin could be openly 'out of procedure' when he wanted and our stupidity over-tried him. He had nothing to lose but his Killick, being another pensioner called back for the War. Signal traffic on a frequency changing exercise under him would be something like this:-

Ground(in code): 'Change to xxx cycles.'

Plane (in code): 'Complying.'

long pause

Plane: very faintly calls ground and in code asks what strength is its signal.

Ground: AAA (the code for 'plain language follows').

'Believe I have gone deaf. Try retune your power amplifier and recall.'
Plane: calls again fainter and off the frequency.
Ground (in code): 'Readjust frequency.'
Plane: calls again, still faint.
Ground (in code): 'Retune Power Amplifier.'
Plane: calls again; barely audible so far off frequency.
Ground: AAA. 'Silly bugger leave your oscillator alone. The Power Amplifier is the brown bastard' and so on . . .

In fact, in the end we got quite slick at frequency changes, cyphering and general communication; we had to. By the end of the course, the sort of exercise we did was to leave one ship (representing own carrier) to search for another, which could take an hour or so. Meanwhile 'own ship' would signal in cypher her own changes of course and speed so that, if you could read the signals, you could maintain a navigational plot of her as well as the one for the plane. When you found the enemy you had to change frequency and cypher up a report of her position, course and speed. She would then keep changing course and speed which all had to be reported in cypher as well as being covered in a third navigational plot of her movements. This would last for an hour or so and if 'own ship' felt that your cleverness was enough to avoid being overloaded, they would order a few more frequency changes and do some more course and speed changing. Eventually the great relief order would come, 'Return to own ship.' So, hoping the navigation plots were right one bravely gave the pilot the interception course to find 'own ship' and hoped to find her. It seemed magical when one actually did, but one returned totally exhausted!

Bombing exercises were the greatest fun. The Observer was also the bomb aimer for 'High Level Bombing'. During my operational service it was a technique abandoned in favour of dive-bombing which was more accurate and did not give the enemy the sitting target of stooging along at about 80 m.p.h. straight and level, as necessitated in 'High Level'. We had a hatch about two foot square in the bottom of the plane in which one mounted a bombsight. This was essentially a pair of parallel wires along which a small blob could slide. One fed into it data on wind direction and speed, height, ballistic characteristic of the bombs in use and the wires then angled from the fore-and-aft line of the plane and the blob came to the right position along the wires so that with your eye to the sight, you would hit what was under the blob when you pushed the bomb release tit.

Communication with the pilot was via that great invention, the Gosport tube. This was a pair of garden hoses from pilot to Observer. One tube had a hot water bottle neck mouthpiece at the pilot's end, the other at the Observer's. From the flying helmet earpieces we had a bifurcated tube like a stethoscope which terminated in a piece of aluminium tube which one inserted into the non-mouthpiece hosepipe end in one's cockpit position. Besides talking to the pilot reasonably well, the facility allowed one to annoy him if one inadvertently (?) put one's mouthpiece end out into the slip-stream. He got more than a puff in his ears!

So, for bombing, one had to talk the pilot into a straight line on to the target (not easy if across the wind, which we had to learn) by simple commands like 'Left, left' or 'Right.' (We must have learned this from the RAF because I have always marvelled that the Navy did not go 'port' and 'starboard' to high level bomb. It was always hell with Lt. Malet, who was not a pilot who could hold a straight course any better than containing his impatience. After two or three abandoned runs, one would be giving him the careful 'Left, left' . . . 'Right' and just as the target was coming into the wires he would bank away and shout furiously into the Gosport,

'First you say go left, then go right; which fucking way you want me to go? Next time if you not go straight, I go home.'

It was much more fun diving on the fishing boats and dropping oranges on them; at that we got quite good shots.

The arts of navigation, or rather the requirements, have already been dwelt upon. The first thing was that we never had planes with a sufficient range for us to need astro-navigation; it was all dead-reckoning – the drawing of vectors representing aircraft speed and direction being added to those of the wind. Essentially the most usual 'chart' we used was a plain piece of paper with a compass rose on it. The first thing to do when airborne was to find the wind speed and direction – you could never rely on the Met. Officer's estimate (except in Trinidad but there you had to find the wind anyway as part of any exercise). To do this you dropped a smoke float (but only if over the sea! over land you picked a landmark beneath you). Simultaneously you started your stopwatch and told the pilot to make a steady rate of turn through 180 degrees (i.e. to a reciprocal course); after two minutes on the watch he was told to do the same again. (Lt. Malet: 'Can't you make mind up which fucking way you want to go?') You then took the timings of the smoke float coming up on the beam and on the quarter. Plotting all that revealed the wind data: annoying after all that effort (and known all too well by Malet) that the wind in Trinidad was always 090 degrees – due east – at 15 knots. Later one dropped another smoke float and took a back bearing on it as a check that one had got the answer right. In fact after a time flying over the sea one learned to make a good estimate of surface wind speed and direction from its visual appearance.

It did not always work out right; one of the commonest errors was to give the pilot the reciprocal of the course one wanted, as a result of reading off the opposite side of one's protractor. Equally easy was it for the pilot to steer the reciprocal of the course he was given by setting his compass to the opposite side to that intended. Thus when inevitably the mistake came to light, there could be fierce debate as to who had been the clot. Basically, it was always the Observer's fault because he was trained to believe that the pilots could not be relied upon in such matters (not far off the truth in Trinidad) and it was always his responsibility to check that the pilot had set the right course. One friend, Maurice Brown, went missing with his crew for this reason. They came down through cloud to find themselves in Venezuela and under orders from the local Air Force to land. Under the regulations of war, if you stray into the territory of a neutral, they are bound to intern you for the duration.

Much was the joy when a week or two later they turned up after much diplomatic pulling of strings had secured their release. He was one of the more respected members of the course, not because of behaviour but he was older than most of us and had a certain dignity even when quite pie-eyed. As a result, his nickname became 'The Colonel'. At first he disowned it, as inappropriate to a schoolmaster – he claimed to have only joined the Fleet Air Arm as something to do after being sacked for drinking his pupils' milk one morning when the vast thirst of a major hangover had overcome him.

Besides learning to do the telegraphy in the air we had to learn air gunnery. In a normal aircrew carrying an air-gunner, he would look after both these functions, but in some types of aircraft (two-seat fighters) he was not carried. Also, if TBR (Torpedo-Bomber-Reconnaissance) aircraft were required to fly extra long range, the Observer's normal seat was replaced by a supplementary fuel tank and he sat in the TAGs seat with it for company. At least it grumbled less when you got lost! For the air firing exercises, the Swordfish would tow a drogue (like an airfield windsock) over the sea for us to shoot at and in succession several of us in Sharks would shoot at it (or at each other, if we got the procedure wrong – no damage, we were not good enough shots for that!).

Another of the arts we had to learn may have had historical importance which makes it worthy of mention. Taking aerial photographs is an essential intelligence activity, either for assessing damage to the foe after attacking him or for getting information on his dispositions before having a go at him. (Summed up by some as getting shot down trying to record what would have shot you down on the great day of the attack.) This was another task entrusted to the Observer, and therefore learned in Trinidad.

A large RAF standard camera was used; I cannot remember its model designation, nor its specification. It may have been suitable for use in large and palatial bombers, but was an awkward brute to handle in a FAA open cockpit. The easy exercise was the taking of oblique pictures, holding the camera over the side of the cockpit. Easy that is if you are handy at holding a thing the size of a portable television set steady enough in a 90 knot slipstream to take a clear picture on a pretty slow exposure. Just like taking snapshots, but on the basis of steam hammer nut-cracking.

The difficult game was making mosaics, as we called them: this meant flying in straight lines, taking vertically downwards views of the ground at intervals so timed that the edge of one shot only just overlapped that of its predecessor (so as to be economical with film). The camera was mounted in the bomb-aimer's hatch for this. It had a motorised attachment to operate the shutter and film wind-on at set intervals. The first requirement of the exercise was to fix a course to steer so that the track along the ground was that intended. This demanded very precise wind determination by the Observer and ability by the pilot to steer an accurate course, holding the plane level at all times in spite of the buffeting involved in flying at our levels in the tropics. Naturally, the start had to be precisely over the chosen start datum on the ground. The Observer had to calculate the distance on the ground represented to the plane's speed over the ground. (Speed over the ground would only be accurate if the wind finding were accurate; barometric correction of the altimeter had to be accurate in order to know the frame size.) All in all, it was an exercise making the highest demands on navigational skills and, please remember, when you had done one line of photographs, you then had to repeat the exercise for the next line, ensuring that its strip of pictures would only just overlap the strip for the first line. Unfailingly, you took back to base uncontrovertible evidence on the extent to which the necessary skills had failed to be displayed.

The historical aspect of this, I mentioned at the beginning, was that our mentors had the imagination to set each of us different bits of the island to cover, so that by the time the last course had been through Trinidad, most, if not all, of the island had been covered and the result is the first complete aerial survey of Trinidad. Sometimes the Navy shows quite uncharacteristic capability to use its imagination.

Memories are much clearer of our free time than of the training. There was the magnificent beanfeast when the cinema was opened, when we were all allowed to bring in our shoresides friends to the party. Their Lordships of the Admiralty had provided a sum for this construction, but in terms of what it would have cost in the UK. In Trinidad, it provided a magnificent hall with full stage and dance floor as well as the cinema arrangements. For the opening we had a (thankfully) brief visit from the Governor and his wife (I suppose one of them opened it officially) and the Trinidad Police Band, the best band in the West Indies, apart from being one of the smartest of military bands on parade. And the rum, it flowed and flowed.

A feature of evenings on rum seemed to be a lack of hangover the following morning, but a noticeable continuation of inebriation. We had Sunday Divisions the morning after the 'opening' and I recall our lines gently swaying like palms in the breeze as we stood at attention for inspection. Leading Telegraphist Tomkin distinguished himself on the way to the parade. Not noticing Lt. Bush, he passed without saluting.

'Come here,' said Bush, 'Just who do you think you are?'

'POW, sir,' says Tomkin.

'What the hell do you mean by that?'

'Finished my time in '37, sir, and went ashore. Now I'm pulled back for the duration and stuck here, sir. Prisoner of war, sir.'

Bush was not to be outdone:

'Commander's report, Tomkin.'

No messing about with Tomkin, though, in for a penny, in for a pound. Having worked up his party spirit with Bush, it spilled over when we got down to Mattins in our new cinema, which was also to serve as church. Our Padre like to sing the versicles and responses and adopted a curious warbling tremolo for his part. When it came to 'The Lord be with you', Tomkin, in perfect mimicry of him and at the top of his voice, chanted: 'And with thee, Chum!' Finally, the service ended with the National Anthem in full. Throughout, fully audible against our fainthearted efforts, Tomkin was to be heard doing the Red Flag fortissimo. It was a week or two before he reappeared to conduct our signalling exercises.

Another major beano was a big Ball at the Pereira family mansion. They represented the top peak of Island society, the family having invented, or purloined, the recipe for Angostura Bitters in ages past. Not many of us got invitations and most of them declined as the Ball was the night before the start of our course-end examinations. I remember little of the party but vaguely recall a feeling of shame that our group put more effort into enjoying themselves than into comporting themselves. The outcome of that was rather serious; six of us who attended failed the papers set the next morning and we were the only failures. Thus, we had to face watching the rest of the course pack and depart for home a few days later, whilst we had to be confined to camp to revise and retake our papers a fortnight later. We were lucky to get this chance instead of just being sent to sea as ratings. In part this must have been the charity of our officers, many of whom had been at the Ball and knew why we had failed; in part it must have been that having lost two successive Courses, the Navy could not afford to throw away any potential Observers.

I was glad we did not have practical exercises in a skill which Observers have to have if sent to a battleship or cruiser carrying a plane. This is to play a major part in the manoeuvre of being picked up by the ship. I am everlastingly grateful that I was not sent to such an appointment. The Walrus (the standard machine for such ships) is a biplane, the lower of the wings being level with the top of the hull. The engine is slung between the mainplanes, facing aft so that the airscrew pushes the plane instead of pulling. For a landing out at sea, the 'Slick landing' technique was adopted. By this, the ship took a sharp turn thus flattening the waves on the side its stern had moved away from. (This calm patch is called the Slick.) Quickly, the Walrus must land and hook on to the ship's crane hook to be lifted clear of the water before the surface returns to normal. If you miss the hook, you taxi round again, but have much rougher conditions for the subsequent attempt. You will have guessed it; it is the Observer who must get hooked on. To do this, as soon as the plane has landed, he climbs through the upper hatch and from there on to the leading edge of the upper mainplane. If he slips back from here – and it is wet, slippery and rocking – he becomes mincemeat as he goes through the airscrew. With one hand he lifts out the hoisting strop and ring from its stowage in the wing; he calls instructions to the pilot over the engine noise to con him towards the crane hook. At the right moment he must reach up and grab the hook and get it through the ring and avoid being shaken off as the plane is jerked from the water. Rarely is there a second shot if the hook is missed at the last minute because that has left too little time for the crane operator to jump the hook clear of the airscrew. We were content to finish with only a theoretical knowledge of the procedure.

In due course we resat our exams and passed with flying colours as was appropriate. We then waited in camp at a few hours' notice for any ship which might call into Port of Spain and pick us up for home.

Quite suddenly, the call came and with all our kit we boarded the jitney for a last dash into the town. We left as we arrived, by a lighter to a ship out at moorings. In fact, she had only dropped a hook and had not moored as she was only in for as little time as it took to pick us up. She dropped a cargo net down her side to us and had a good laugh at us struggling to get kit, hammocks and selves up the netting. She turned out to be *Highland Princess*, a passenger/refrigerated cargo ship of Royal Mail Lines, homeward bound from Rio with a cargo of good red meat and many young ladies from the British community who were coming home to volunteer for the forces.

Compared with those who passed the exams the first time, we had done well. They went back in conditions like those in *Georgic* outbound. We shared cabins (but not with the ladies) and had to do only occasional U-Boat watches. Our main duties were to teach the young ladies morse code and the tying of knots (and anything else they were wanting to learn!). She was a fast ship for those days, being capable of 20 knots, so we were thought capable of getting past the U-Boats without being in convoy or escorted, but what a route we had to take! From tropical heat we grew colder and colder as we went past Greenland and through the Denmark Strait to leave Iceland to the south. If I remember aright, it took about a fortnight to get back into the Minches and so into the Clyde.

On arrival at Gourock, our days as ratings were numbered. All we had to do now was go to Lee-on-Solent to report (we had no officer or petty-officer in charge of us *en route*, for the first time) before going on leave to buy officers' kit and await appointment. One had grown quite fond of ratings' uniform and it felt a little as though a stage part were growing to its end. The Customs at Gourock were harassed by the RTO (Railway Transport Officer) to let us through unchecked because he had a special train for Portsmouth and Chatham just about to depart. (Pretty good from Gourock Pier?!) This was also good news because we were well loaded with dutiable items of which there was a shortage in England.

As luck would have it, the train arrived at Olympia Station, of all places, during the following morning. There the Chatham part of the train was detached and went on. We were told that it would be some two hours before we got a locomotive to haul us to Portsmouth, so could leave the station for that period. Just nice time to call at Princes Gate and announce my arrival and give warning of my likely return on leave next day and to dump all my dutiables and heavier items from my kit bag.

At Lee, we were in time to do station 'joining routine' that evening. This had to be done even if you were only to be on their books for ten minutes. It was a matter of rudimentary kit inspection and filling in a form about next-of-kin and a medical – a look round your mouth with a torch by the quack and a glance at your genitals. (If you look capable of eating and fucking, you're good enough.) After breakfast next morning, 'leaving routine' (the same thing in reverse, complete with the same doctor) was conducted and we were discharged on leave. End of training; after leave, probably serious business!

Footnote on Trinidad: Our period there saw the beginning of the biggest change the Island of Trinidad experienced in the last couple of hundred years – colonisation by the USA! During our training Churchill and Roosevelt had one of their historic meetings on a battleship. The United Kingdom was at that time, like perhaps at all other times, desperately short of small ships for convoy escort duty. The USA was keen to support our war effort just so long as they kept out of the War and could make a few bucks by so doing, and they had masses of World War I destroyers in 'mothballs', of no visible use to anyone. Thus the deal was struck: fifty useless destroyers for the RN in return for rights for the USA to set up military bases in the British West Indian colonies – something they had always hankered after, in pursuit of the gospel according to Munro. The destroyers proved utterly unreliable in the deep sea, where they continuously broke down; they pitched and rolled in the calmest waters sufficiently to sicken the hardiest sea-dogs. In anything of a real Atlantic lop, they were almost uncontrollable. It is not thought that Churchill consulted the Navy about the deal any more than he did the inhabitants of the West Indies. One of Roosevelt's better cons!

During our latter weeks in Trinidad, up to then a very pleasantly unsophisticated place, the advance guard for setting up the first US base arrived – a battalion of the US Marine Corps. No country could have sent better ambassadors. They were the cream of the US peacetime forces – it was to be nearly another year before they were at war. We got on with them extremely well and shared Piarco airfield with them until they built their own base. They were proud to claim that their Corps was very much modelled on our Royals. Trinidad citizenry were intensely pro-British at that time and fearful that the great USA would come to dominate their lives; Churchill had to some extent sold them down the river. Thus all was not honey ashore for our friends in the US Marines and we did much to help them over the hurdle by being seen with them relaxing in Port of Spain. We had great all-day sporting contests with them. I recall the first time we beat them at baseball, and their first soccer victory over us. They were not so hot at cricket; a certain lack of patience with it, combined with a desire to use a cricket bat like that for baseball, was the problem. If they connected, the result was spectacular, but how rarely did they connect.

What staggered me was not just how profoundly the Americans affected the whole of Trinidadian life, but the speed at which it happened. I went back in *Indomitable* only months after the first big base was fully occupied and the whole atmosphere had changed. They had earned some local popularity for bringing in all the dollars they did; everything was going madly americanised. The calypso, that barometer of cultural development, had totally changed. It had been simple folk music, if with very salacious lyrics, commenting on events of the day such as Test Matches. One was composed shortly after the US arrival: 'Working for the Yankee Dollar', which went to extremes of anti-American leg-pulls. Quickly it was sent to the USA, given new pro-American lyrics and recorded with a sophisticated band; then re-exported to Trinidad. The calypso never regained its innocence.

The US Army and Navy brought in thousands of wives and families; they married many Trinidadians, so Trinidadians started to discover that it was easier and cheaper to visit USA rather than UK. After the War, so many Americans knew Trinidad, it was easy to found a monster new tourist industry.

Chapter 5

Becoming Operational

I CANNOT REMEMBER how long a leave we had on return from Trinidad; it seemed generous for those times, so I imagine it was about a fortnight. Most of it was spent in London, although a few days were taken at the small house near friends in Hove, which my mother had rented at family instigation so that she had somewhere to go when bombing sessions became too frequent. I saw little of my brothers; Sandy was at the Middlesex Hospital, Kenneth a private in the Hampshire Regiment and Ian still at school. My main girl friend, Jean Anstruther, had both joined the WRNS and found a new boy friend in the interim.

The main duty during leave was to obtain uniform; this I did at a small bespoke tailor opposite the Law Courts, who was subsequently bombed out of business. The tropical stuff was ordered from Austin Reed, who promised to send it on once I had an address as they could not supply it all in time. It must have got lost at sea on the way, because I never got it. Give them their due, it took me some four years to point out the deficiency to them, but they still gave me full credit for the missing items! A great irritation was that it was only a midshipman's uniform that I was buying whereas all the rest of the course, except Dicky Dyke and me, were becoming Sub-Lieutenants. It was a matter of age; Dicky and I were not yet twenty.

In due course the signal came: appointed Observer in 827 Squadron; proceed by 09.30 train Euston/Thurso on date stated and report to NOiC's office, Thurso. (This just to ensure that you would not know where exactly you were bound.) The Monday morning 09.30 from Euston was a standing naval special train for catching ships in Scapa Flow; it even had a name, 'The Jellicoe'. It reached Perth by evening and stopped there long enough for everyone to get their first meal. There were not many unscheduled stops *en route*. Then in the early morning it chuffed down the hill into the little station in Thurso which had never known such crowds – well, not since 1918.

NOiC's (Naval Officer in Command) office put us straight into requisitioned fishing drifters which took us out to the 'Depot Ship'. This was the old Union Castle liner *Dunluce Castle*, moored as she was in the middle of the Flow and used as the distributing point for personnel going to or from ships. The various ships' boats plied regularly to and from *Dunluce Castle*. There we got quite a good breakfast, and I learned that 827 was not in a ship, but at RNAS (RN Air Station) Hatston which was outside Kirkwall. I had met Colonel Brown – the wanderer to Venezuela – and Dicky Dyke at Thurso and discovered we were all going to 827. We were loaded onto another drifter for Kirkwall pier.

There was one good laugh as we waited for the drifter. Watching a Commander embark in the boat for his ship, we saw the ratings transferring his gear slip on the foot of the brow (the gangway over the side) and drop his tin trunk into the hoggin. Off it went in the quite brisk tide. The Naval Officer's tin trunk is a good article, being airtight with a well sealed lid, so the gallant Commander's trunk floated well and in spite of his wrath I doubt very much if any of his gear was wet by the episode. (I miss my trunk, which I kept for many years until we were misguided enough to lend it to a nephew to store books and he never saw fit to return it.)

A truck took us up to Hatston, just in time for a pre-lunch drink in the Wardroom. There we met our CO, Lt.Cdr. Sydney-Turner, the Senior Pilot Lt. Jock Read and the Senior Observer Lt. Leonard Williams, and all the other officers. There were quite a few newcomers; the Squadron had been decimated in a raid on Kirkenes when it had been aboard *Victorious*. This raid had been set up to help keep Stalin convinced that we were trying to help his war from Britain. Kirkenes was an iron-ore shipping port in northern Norway sufficiently important to the Germans to be well defended. They had had advance intelligence that 827 were coming. Now they were reforming at Hatston, awaiting a new ship to fly from, still in Albacores.

The Fairey Albacore was supposedly the latest improvement on the famous Swordfish. The crew stations were similar: pilot up front and the Observer behind him with the air-gunner abaft him. However, whilst the pilot had a separate cockpit as in the Swordfish, he was out of reach in that the cockpits were not adjacent in the Albacore, the Observer/Gunner one being some five feet behind the bulkhead forming the back of the pilot's space. The fuselage between them was occupied by a large fuel tank. No longer, as in the Swordfish, could the Observer tap the pilot on the shoulder or yell into his ear to attract attention; all contact depended on the Gosport tubes described in the previous chapter.

The Albacore had a more solid appearance, with a fuselage of sheet aluminium instead of doped linen fabric. The bi-plane wings look better strutted and wire braced than a Swordfish's, but were still in fabric. (Fabric should not be derided; it was good stout linen with the practical advantage that damage was easily patched at sea.) The biggest advantage of all was that the aircrew were all 'indoors', as compared with the Swordfish, being enclosed under perspex greenhousing. The Observer and Gunner got in through a small door in the side – very hard to squeeze through in full kit and with a 'Mae West' on – and had optional exits for emergencies: a hatch through the roof, the bomb-aiming hatch in the floor, the rear flap which the Gunner folded back to bring his rear gun into action. This was a .303 Vickers Gas-Operated, fed with drums of pre-loaded ammunition stowed all around the cockpit walls.

One convenience was a bottle to pee in if required. This was a rubber bag like a black bladder of a rugby football, attached to a chrome mouthpiece with a stopper. The biggest crime was to use it and forget to empty it on return and get the rigger to wash it out. If left with contents in, the rubber would perish whilst the contents matured; as soon as the next user grasped it, it would burst, leaving the most God-awful stink in the cockpit for days. (Observers seem worse than tom cats!) Author muses: 'I wonder how today's Navy provides for WRNS Observers?!'

Unlike the Swordfish with the Bristol Pegasus engine – about the most reliable radial there ever was; it was said you could still keep going with a cylinder shot off! – Albacores had the more powerful Bristol Taurus. This had a nice deep-throated roar when running well, and a whole Squadron of Albacores flying by sounded quite like RAF heavy bombers. It had more power than the Pegasus, but I do not remember that it allowed a larger bomb load. I seem to recall that both planes' basic load was four 500 lb bombs (or eight 250 lb) or four depth charges or, on the fuselage bomb rack, one 2000 lb bomb or a torpedo.

I think I am right in saying that the Taurus was the world's first sleeve-valved radial engine. Whether or not that is correct, there can be little doubt that it was the world's least reliable engine and our fitters had to labour hard to keep us airborne. (Fitters did the engine, riggers the airframe, armourers the guns and bombs.)

It was nice to be 'indoors' for doing one's navigation, albeit still perched on a little stool seat, with the chart-board (about two feet square) on one's knees. Quite often one did not bother to clip on the floor strap to one's parachute harness, as always was the case in open cockpits to avoid being chucked out altogether in a severe bump. It was, of course, another thing to remember if one decided to 'bale out'; that is not an effective manoeuvre if you are still linked to the deck! (This little strap had a good name, but it now quite escapes me.) The seat had provision for harnessing oneself in like the pilot; this was pretty necessary for resisting the forces of the arrestor wires on deck-landings, or those when being catapulted off.

We had a pleasant bunch of aircrews; as the Air-Gunners were all ratings, they lived separately and at this distance of time one cannot remember them as well as the fellow Observers and pilots. My usual A/G was Ed Ward, a big fellow from the Midlands, older than me with a rather avuncular attitude in spite of my superior rank. He was always even more pleasantly surprised than me when I found the way home – not I think in any disparagement of my capabilities; he thought it pretty miraculous that anyone could do it; so do I. Later, flying in another crew, he got wounded by the Japs and went ashore.

Pilots I remember: Sydney-Turner, the CO, was rather aloof and not too well-respected; there was an ever-growing suspicion amongst us that he was rather to the back of the queue when courage was doled out. Jock Read, the Senior Pilot: small man, dark angular face, hot-tempered with us juniors, very capable and had obviously been at the front of the just-mentioned queue. Bill Bailey, red-bearded, also straight striped (i.e. RN, not RNVR as we Hostilities Only people were, with wavy gold stripes on our jackets if we were above being midshipmen). Bill was an excellent pilot and seaman; he had started in the Merchant Navy and in the course of his training for that had been out to Australia and back in a sailing clipper. Richard Meakin: my first pilot, blond, flashy, hot-tempered but massive sense of humour and enjoyment of smut. I give him top marks as a driver. Terry Blank: serious and quiet (who wouldn't be after surviving forty days in a provisionless lifeboat after a torpedo-ing, seeing the whole boatload steadily die except for two others?). Robin Grant-Sturges: pre-War young man-about-town and Deb's Delight, first class pilot and Squadron mate. Charles 'Cass' (nickname from his initials C.A.S.S.) Gordon: suave Wyckhamist, elegant talker of very salacious bent, he had the most remarkable laugh; it was distinct separate syllables, almost as though he were speaking it: hee-uck, hee-uck, hyuck, hyuck . . ., rather like a duck with an aspirated quack.

Charles Gordon finished life as Clerk to the House of Commons and with a knighthood. Then there was 'Prangle' Pike, my last regular pilot in 827: enormously goodnatured; for him life was not just for living, he had to extract the last possible bit of enjoyment out of it. Similar, brighter and a better pilot but even more disreputable, Jock Smith: the Scot with the greatest capacity for the wine of his country – or anything else alcoholic – that could be imagined in a small man.

The Observers: Len Williams; the Senior Observer, was a charming and apparently easy-going fellow of the regular Navy, but in fact very professional and a good and just disciplinarian. He took part in all our parties as an equal; he was the only straight stripe among our 'O's. 'Colonel' Brown, I have already mentioned, as also Dicky Dyke, my fellow midshipman. Another junior was George Measures, a little older than us, coming from the last 'O' course before the two which were lost at sea. George was regarded as a man of the world as he had spent some time on the *Rive Gauche* in Paris studying music. He claimed acquaintance with Mistinguette, which put him right out of our class of experience. We later became great friends and I think he taught me a lot, but I cannot think for the life of me just what. He tried to teach me Gregorian Chant, to which he was devoted. Each morning he made me join him in chanting through the Squadron Daily Orders. Then there was 'Hutch' Hutchinson, RNVR but RN in outlook and of middle seniority. He was very competent and extremely pleasant. Whilst those I have not mentioned were perhaps more nondescript, we were a particularly happy bunch of companions and became a very well-knit team. Off the cuff, I cannot remember any of the others.

First reactions at Hatston were enjoyment at joining such a pleasant team and at the general comfort in which officers lived. It was a hutted camp, but the Wardroom consisted of a spacious ante-room with good drawing-room style furnishings and a bar. The Wardroom itself had long mess tables with immaculate linen and quite good three-course meals, although we all got bored with beef olives on which the Chef seemed to have a fixation. The evening meal could not be taken after 8.15, and well I remember the acute disappointment of arriving breathless from the three-mile run over the causeway from Kirkwall, bellies awash and gurgling with beer, only to discover it was beef olives yet again. At that time we were guarded by the Army and had a battalion of Gordon Highlanders to keep the Hun from bothering us.

One evening as we rushed the gates in pursuit of our beef olives, the

Jock sentry failed to salute. 'Colonel' Brown, a large man, taller even than the Jock, went up to him and, pointing to his shining new stripe, said, 'What do you think that is?' Quick as a flash came his answer: 'One wee thin wavering ring, Sorr.' Beef olives called too much that night for it to be practicable to take the matter further.

Another afternoon we had lent the Army one of the hangars in which to hold their Divisional Boxing Championships. It was a time when the Navy had little respect for the 'brown jobs', so a few of us went along to jeer. Blow me down, the first Army officer I bumped into was Freddy Bryan-Brown, a boxing adversary at school and a colleague in the 1st XV (we always said that we enjoyed the rest waiting for him to arrive for scrums). He was commissioned in the Middlesex Regiment – the celebrated 'Die-Hards', he incessantly reminded us. He too was nothing to do with the boxing contest; seconded to the Royal Artillery, he had come to guard us, arriving just that day. He was to reside out on the airfield perimeter with his Gunners and weapons, but mess with us, so he became a sort of adopted member of 827. The weapons he brought were one of the War's less brilliant inventions; they were batteries of rockets which, when fired, took up a length of wire which would hang on a little parachute. The idea was that Freddy would fire them in the path of any low level raiding plane and thus wreak havoc. Jock Smith remarked that even if well fired, it could not even be expected to bring down an Albacore; why had Freddy come from his famous regiment to play such games? Charles Gordon opined that maybe the famous regiment had thought that he might die too easy.

We gave a Wardroom party to the Gordons (the Jocks, not Charles' family) on the eve of their departure for more exciting things, which was a minor disaster for me. First, coming up from behind what I took to be Freddy, I delivered a great thump in the back, spilling his drink all down his best uniform, as I asked him what he would drink. It was not Freddy but the Gordons' senior Major and such men do not take kindly to being thus smitten by midshipmen. Eventually when all of us had had more than enough, I toddled off to my cabin. (Another joy in officership was a nice little cabin all to oneself.) Just asleep, I was rudely awakened by Colonel Brown, just as infuriated as he was inebriated:

'Your fucking Die-Hard chum has gone and died on my bed. Kindly remove him so that I can get some fucking kip and that's a fucking order.'

On with the greatcoat and off to the Colonel's boudoir to find Freddy out to the wide. Freddy is not tall, but had a generous circumference and was all solid meat. The Colonel was not disposed to help with the removal of other people's friends and to do it single-handed was no mean problem. In the end the Colonel relented and assisted in getting the corpse on to my back in a fair imitation of 'the fireman's lift'. Thus I staggered across the airfield to dump Freddy amongst his own fond soldiers. Next day he told me he had 'felt a little weary' so had taken a short rest on the Colonel's bed before trekking home 'but must have drifted off'!

It was just before this that Prangle Pike earned his nickname. (To prang is to crash or otherwise break an aeroplane.) Our aircraft were parked at dispersal points all around the periphery of the airfield as an air raid precaution. However, on the day we were to be inspected by the First Lord of the Admiralty, the planes had to be lined up in front of the hangars, with us to parade in front of them. It was a long walk out to most of them (or cycle ride, if you could borrow one); thus Sydney-Turner told Pike, who was duty Pilot, to bring in his plane as well as his own. A somewhat angry Pike revved up the Boss's Albacore and swung it out of its dispersal concrete circle a mite too swiftly; a wheel went off the edge and sunk into Orkney soft peat; the lower wing tip that side hit the ground and crunched. So Pike had to walk all the way back to tell the CO that he now had a bogged and bent plane. The infuriated S-T, as he was obviously called, then ordered him to bring in all the remaining planes. As he arrived with one of the last ones he swung it into line with a flourish, managing to hit two others already there. Total score four bent Albacores. So our Squadron had to parade for the great man (Mr A. V. Alexander, a Labour MP and very good First Lord) with twelve crews in front of eight planes. Thank God for the stupidity of politicians: no questions asked!

We spent our daytime and some nights on flying exercises, coming to terms with the Taurus's unreliability. It was a new experience, and a frightening one for me, to fly in close formation. Close meant just that: if you were fool enough to go out to the wing-tip of one machine, it would not be difficult to step across to the next. The machines moved up and down and banked to and fro in the air turbulence and it remains a matter of amazement that we had no collisions. I started praying most when we went into cloud and the others all disappeared and began to appreciate that pilots too had some essential skills. Unlike the RAF, we also flew close formation at night. The pilots could just see the blue haze of their neighbours' engine exhausts and unless close to the enemy, there were very dim blue 'formation' lights at the wing-tips. We had quite a lot of dive-bombing practice, another new experience for me. Fascinating as we peeled into the dive; in my plane one of the Vickers magazines always came adrift and as we were momentarily dropping/turning at one 'G', it would float weightless for an instant before falling to the deck.

Returning from one such exercise we had our first casualties since I had joined. One plane had to ditch with engine failure at low level. As we flew round we saw the pilot get out and struggle in the water to get the fast-sinking rear cockpit door open, to no avail. Both men in the back went down with it; we guessed the Observer was stunned by the impact of hitting the water and thus jamming the door; the Gunner was either in the same condition or went in his efforts to help the Observer.

Whilst I have written a lot about it, we were only about a month at Hatston before getting a week's embarkation leave. This involved the reciprocal of the 'Jellicoe' journey northwards which I have described. The train started at Thurso at 9 p.m., which allowed time for a meal and to get rollicking drunk in Thurso before starting. We got to Perth for a breakfast stop in the early hours. One of us had a brainwave, to 'jump train', get the local into Edinburgh and the morning train from Waverley to King's Cross. It would be a gamble because we didn't know train timings but three of us decided to chance it, allowing for the slowness of the 'Jellicoe'. We bet the others that we would be in Kings Cross before they were in Euston and won handsomely, being there over an hour before 'Jellicoe' was due into Euston. We also had the bonus of a nice full breakfast at the North British Hotel before leaving Edinburgh.

In less than a week after return from leave we had orders to fly down to Machrihanish, at the tip of the Mull of Kintyre, as a stepping stone to going aboard. I remember a glorious fine day for the flight down the west coast of Scotland. At that time, Machrihanish, which was to become a major Fleet Air Arm station (and is now Campbeltown Airport) was just a grass field; you just missed tangling your wheels in the adjacent cabbages as you came in to land on a golf course fairway. The Wardroom was very comfortable for our one-night visit, being the requisitioned Machrihanish Links Hotel.

Whilst to date the old hands had expected the 827 would re-embark in *Victorious*, it was here that we learned that our new home would be *Indomitable* – the newest carrier in the Fleet, preparing for her first commission. The sunshine for our flight south was the last of the Scottish summer, as the weather now closed in to thick mist and drizzly rain. This was deemed unsuitable for an almost raw Squadron to land on a brand new and untried

2. HMS Indomitable, *steaming at about 20 knots (Taken from one of her own Albacores. Another Albacore flies up her starboard side; a Fulmar is ranged on the flight deck preparing to take off.)*

Fleet carrier, so we were stuck at our club house until 13 October, an unlucky number, when we landed on *Indomitable*, which was to be our home for the coming year.

Chapter 6

At Sea at Last

A ND SO ON 13 October 1941, after a hearty Machrihanish breakfast, we flew off into weather not much improved from the day before. It was now typical Clyde weather, a gale of wind, low cloud and steady drizzle. I flew behind Bill Bailey, which reduced the apprehension; he was the most experienced in deck landings in the Squadron.

Fortunately I had given the right course for the rendezvous – as the ship was not far off shore, we flew out in succession, not in formation, and gathered into formation as we arrived. Then we did a 'fly past' our new home and broke into line astern to land on.

As we had broken cloud for our first sight of her, she looked quite magnificent, gliding through a fairly heavy lop. I had only once before seen a Fleet carrier (*Illustrious*, calling in Trinidad on her way to the States for repairs after her pasting at Malta). *Indomitable* was slightly less sleek and more powerful looking; she had more freeboard, having two more decks, as she had a second hangar (for half the length of the ship) under the main hangar, which enabled us to carry an extra Squadron. *Illustrious*, *Formidable* and *Victorious* had only the one full length hangar.

Landing on was a quaint procedure; instead of the conventional glide approach to an airfield, the pilot holds the plane in a tail-down attitude, in a nearly stalled position, and hanging on the engine. Thus the tail hook is well-positioned to catch an arrestor wire but, more important, the pilot is in a position to open the throttle and go up quickly if, owing to ship movement or his misjudgment, he is out of position to land at the last instant. The aft half of the Deck was all that could be used for landing in those pre-angled-deck days. The forward half was used to park the planes already landed, which could not be put down the hangar lift as fast as planes could land on. To protect the parked planes and crews, two barriers traversed the midships part of the deck, which could be lowered to allow aircraft to pass when taxi-ing forward. These consisted of wire hawsers: three about a foot apart, with cross-ties between them forming a sort of

netting. When up, the barriers were at about
propeller height to the
plane; they would stop a
plane which had failed to
catch an arrestor wire very
abruptly and with a fair
amount of damage. Fur-
ther aft, there were about
eight arrestor wires. These
were cables strung across
the deck about fifteen feet
apart on little support jacks
which held them about
nine inches above the deck,
so as to be a fairly easy
catch for the tail hooks the

3. HMS Indomitable: *Albacores on the flight deck*

planes lowered for landing. The ends of these cables went over pulleys
through the deck plating whence they were rove through sheaved blocks
on the piston ends of hydraulic cylinders. These provided a sharp braking
force as the piston extended and after the aircraft hook had been disengaged
by the Flight Deck Party, return of the piston tautened the cable. It was
always an unpleasant deceleration when you caught the wire, noticeably
more than being in a car applying full brakes at speed, though much less
drastic than hitting the barrier.

This first landing was just in nice time to report to Commander Flying
and Commander 'O' in the Briefing Room below the bridge and then find
our flying kit lockers in the Crew Room below it at Flight-Deck level. Then
the Bosun's mate piped, 'Stand Easy; Hands to place Spit-kids.' So, off to
the Wardroom for morning coffee.

The Wardroom and its anteroom were unconventional in *Indomitable*,
being amidships, instead of being in the stern, as tradition dictated. The
two rooms, with a fore and aft companionway between, took the whole
width of the ship (some 150 feet). By convention, the ship's crew lived
forward. They, unlike the Army, Air Force and Royal Marines, have never
been required to take the oath of loyalty to the Crown. (Pretty pointless in
the Press Gang days!) To get protection in mutinous conditions, the officers
traditionally lived aft, with the Royal Marines' 'barracks' amidships.

After coffee, we learned our way about the ship. Our stewards had been embarked with our gear the day before in the Clyde, so they had all our stuff stowed in our cabins. Junior officers were given double berth cabins. These were bigger than you'd get in a cross-Channel ferry, but less grand than the cabins of a cruise liner at the top end of First Class. There was a washbasin in each cabin and cabins were usually not far from an officers' bathroom and an officers' heads. The bathrooms usually had about four standard baths alongside each other. In the bottom of each bath was a duckboard (rather uncomfortable to sit on) under which was a steam pipe with jets in it. You ran a bath of cold seawater, then injected it with steam to get the right temperature. It had all been plumbed for hot and cold fresh water, but when we were planned for longer sea times than envisaged when she was laid down, salt water was put in and we were issued with seawater soap.

The ship also had such facilities as a dentist's surgery as well as a sizeable sick-bay. I had what seemed a good cabin for a 'snottie', shared with Dicky Dyke. It was over the starboard screw (she was a three-screw ship, which was rather unusual), and the cabin deck was exactly at the waterline. Whilst we looked around, the ship came back to lie off Gourock to embark last minute stores. The hangars took up a great deal of the inside of the ship. The upper one ran the whole length from the after lift to the forward one. The lower one was just over half that length, accessed by the after lift only. Both were the full width of the ship, apart from space for a few narrow weather decks and boat stowages outboard of them. The hangars had rail fittings across them, on which could be run 'skates', little bogies on to which a plane's wheels could be run for moving it across the line of the ship. Moving planes around the hangars was a difficult and dangerous game in anything of a sea; if a plane 'took charge', great damage could be done to other planes and to personnel. The hangar decks were amply provided with eyes for lashing down the aircraft.

The other Squadrons had landed on before us. 831 Squadron, our fellow Albacorists, a Fulmar (2-seater Fighter) Squadron (800) and, a novelty for the Fleet Air Arm, a Squadron of Hurricanes (880). At sea, the aircrew had no allocated ship's duties, although they could volunteer to go on the bridge roster and study for a watchkeeping 'ticket'. We did, of course, have an action station to man if Action Stations were piped whilst we were deck-bound. Mine was in charge of a 20 mm Oerlikon (light AA) gun position on the starboard quarter. Flying in harbour was thankfully rare, so we had allocated duties in harbour.

Most aircrew were on the 'Officer-of-the-Watch in Harbour' roster. This was a matter of being in charge of the Quarterdeck and ensuring that all who came and went showed it a proper respect. The Quarterdeck had the same reverence as it had on ships where it was a true weatherdeck. It had to be saluted; in days gone by, it had housed the ship's crucifix. It was where the larger ships' divine services were held, though there was an inboard chapel for Holy Communion etc.; it was also where the Commander marched up and down with officers he was reprimanding. It was where the Officer of the Watch and his Side Party were stationed in harbour, at the head of the brow (gangway). Against a wharf, the brow was usually rigged to a weather deck somewhere around midships. The party included a bos'n, complete with pipe, one or two members of the 'Jaunty's' staff (the Chief Regulating Petty Officer or Master at Arms was nicknamed Jaunty; the nearest Army equivalent would be RSM), and a duty signalman. He had to watch who was allowed on board and make sure the correct pipes and salutes were made for senior officers boarding or leaving the ship. He was also responsible for sending boats away and for the correct turn-out of libertymen. Perhaps more important, he had to supervise returning libertymen and ensure that drunks were properly dealt with. It was a minor offence to return drunk, so they had to be entered for the next day's Commander's defaulters' parade. It was imperative that any man likely to hurt himself getting back to his messdeck (easy for a drunk to do) was taken care of, usually by being put in the cooler. If the ship was at anchor or a mooring buoy, bearings had to be taken periodically to confirm that she was not dragging her anchor or moorings.

As a 'snottie', I was made a sea-boat's coxswain in harbour. This was quite fun, but getting into and out of the boat was a matter to get used to. When lowered in harbour, the boats were moored from a boom projecting from the ship's side about half way along the length. It was about twenty-five feet above the waterline, pivoted to the side, braced by a jack-stay from the outer end to a point two decks above the pivot. Also, of course, braces ran fore and aft from the outer end. On the underside of the boom hung blocks (pulleys), through which were passed heavy warps. The one end of these was made fast to the ship's side some 150 feet forward of the boom. The other end had a stop knot to prevent it running back through the block, leaving enough free end to hang down to about three feet above the water, where it terminated with a spliced eye. To this eye, the boat's painter was made fast; thus, the weight of heavy warp made a spring to take up the boat's movement, which could be quite severe if we were moored out in an estuary. Beside each block, also suspended from below the boom, was a rope ladder, whose bottom end was also tied to the boat with plenty of slack. To get from ship to boat, or vice versa, meant walking the top side of the boom; only at the outer end was the jack-stay available to grasp and, under all eyes, no-one would dare to be seen touching it. Getting from boom to ladder beneath it was another gymnastic feat, particularly in a fresh wind with everything moving about. Getting from ladder foot to boat involved leaning across to get hold of the boat's painter to pull the boat up to the ladder bottom and then hopping into the boat. The essential thing was to do it all in a manner as though one had done it all one's life. Plate 12 shows a similar boom on the side of HMS *Archer*.

I wonder if the Germans would have noticed if my little Oerlikon had not been there. It was little alongside sixteen 4.5 inch guns and eight mountings each having eight Vickers Two-Pounders (Pom-Poms). Between all these gun mountings were walkways along either side of the ship on which you were a bit below shoulder height to the Flight Deck. These were called the 'Nets' – remember how Nelson's men put their hammocks for action and you will see the reason. Unlike American carriers with teak flight decks, ours were of steel; in fact, apart from the most forward and after parts, it was of 1.5 or 2 inch armour plating. It was a major feat of naval architecture to be able to carry this weight of steel so high above the waterline – I should think it was sixty to eighty feet up. We carried fewer planes than the Yanks, but the justification of our system came later, when Kamikazes turned up (or was it down?) in the Pacific. If the Yanks sustained a hit, it was either curtains or, if the ship was saved, some nine months' dockyard rebuild. They were flabbergasted to see *Indefatigable*, the first of ours to receive a Kamikaze, operating its aircraft ten minutes after it.

The ladders between decks took some getting used to if you had never been to sea in the Andrew: like a passenger ship stairway, but so steep that each tread was virtually out of sight below the one above. Again, one had to go down forwards and just as easily as one would on the stairs at home, if one did not wish to appear a landlubber.

The ratings' mess decks were something of a contrast to the officer luxury, but only really looked cramped when there was a watch and a half all slung in their hammocks. They were surprisingly similar to the crew quarters which can be seen in *Warrior*, on view in Portsmouth harbour. Even much of the equipment was the same! That's enough description for now except perhaps for dimensions. She was a box 750 feet long with a beam of 150 feet and she drew about 32 feet fully laden – which we learned before long was too much in some circumstances!

There were some new friends in the other Squadrons: particularly do I remember Hamish Muir-Mackenzie, Fulmar pilot of pre-War RN vintage, who will turn up later in the narrative. Jack Stamper, our scrum-half at *St Vincent*, was also a Fulmar pilot in 800. Little Hugh Popham, who has written a book about it all (*Sea Flight*, published in 1948), was bearded like Jesus but much wittier and, like the rest of us (but closer to him), terrified of Lt. Commander Judd, his CO, a truly formidable man of ghastly rages. They flew Hurricanes, both of them rather well.

Our Captain was a quiet man, and like most captains of big ships, one did not often encounter him; later, as you will see, I had some degree of contact. Name of Morse, but not old enough to have been the inventor of the Code! The Commander, the senior officer in the Wardroom (the Captain can only go into the Wardroom on special invitation of the members), was a pleasant stickler for discipline. Short and square, with high blood-pressure complexion, he rejoiced in the name of Commander Wootten Wootten-Wootten. Looking after the flying side of the ship was Commander 'F', whose name has gone. Under him came Commander 'O', the officer responsible for all Observer matters – briefing aircrews before flight and de-briefing them after – thus our main purveyor of intelligence. He was Commander Geoffrey (Hank) Rotherham, a very professional and particularly kindly man. He had won renown by flying from Hatston to Korfjord in a target-towing aircraft to confirm that *Bismarck* had sailed, in weather which made it 'impossible' for RAF's Coastal Command (who had the responsibility) to fly there and more suitable planes for doing it. Under him, as Intelligence Officer, was Lt. Commander Everett. Never was 'Intelligence Officer' a greater misnomer. Nice guy; utterly stupid; always in a muddle; axed from the Navy years before and brought back for the War. Probably the best known of the ship's officers to do with flying was Stuart Morris, Lt. RNVR, who was the Fighter Direction Officer. He had won an Olympic medal sailing international 12 foot dinghies.

Lt. Commander Pears was 'Bats', the Flight Deck Control Officer, who had all our lives in his hands and commanded the Flight Deck Crew. The most responsible part of his duties was to stand on the port quarter of the Flight Deck, signalling with his bats (like the ping-pong bats now used to signal to airliners parking at airports) to guide the pilots into their deck landings. He had to be a very experienced pilot and our pilots had to have absolute faith in his signals. He could indicate need to climb or fall faster, to go left or right, and most important, the exact moment to cut the engine. The stern of a carrier can be moving up and down some forty feet, which cannot be seen by the approaching pilot; 'Bats', of course, could appreciate the rhythm of the movement standing on the deck, so he aimed to make the landing plane come on or hold off to make the 'cut' at the right moment; a stall from forty feet above the deck can be rather debilitating for the crew and expensive for the plane.

He also had the exacting job of supervising the 'ranging' of aircraft. If, for example, a couple of Squadrons were to take off, they had to be pre-parked (ranged) at the stern end as tightly packed as practicable, so as to leave the maximum length of deck for the take-off run. (In rough weather, it was a fairly formidable job to get to one's aircraft; chart-board and navigating instruments, parachute, etc. to carry, deck slippery; only just room to squeeze between one machine and another; propellers whirling lethally to warm up in all directions. Horrid in daylight; terrifying in total blackout at night.)

He did us all proud for nine months until he met his end. He was landing on a Squadron whilst our own guns were firing on the Malta Convoy. One of the guns just by his position had a 'premature' (shell exploded virtually on emerging from the gun muzzle) and he was cruelly torn to shreds by the fragments.

The great thing about carrier operation is that planes must be got off the deck and back on to the deck in the shortest possible time. The ship has to hold a steady course throughout either operation, making her a sitting duck for any enemy U-Boat or bomber; she wants to minimise the time when she is so restrained. Bats could get us landing on at only thirty seconds between planes; bear in mind that this means plane lands; deck crew unhook the arrestor wire; barrier is lowered; plane taxis forward of the barrier, which must be up again in the thirty seconds before the next plane lands. It requires a lot of drilling of ship's and aircraft crews to achieve it.

Thus the first assignment for the brand new *Indomitable* was to seek quiet waters far from enemy interference in order to perfect the drills as quickly as she could. For this we sailed on a gloomy autumn evening; we were to 'work our passage', however, escorting a west-bound convoy across the first leg of the Atlantic.

Chapter 7

Operational at Last

I REMEMBER a feeling of pride in the ship and *esprit de corps* developing immediately amongst us although we were a collection of units from a variety of sources. Ship's crew were largely from Chatham Depot, but there were quite sizeable contributions from Portsmouth (Pompey) and Plymouth (Guz) – the 'Tiddy Oggies' (anyone from Plymouth was a Tiddy Oggie, the local name for a Cornish pasty) – as well. They and the Marines had been with the ship for a few weeks. *Indomitable* had only been commissioned at Barrow on 1 October 1941; the basic crew must have boarded long before the commissioning, in order to man the ship for trials before official handing over by the builders and official 'commissioning'. The Squadrons each had their own history of independent activity until we met with *Indomitable* but quite amazingly quickly we all got to know each other and all felt part of the carrier. She was a truly majestic ship and whilst the mess-deck lawyers rumoured that she was destined to be an unlucky ship, we were all happy to be with her. The ill-luck originated, it was said, because she had launched herself; she had started off down the slips at Barrow a day or two before being blessed by the traditional launching ceremony. The truth or otherwise of this I never heard. She certainly never turned out to be one of the great lucky ships, but she was less unlucky than some in wartime.

We sailed on 15 October 1941, and although doing Anti-Submarine patrols for our convoy from the start, we were given plenty of flying exercises as well. Anti-submarine patrols were a matter of flying to and fro across the ship's path and about five or ten miles ahead of her. Usually two planes were used, one covering the port side of the track, the other the starboard side. Normally we were only up for about three hours, so it was not very arduous. By now I was more or less permanently crewed with Richard Meakin as pilot and Ed Ward as TAG. Richard had refused to accept me at first; in a navigation exercise before being out of the Clyde in thick weather I had told him that at any minute we should see the ship, at what should have been the end of the exercise. He broke cloud, nearly hit a mountain and then recognised Belfast beneath him. It took a day or two to make him believe that the fault was largely his; my plot and notes proved that he had steered a reciprocal course to that which I had given him somewhere around Ailsa Craig. Admittedly, I should have spotted his error earlier. Thereafter mutual confidence grew, although I was always slightly narked that he expressed the surprise I secretly felt when we did actually find our way back to the ship first time.

As we crossed the Atlantic, we opened our casualty list. On 24 October we were scrambled for a search in lousy weather. One of the 800's Fulmars had ditched with engine failure; only a very rough position was known. We searched for as long as our fuel would last, but found nothing. It was only after landing back on that I learned that the missing pilot was Jack Stamper. A day or two later, one of the Artificers went down with appendicitis. This should have been no trouble; the ship had an excellent theatre and sick-bay and we had one of the top surgeons from Birmingham as second in command of the medical team – now a Lt. Commander RNVR. In command was a Surgeon Commander RN who had been in hospital administration for years and, like many of the Navy's medical fraternity, qualified in Dublin, which was regarded in pre-War days as the easiest road into medicine. The gallant commander decided that this was a nice simple operation for him to use as opportunity to get his hand back in. Whilst he had no specialist surgical qualification, it was quite common for naval doctors to operate at sea – it was often essential, because most ships did not carry an FRCS.

Doctors, as you know, are prone to cover up for each other, but as we arrived from our various duties into the Wardroom for our pre-lunch 'pinkers', Mather, the RNVR two-and-a-half surgeon, was already high and muttering 'sheer butchery' and suchlike. 'Wouldn't have expected even a Wardroom cook to make a fuck-up like that getting out a simple appendix; I had to watch as assistant, not allowed to assist, while he cut the bugger up like strips of tripe.' 'How's the patient doing now?' we asked. 'Plumb bloody dead,' was the answer. So, next day, up came our first funeral at sea. Even this was a fiasco, occasioned by inexperience. For burial at sea, the corpse is sewn into a sailcloth shroud, suitably ballasted with scrap metal (cannon ball in Nelson's day). At the appropriate moment in the Service ('Ashes to ashes . . .'), the board on which the corpse lies at the side is tipped by the side-party, who must be careful to hang on to the covering White Ensign, allowing the body to slide out from beneath for its last plunge into the briny. This part went to the book, but those of us near the side were surprised that it did not immediately sink from sight. So far as we knew, it never sank and was last seen as a speck in the distant wake like a well-inflated white Li-lo. The awful truth dawned: the Bos'n had forgotten to include ballast in his parcel.

Meanwhile we continued our patrols, got more used to the ship and got initiated into such new pursuits as deck hockey. This was a fast and furious game rather akin to ice-hockey but with fewer rules and no protective padding. The stick was rather like a small Irish shinty stick and a very handy weapon it made; the 'puck' was a small strop (about 4 inches diameter) of rope, rather like what liners use for deck quoits. It was a tough ship's league; the most feared team were the stokers, who were awe- inspiring in their enthusiasm for getting at officers when they played all-officer teams, which 827's team happened to be. Looking back on the game, I cannot see how we avoided killing a few players daily, but all I recall were heavy bruises and the occasional few stitches and those not that frequent. Stokers did not specifically hate officers! They were recruited from the least privileged strata of society because up till the relatively recent introduction of oil-firing, theirs was the devil of a job. Thus, they tended to be the toughest bunch on board and the ones least sympathetic to authority in any form. It went no further at deck hockey than good- humouredly taking every opportunity offered to thump an officer, but their main objective as a team was still to win the game, not to murder authority. Imagine the stoker's job in coal firing days: for a four hour Watch you continuously shovelled coal into the boiler hearth. You breathed coal dust; you worked on a steel plate deck slippery with coal dust; the deck heaved all over the place with every movement of the sea. The working temperature would be between 120° and 130° Fahrenheit. To push the air draught through the boilers, the boiler-rooms were pressurised – you could only get in or, much more importantly, out via double-doored airlocks. In action you had to keep shovelling all the harder as more speed or smoke were called for; all you knew of what was going on was the noise of guns and, perhaps, arriving shells. You knew that you were below the waterline and that in the event of the ship being holed, almost certainly all exits would be sealed regardless of personnel within, in the interests of keeping afloat. It is a comment on the social circumstances of the early part of this century that the Navy was able to maintain its full complement of stokers without national conscription and without resort to the Press Gang.

I remember being most impressed by our first Sunday at sea. First, 'Divisions', a church parade for all not on Watch except that Roman Catholics got their 'Fall out Roman Catholics' before we got down to Anglican business. In *Indomitable* Roman Catholics were out of luck because we carried an RC padre too, so they had to get down to their business instead of having a bonus stand-easy. Then we repaired to the Wardroom for rather more formal pre-lunch drinks than on weekdays. We were in uniform from Divisions, instead of wearing what we liked as was the case most days at sea. The Royal Marines band formed itself into an orchestra playing light music, sitting in the companion way between the ante-room and the Wardroom. For Bandsman Shacklady, normally a trombonist in the band and a ship's Drummer (that means bugler), it was dreadful; first he became a violinist in the orchestra (a bit quiet for his taste); second the Bandmaster invariably put in a bit from *Caballera Rusticana* which he absolutely loathed. He was always chatty to junior officers and, as one picked one's way through the orchestra to the ante-room, he would mutter in his Geordie accent:

'We got the fooking caboleera agin todeay,' with a lugubrious look at the bandmaster. One of our number asked the bandmaster for something else one day, but he had Shacklady's measure:

'Sorry, sir. We are not here to please Bandsman Shacklady, but to play the music the Commander has approved.'

(The Commander wouldn't have known Beethoven's Ninth from 'Good King Wenceslas'.)

I suppose the light music on Sunday lunchtime seemed faintly ridiculous in the circumstances. In the main it seemed a good thing to maintain peacetime habits, so far as that was practicable; it was nice to be following BIG SHIP routine! A deck officer pointed through a scuttle (porthole) at our escorting destroyers which seemed to be submerged for more than half the time during a mid-Atlantic storm on one such Sunday:

'Poor sods; soaked through; frozen; no gin and music; not even a hot meal until we get to the other side.'

The concerts were (via the Tannoy) relayed throughout the ship. 'Keeping the Crew amused' was not a problem. At sea in wartime if they were not on Watch or exercises, they were lucky to find enough time to get in some eating and sleeping. If still aboard in harbour, if not on watch or on more exercises, it would be usual to sleep off the rigours of having been at sea and the greater ones of having had a run ashore! At sea, apart from where we lived and messed in the ship, there was not the sort of officer/rating split you imagine. There were afternoon amusements such as deck hockey and a little boxing (not very popular) and soccer, hockey and rugger when facilities ashore were found. There were occasional amateur variety-show type concerts aboard. All these activities were participated in as equals as near as could be done by all on board who wanted. At sea, remember, we did not dress as officers and ratings; we more or less wore what we wanted unless on on the bridge, when uniform was worn. Likewise for the rare parades like Divisions we spick and spanned into our very best uniforms to remind ourselves that it was the Navy!

There was no rationing of letters home. All letters had to be censored. This was done by one's seniors – I don't know who did the Captain's. It was obviously one of the nastiest jobs an officer had to do. Only if a whole letter was taboo did it go back to the author; you just cut out offending bits with scissors; if that lost text from the reverse side of the paper, bad luck. The author knew not who had censored his letter nor what had been scissored. As censor, one came upon the occasional pearl – e.g. seaman newly arrived in his first ship in Scapa Flow: 'Dear Mum, You probably don't know what the Navy expression Fuck All means, but there's miles and miles of it here . . .' 'My friend had done what he calls catching a dose, but he won't tell me what that is . . .' Before we had finished in *Indomitable*, they introduced a new letter system for all overseas forces. The letter was on a single sheet of foolscap; after censorship it was microfilmed, then put through an enlarger/printer in UK at the Forces' Post Office, enveloped and delivered. In *Indomitable* a letter home took about three months and the reply a little longer if the ship had been flitting about a bit. I got some mail in Algeria, when on loan to the RAF, which had been sent from home to *Indomitable*; I had been home on leave in the interim. You could not say where you were or whether or not you had been in action. You could not comment on other ships in company. You could say that the climate was very hot, for example and describe a run ashore if that did not identify the place. There was a natural tendency to drop hints as to where you were: 'Very hot ashore last night, ate a fruit I had not met before called pawpaw . . . also drank some excellent old rum.' 'Marvellous local hospitality here . . . superb climate . . . very beautiful coast . . . dinner in the local business club . . . it was just like the Carlton.' 'Allowed ashore here for several days, so took the train into the hinterland . . . just like a train ride through Whipsnade.' Thus could a family of only Mackenzie intellect plot

Indomitable's progress from the Caribbean, round the Cape and up to Kenya. You had to avoid reporting some real events which were not censorable, in case you threw them off the scent. For example, you did not comment on the game of rugger in Colombo because you knew all the family thought rugger was only played in temperate climates and might guess you had turned for home!

We kept pretty up-to-date with world news. The ship could use its radio receivers, so could pick up the BBC world service. As soon as there was anything momentous, the Captain (usually) broadcast it over the Tannoy. Once a week the Captain gave a half hour talk on the week's news and his own interpretation of its significance to us. In the history you have so far had, the Japanese did not figure in world news; they had not begun to do more than bicker diplomatically with the Americans and who, we thought, could blame them for that. They had virtually finished their conquests in China and Korea. (Those we did not regard as our affair at all, although totally deploring their reported atrocities.) Singapore was still the British bastion of the Far East to which quite a few of us guessed we were bound after the 'work-up'.

Anyway, it was a grand feeling to sip one's gin prior to an excellent lunch and look out of the scuttle at convoy and escorts labouring through the winter Atlantic. The escorts were taking it green every time their bows dipped to the sea. Wartime convoys were one of the world's truly majestic sights, but were undoubtedly best appreciated from *Indomitable*'s Wardroom rather than on the wet bridge of an escort in which they had probably not been able to produce a hot meal for days.

The Royal Marines' Band all had ship's duties. An obvious one was providing 'Drummers'. These, as you know, were buglers. Always one on Watch; the last resort communication in action was bugle calls; everyone had therefore to be kept familiar with them, so they were used continually through all days to punctuate the ship's routine and non-routine doings. Some of the Band, as in Army regiments, were first-aid men and stretchermen when in action. They had full Royal Marines soldier training, so if we had to put a detachment ashore they were available. Some of the ship's main and secondary armament was manned by the Royal Marines detachment, and these duties no doubt absorbed some bandsmen.

As the weather warmed we shifted into tropical rig and Dicky Dyke's hot weather funnies began. (My cabinmate, remember?) First, he appeared at Divisions with black boots and tropical uniform instead of officers' white shoes. When the Commander remonstrated, this little RNVR snottie pointed out quietly that his mother said he had weak ankles and must wear boots. This so floored the Commander, Dicky wore his boots for the rest of the trip. The other funny was mother's precautions against prickly heat. Every spare moment, Dicky would strip and lie on his bunk. He had a trayful of powders (I called it The Cruet), which had to be applied to the most private parts in a pre-ordained order. Never did a chef season a sausage and two dumplings with such loving care; the sausage would be lifted and its underside dusted with several condiments; then the topside; then with legs in the air the most careful attention had to be paid to the dumplings with each item on the tray in turn.

Another recreation when others were landing was to loll on what we called Goofers' Gallery. This was a small weather deck at the after end of the Island, about two decks higher than the Flight Deck level. From it one got a very good view of the landing planes and could poke fun at the shortcomings of everyone else. Invariably someone bent something when a whole Squadron came in, it seemed; there were times though when it all went like clockwork and the Goofers would retire from the Gallery complaining to each other 'nothing to laugh at at all!'

Eventually we left convoy and next day picked up moorings in Glassy Bay, Bermuda, scene of our departure some months before in the St Lawrence River steamer. Here we had to lie for some days for some reason I forget – it could have been awaiting stores or machinery modifications. So my duties began in earnest as a boat's coxswain. The first night I was on the 'Sea Plane Tender', a super boat of speedboat lines and two hundred horsepower engines. She could do thirty-five knots in an emergency. I was taking officers ashore to Hamilton (about a half hour's run) and then bringing them off again. One had to be careful in the dark and read the buoy lights correctly; the course for Hamilton ran up the left hand side of a Y, the right side of the Y also being a buoyed channel. In the middle was a coral bank only a foot or two below the surface.

One night, when not a coxswain, I was able to go ashore in Hamilton. We had a good Squadron piss-up with our maintenance ratings, so much so that one or two petty officers missed the last ratings' boat back. We adopted the device of several of us returning bareheaded, lending our officers' caps to the POs and getting them aboard with the later officers' boat. Everyone was very tickled that Petty Officer Pyke was wearing his near-namesake's cap (Prangle's).

The next night, when I was ashore, a snottie from 800 Squadron had the tender and took her away, with all his fighter pilot's panache, at the 35 knots we were only allowed in emergency. He tore the bottom out of her on the coral bank, which was not popular with his boatload, who never saw Hamilton that night. They stood, wet up to their knees in the wreckage and water, waiting half the night until it was realised that they were missing. He was definitely not popular with the Commander, whose best sea boat had been totally written off and all Bermuda Dockyard could supply as a replacement was a standard motor boat. This did me some good, because it led to a reallocation of boats and coxswains and I became coxswain of the Captain's galley. A fairly pedestrian little boat, but the honour of it! It turned out to be a very interesting job. He (Captain Morse) had held a shore appointment in Bermuda not long before, so knew lots of people and nice places to go for bathing picnics. I saw a lot of the coast as a result; he was always good enough to tell me a good place to take the boat's crew to picnic and take it easy for the day whilst he entertained his guests.

I remember USS *Wasp* came in one evening and Morse was asked over to her. As we arrived near her stern, there was a hideous mess of boats circling at full speed. *Wasp* had all her boats out to take her crew ashore and half the boat owners of Hamilton were there too, trying to see what business they could pick up. To get through it all and win the competition to be next at *Wasp*'s brow took nerve as well as seamanship and it was warming to receive the skipper's congratulations when we made it. Even better when we got him home on the return trip some hours later; by then it was dark and the wind had blown up somewhat. *Wasp*'s boats had stopped operating and they were quite surprised to find us arriving on time at the foot of their brow to pick up the Boss in so small a craft as *Indomitable*'s Captain's galley. He managed to jump in and off we set into a fearful lop. We seemed to take hours against the headwind to make the few cables which separated the two ships. On return to *Indomitable* we again received his particular thanks and congratulations. Not much of an achievement, when one looks back, but it is amazing what a sense of success he managed to convey, which is why it sticks in the memory. Not every 'snottie' gets the Captain's congratulations – it's like a pat on the back from God.

In due course, we set off for Jamaica, which was to be our base for the final 'work-up' of the carrier and its planes. My only memory of the passage was doing an anti-submarine patrol ahead of the ship as she went through the Windward Passage and the Jamaica Channel. It was hard to remember to look for submarines; the beauty of the Haitian, Cuban and Jamaican coastlines was beyond belief.

And so we came up the channel for Kingston, Jamaica, little realising the significance to the Navy of what we were doing. The channel was marked with a few unconventional beacons instead of the usual port and starboard hand buoys and it was not obvious on which hand these beacons should be passed. Our Captain and Navigating Officer took the easy way – instead of looking up the Aids to Navigators, they followed a locally based Flower Class corvette who was going in ahead of us. Too late in the day, they realised that we were overhauling the corvette fast, because she was stationary – grounded. Thus, in perfect calm evening weather the latest pride of the Navy ground with a ghastly thump into the coral bank upon which the corvette was already perched. And were we stuck! The tide was only just on the turn to ebb, so quickly a kedge (stern) anchor was boated out. She went full astern, winching madly on the kedge to no avail. An hour later, coral broke surface either side of our bows, which normally drew about 30 feet. By the next full tide, in the early hours of the morning, the entire ships' company were fallen in on the stern of the Flight Deck and Quarterdeck below it. Our orders were to jump in time to the big drum of the ship's band. (Sounds silly, but two thousand men all coming down together on the deck gives the ship quite a thump.) Meanwhile, we had put out two more kedges to haul on and every tug in Kingston to pull. With a steady growl from beneath we came clear and went to our mooring in the harbour.

Here it was found that we had bent our stem badly; about fifteen feet back along the keel and twenty feet up the stem was bent out at around thirty degrees. Only drydocking could repair it. Whilst USA was not in the War, they were not averse to making a dollar or two mending our ships, so off we sailed for Norfolk, Virginia. Our stay there deserves its own chapter, but first I must mention the horror our grounding turned out to be. Naval plans were that following our work-up, we would join the Far East Fleet. Had we done this in time, we should have been with *Prince of Wales* and *Repulse* when, the Japanese War having begun, they did their fateful sweep into the China Sea. Our fighters could certainly have held off the Japanese bomber force who found them by chance and overwhelmed them. Naval historians have asserted this, because the Japanese were so much at the limits of their range. I had a more personal confirmation of this in recent years. A Japanese business contact turned out to have been one of the pilots involved; he said that they just would not have had the fuel to manoeuvre away from fighters and attack; they were so low on gas that they were in two minds about attacking until they realised that the target was Britain's newest battleship and her finest battlecruiser.

We blamed the Captain and his Navigating Officer for the grounding; we didn't like 'Tanks' anyway (the traditional name for the Navigator in the Navy for obvious reasons). I think we had a corporate sense of shame about the episode. However, our shame and annoyance was tempered by the interest and excitement of going to the USA for repairs. It was not a country as familiar to lots of British as is the case today, and was the reputed land of plenty and of super sin – our picture was Hollywood's. Only the equivalent of today's 'Jet-Set', the tiny *Queen Mary* set, and the impecunious immigrant, ever penetrated there before the War.

Chapter 8

The Land of the Stars and Stripes

I HAVE TO SAY at the outset that my memory is not good enough at this range of time to be sure which events in our visit happened in Portsmouth, Virginia, in Newport News or in Norfolk. A look at the map will indicate that these three are not that far apart on the southern side of the mouth of the Chesapeake Estuary, so my inaccuracies are not that pertinent. If I do remember correctly, we first came into Portsmouth but went across to Newport News for the drydocking. For part of the stay, we aviators took our planes ashore for exercise flying from the Navy Airfield at Norfolk.

Never had one imagined in advance that the USA would be so utterly 'foreign', or so full of contrasts. Marvellous hospitality from individuals contrasted with quite vicious antipathy to and insulting of the British by the general public. An old world courtesy in general manners with a more appalling apartheid treatment of blacks than anyone has ever seen in South Africa. All these differences seemed to come from absolutely sincerely held views. In talk of the 'Yankees', it was hard to believe that the Civil War had finished some hundred years before. Visiting the South in subsequent (business) years, it was equally amazing how fast it has all changed; they are USA now, and Dixieland had, perhaps, thank goodness, gone for ever.

We were carefully briefed before arrival that we must 'show the flag' with discipline and dignity; we were to be in the heart of the US Navy-land at the height of peacetime efficiency and not let it show that we were fifty per cent wartime amateurs coming from ports and depots which had lost their spick and span discipline in the hard school of war and air-raids.

Indomitable tied up first at the premier berth in Portsmouth; it seemed incredible how tidy and shining everything around us was, how punctiliously exchanges of salutes and other disciplines around us were conducted; it was like being a private in the Pioneer Corps suddenly finding himself in the middle of Chelsea Barracks. Small wonder, then, that our first day in saw Marine Shacklady condemned to a few days' cells. (He will be remembered for his dislike of *Caballera Rusticana*, in the last chapter; his most endearing – and enduring – characteristic was an inclination to 'take the mickey' if he found himself in circumstances where the bullshit was thicker than he liked.) He was the duty drummer for bugling 'Colours' our first night in. Finding himself the star performer midst all this bullshit and in the heart of Dixie was too much for him, so as the White Ensign sank down its mast, the familiar bugle call was 'swung' outrageously and most skilfully – no-one could deny his musicianship.

At that stage of the War, the Americans were making such a killing out of it that poor old UK had hardly a dollar left. For a run ashore all we junior officers were allowed was one dollar each and, in those days, that was one fifth of a pound, not about half, as these days. A group of us on our first 'run' walked down the main street wondering what could be got for a dollar. Finally we entered what looked most like a tea-shop. (Come to think of it, you don't see them in the UK either these days.) A quite gorgeous girl came up and said in beautiful southern tones:

'Good afternoon, gennelmen. What would yo'all requier?'

Taken aback, we asked limply whether they had afternoon tea.

'Just a minute, gennelmen, I'll enquier for yo'all.'

Few minutes later, back she came and intoned:

'I'm sorry gennelmen, we have India tea, we have China tea, but we jus' don' have affernoon tea.'

So, we asked, what could we get for a dollar?

'Well, seeing as yo'all are visitors an' we can' do your affernoon tea, we will serve any choice you'all care to make off the card.'

So, the first good meal was had on Southern Hospitality.

The dreadful shock ashore was negro segregation; buses, seats in the park, even on the cross-harbour ferry they were not allowed where the whites went. They were treated like dirt all round and slunk around the streets as though trying not to be there. By the time we had had enough of America (about the second day!) we took to crossing the harbour in the negro compound on the stern of the ferry, but it does not do to protest in other people's countries. The negroes crouched away from us, embarrassed; the whites shouted out; 'That's where the Limey Officers belong!' Later, in social encounters with our hosts one learned that the blacks had truly no rights. You could shoot one with impunity, if you wanted. It was always a white jury; all you had to say was that he was making eyes at your wife or friend and that was accepted as justification. All credit to the Americans, for the distance they have travelled from there in half my short lifetime.

About two days after arrival, we sailed into Chesapeake Bay and the Squadrons took off for the NOB (Naval Operating Base) at Norfolk. Compared with FAA airfields in UK, it was vast. We seemed to them to have come from a different century; they found it impossible that we were fighting a war in bi-planes, which they had not used for years. The US Navy were marvellously hospitable to us. We were made full members of their Wardroom and accommodated sumptuously (free) in the BOQ (Bachelor Officers Quarters). There was much comparing of notes about our navies; they were amazed that we were allowed to drink at sea.

'Why, if we were allowed hooch at sea, first thing you'd know we'd be aground.'

To us this was unanswerable. How our ship had been damaged and what damage we'd sustained were secrets we were not allowed to divulge. We felt rather bad about the general assumption of our hosts that we had sustained our damage bravely fighting the Hun.

They went on so about our bi-planes that we demonstrated to them our skills in combat (mock, that is); just as with a Me109, one fighter could never get an Albacore because of the latter's turning circle and ability to fly low (wheels wet!). We did one big show-off to them; one morning 827 – the whole Squadron – taxied in formation to the side of their main runway and faced across it. We then did a formation take-off on the width of the runway. They still felt that they would rather fight a war, if they had to, in American Navy planes. We did too, really.

Indomitable was not the only Limey in port. *Formidable* was there without Squadrons, completing the major refit she had needed after encountering the Luftwaffe off Malta. The US Legion asked the two ships to give demonstration games of soccer and rugby for charity. In those days, rugby was more an officers' game than it is today, because it was only learned in public schools and a few of the grammar schools. Thus, with our Squadrons aboard, some seventy officers, and an operational complement of ships officers, we had rather more to pick from than *Formidable*. On the other hand, we had never selected and played a team; it had to be done on paper form. Johnnie Forest was top of this list – capped for Scotland in the centre, now a Hurricane pilot with 880. Somewhere at the bottom came me, on the strength of having been asked to train with the Sussex team just as War broke out.

Just before we set off for Hampton, where the game was to be played, *Formidable* asked us to lend them a scrum-half. We had two hookers, at which position I had been picked; as the junior officer of the two I had to go to the opposition. On arrival at Hampton, I was taken over to *Formidable*'s team to meet my partnering fly-half; it turned out to be none other than Basil Gourlay, now Captain of Marines, whom I had last met as our fly-half in the school team at Eastbourne. The game was fast and furious and I cannot remember the result. We all got very sore because the ground was like concrete, baked hard in late autumn. The stadium was huge and packed to capacity; I could not see the ball within the scrums because of the dust being kicked up; the Americans had arranged a running commentary over the Tannoy and it was most off-putting to hear what you were doing as you did it. I think we were all glad when full time was blown, but quite unprepared for what followed.

The audience, used to the American game, were astonished that we played with no padding or crash helmets and that the teams played right through the game without substitutes to allow the occasional rest. We must be supermen! As we came off the pitch, we were mobbed by all the womanhood of Hamilton. All of us were carted off to private homes for family evenings after dressing. From those encounters ensued for most of us invitations back to the family to spend Thanksgiving Day which was in the offing. It was marvellous hospitality from most charming and courteous people.

By way of contrast, our ratings were having a deplorable time ashore. A small proportion got invitations to private families where they fared just the same as we did on such occasions. The trouble, which we shared, was around the restaurants and bars of Portsmouth and Newport News. There the locals set out to be as provocative as possible:

'What colours are your flag?' you would be asked.

First time round you would reply, 'Red, white and blue, same as yours.'

'Well, what's the dirty yellow streak I see running through it? Why are you guys always running away from the Germans?'

Hard to keep your cool against such childishness; hard to bear from those who were profiting in safety from the War we fought on their behalf as well as our own; the truth about running away from the Germans – about all we had done up to that time – struck particularly hard. All the time we were reminded that we would be nowhere without them supplying arms, food and so on. They did not like the reverse view; we were having to give our lives, they were taking every dollar we had got whilst we defended them.

In ratings' bars the fights became frequent; for their own protection our men were not allowed ashore in groups of fewer than six. Finally, just before we sailed, one of our men was arrested for murder – someone had been killed in a bar fracas. Immediately, up came again the great contrast of that part of the world. Locally a fund was launched for the defence of the British seaman; generosity of contributions was quite staggering – enough to get a man off if he had assassinated the entire American Government. But, by that time, we were wishing that someone had!

Chapter 9

Back to Jamaica

A S WE SAILED OUT of the Chesapeake, the Captain addressed us all over the Tannoy and clarified that we now had to catch up the training programme by hard work which would begin immediately. So we had exercises, exercises all the way to Kingston. This time we managed to get to our moorings in harbour without hitting anything. Then began one month's work-up which was truly exhausting. All the week at sea on exercises; the week-ends in Kingston in the most colossal whoopee.

On arrival at Kingston, our Captain and Navigating Officer were sent home and replacements arrived. We had the great luck to have as new Captain Tom Troubridge, one of the great characters of the RN. A direct ancestor had been a Captain at Trafalgar and all generations since had served the Navy with distinction. He was a vast man with cherry-red complexion veering towards Bishop's purple here and there. His waistline was bigger than it should be by a margin which would make most men look ridiculous in tropical rig (white shirt and shorts); he, however, always seemed as dignified in the rig as any archbishop does in his array. At deck hockey, a passion of Tom's, the dignity vanished; the dexterity and energy with which he cleared all before him were formidable; even the stokers respected this officer on the hockey pitch. Loud booming voice; strict disciplinarian full of the factor which makes discipline tick – humour. He was a real twentieth century Hornblower. I recall once he was involved in a desperately fought deck hockey match; the ship was banging along at some twenty knots in the charge of Bill Bailey as Officer of the Watch. Bill had miscalculated on his zig-zag pattern, so to correct had ordered full helm. The resulting list, superimposed on the already lively motion of the ship at that speed, made hockey almost impossible. Tom stops playing and roars from the Flight Deck: 'Officer of the Watch!' (not many men could make themselves heard from Deck to Bridge). Bill's head appears from the side of the bridge:

'Don't be so bloody split with my ship; we are not I think in action and you have ruined a perfectly good game of hockey!'

Then to the referee and those in the game:

'Play on, damn you. Frightened you'll go over the side?'

Up to the outbreak of War he had been Attaché in the Berlin Embassy, so knew most of the leading Nazis personally. He used to give us regular evening chat-shows over the Tannoy regarding those days and he made them fabulously interesting besides spicing them with a lot of humour. In the summer before the War began, a British Squadron had visited Kiel. (No two Navies got on better in port together than the British and Krauts in peacetime; although there was terrific rivalry, there was tremendous respect.) British ships had taken several of the biggest silver trophies for sailing and rowing in the Fleet Regatta. As they sailed away, a senior German officer said mournfully:

'How are we to get our trophies back for next year if war is declared?'

'Quite easy,' said Tom, 'I will get them melted down and send them back as bullets.'

It was around this time that the virtuous Dickey Dyke found himself having to take a walk on the Quarterdeck with the Commander. (This is the traditional means for the Commander to administer a reprimand to an officer and was a very serious business.) Dickey had exceeded his wine allowance in the Wardroom – a serious misdemeanour at any time – with only five days of the month elapsed! (We were allowed to spend £5 per month in the Wardroom; this may not seem much, but remember that a gin – rather larger than a pub double – cost 2*d*., so the allowance represented six hundred tots over about thirty days.) Dickey's crime had come about because of his willingness to help his Squadron mates. He already helped us Observers enormously; if the weather was rough he used to beg us to let him fly our A/S Patrols for us – anything to have a few hours off the ship's motion. Dickey did not drink alcohol; his mother said it was not good for him. As a few of us had problems stretching the £5 for a month, some genius had the idea of getting Dickey to provide a wodge of signed blank bar chits so we could get a flying start to the month, paying Dickey in cash, of course, which was strictly illegal so he could not admit to it.

The weekends in harbour were very hard work. Just opposite where we lay was the Myrtle Bank Hotel. It had (novelty for those days) a large swimming pool equipped with a bar; swimming and sipping rum and Coke simultaneously were easy to get the hang of; it was more difficult to find time also to pay attention to all the gorgeous womanhood who frequented the pool but drank less. After dark we switched scene to Spanish Town, where stood a notorious open air night club and sin spot called 'The Glass Bucket' where good rum was cheap, the music a pleasure to dance to and the girls a pleasure to dance with. Here we caroused until well after the last Officers' Boat had returned to the ship; our usual return was by local bumboat at around five or six in the morning. Once Colonel Brown and Jock Smith arrived back soaked to the skin. Apparently the Colonel, who was always very dignified in his cups and prone to delusions above his true station in life, had got the idea half way back to the ship that he could do as well as Jesus, so would walk the rest of the way. None of us could understand how Jock, drunk enough for the courage to go to the rescue, had not sunk like a stone.

Many, too, were the parties at private houses; Jamaica society was a very hospitable bunch of people. New phrases came into *Indomitable*'s language – 'Going on a grippo' – 'Strangling the barons' – both meaning 'allowing the locals to entertain us'; both had, in fact, been coined during our Observer course in Trinidad. There was a 'remittance man' who seemed permanently to reside in the bar of the Turtle Tank Hotel and who was so forthcoming with hospitality that you could count on a good evening ashore even if you went without any personal cash at all. I cannot remember his name but will call him James for ease of relating the story. The extent to which he seemed delighted to entertain large numbers of *Indomitable* officers night after night was past belief.

I had met in the club a chap with an Old Eastbournian tie and, getting into conversation, had learned he was deputy head of the Jamaica Police. He was thus so senior to me that I was surprised, one weekend when we were in, to have a personal invitation to dine at his home. I was astonished to find that I was the only guest for dinner. After dinner his very charming wife withdrew and I was then interrogated increasingly intensively about the extent of my colleagues' and my relationship with the man James at Myrtle Bank. Really, all one could say was that he was pretty civilised and much pursued by us somewhat impoverished officers because he was such a surefire 'grippo'.

I was then warned that James was under more than suspicion for being an enemy agent; we junior officers might like to be careful what information we imparted on our 'grippos' in our own interests. As far as he was concerned, the more we kept James going, the better. Island security were confident in their suspicions; they had no evidence on which to secure a conviction and the more we kept James going, the better their chance of getting one. So, back aboard, I did warn my closer friends to be careful.

The point was rubbed home the next weekend when we were in. In the Wardroom for morning coffee we were listening to Lord Haw Haw on the radio. Suddenly he announced:

> 'You think we Germans do not know exactly where the British naval units are. I can tell you, however, that your newest aircraft carrier, the *Indomitable*, is moving this very minute from Berth 23 in Kingston Harbour, Jamaica, to a mooring nearer to Palissadoes . . .'

This was absolutely accurate; top marks to James!

An astonishing aspect of security in those days was the extent to which we could invite civilians aboard to see over the ship. I suppose the Navy felt that it was only proper to return shoreside hospitality. One trick evolved by Charles Morgan for these occasions required the careful synchronisation of one's watch to ship's time. One arranged the tour of the ship to arrive at the foot of the ladder to the Flight Deck just as 'Colours' started to be sounded. Naturally, ladies first up the steep ladder, but a warning to them to stand still for the quite long playing of the Colours. Meanwhile, we stood below, taking in the views above at the head of the ladder.

Believe it or not, someone in the ship invited James aboard for a tour; I wonder what Hitler learned from that?!

Two big personal events happened during that Jamaica phase. First, Cocky Reid, 827's Senior Pilot, got himself engaged and married in the course of three weekends. Nice girl of a leading local family; huge wedding; two day honeymoon. In the event, he did not survive our trip in *Indomitable*. I wonder what became of her. What a super wedding for a marriage which was to last for two days for all practical purposes.

The other was my twentieth birthday. This was important because it meant that as of that day I ceased to be a Midshipman and donned the single golden ring on my arm which defined my dizzy height as a Sub-Lieutenant. Goodbye to my being a boat coxswain; I had two watches to keep on the Quarterdeck on my birthday as Officer of the Watch in Harbour. Anyway, I got ashore before it was too late at night to celebrate and, no doubt, disgraced myself in fine style.

The greatest event of corporate importance to us all at that time was the Japanese attack on the US Fleet at Pearl Harbour. I do not think that Winston Churchill or his chum Roosevelt would have smiled upon the way the young officers of *Indomitable* received the news of this major disaster to the Allied cause. In retrospect, if those officers had been able to foresee what the disaster made possible for the Nips, they might not have celebrated so heavily. It happened like this:

Indomitable was rather proud of its rugger team, which had done well against *Formidable* in Virginia and was quite a strong team on paper. We had a first class string of outsides, led by Johnny Forrest in the centre (a Scottish cap, later to die in his Hurricane in the Mediterranean). We challenged the Island of Jamaica, current Caribbean champions, to a match. Most of our team had had a tremendous 'thrash' the night before the game and were still the worse for rum as we went ashore to the garrison where the match was to be played. A sorry sight we must have looked as a party, in uniforms stained with spilled rum, lipstick and worse. Seemingly we arrived at the wrong gate to the garrison, so there was no-one to meet us. However, we found a rather pleasant alfresco bar alongside the ground, which turned out to be for the garrison NCOs. Here we settled in to prime ourselves. As the second round was being dispensed, a news flash came up on the barman's radio. The Pearl Harbour attack had happened and seemingly the entire US Far East Fleet was sunk. After our experiences in the US our only reaction was, 'Well done, the Nips!' Colonel Brown and I were walking up and down the touchline, still in uniform and glasses in hand as the teams ran out to start. Somehow we were still there in time for kick-off. We played as men possessed as a team, so happy were we, and managed to defeat the mighty Jamaica. They claimed afterwards that it was impossible to live in scrums against us because of the rum fumes.

So ended this happy sojourn; it was with later shame that we realised that if we had not hit Jamaica the first time in, the Japanese would not have got *Prince of Wales* and *Repulse*, that they would not have done so but for their victory at Pearl Harbour which we celebrated so heartily and that what we had celebrated was the beginning of death and misery for millions.

As we sailed I received one more knock. As we were now venturing into more dangerous waters, I was no longer to sleep in my waterline cabin. I could sleep anywhere on the decks above in a hammock to be provided, or in a camp bed in other officers' cabins if any would admit me. I was able to choose the latter on invitation from Colonel Brown, Jock Smith and 'Prangle' Pike who shared a three-bunker. It was very good of them because the addition of me made it very cramped.

Chapter 10

End of Working Up

SAILING FROM KINGSTON coincided with a change in our status; we had been up to then a new ship working-up (though assuredly we would have been called into operations if the situation had demanded it). Now we were regarded as fully operational. We sailed with an escort of three destroyers – their names and class I cannot remember. This was a fairly normal escort for a Fleet Aircraft Carrier; there were always at least two ahead of us as an anti-submarine screen. Whenever we were operating aircraft, the third would take station on our port quarter, some three cables off, so that if a plane went over the side whilst landing on or taking off, there was someone conveniently stationed to pick up survivors quickly.

Whilst keen to get off to the War, I think we all felt a little sad to leave Jamaica where we had had so much fun and RN Air Station Palisadoes who had given us so much help. I was interested to find, as a Metal Box visitor in the seventies, that our Fleet Air Arm Station at Palisadoes had grown to be Manley Airport, handling international jumbo-jets; the same had happened with Piarco in Trinidad, where our camp had disappeared without trace, but our little airfield had grown into the local international airport. However, we were not immediately leaving the Caribbean; we had to call at Port of Spain for certain stores awaiting us there. Naturally, those of us who had trained there were delighted to be making a return visit, however brief.

As we came into through the Bocas (the straits between Trinidad and Venezuela), all Observers were ordered to be ready to go ashore for some training as soon as we dropped anchor. So we found ourselves back in the same old jitneys, roaring back to Piarco where this afternoon's training was to be given. It turned out that Piarco had just received all the data, pictures and silhouettes of the Japanese operational aircraft, so we had a hard afternoon learning how to identify the various types. It will be appreciated that Japanese aircraft recognition had not figured in our original training, as no-one had envisaged them coming into the War.

When the jitneys were going through Port of Spain to get us back to the ship, I put it to the Senior Observer in charge of us (827's Len Williams) that I had friends ashore and asked if I could be dropped off for an evening's shore leave. He gave the OK so long as I promised to be back aboard for the forenoon watch the next day (i.e. by 8 a.m.). So off I went and called on the Ross family, who gave me a great welcome. I took Jean out to the Country Club to dine and dance and then spent a long sentimental evening talking on the Ross verandah. In those days, virginity was respected and so eventually we went off to our separate beds after no more than a good chat and cuddle! In the morning, Harry Ross woke me in good time to get down to the docks. By now he was an officer in the local RNVR at the Dockyard and able to arrange for a boat to take me out to *Indomitable* as she rode at anchor in the bay.

Imagine our horror in finding on arrival at the base that *Indomitable* had sailed in the night! Security was such that no-one in the base could say where she had gone; only that there had been a submarine scare around midnight and she had up-anchored and scarpered. She was known to have embarked all the stores she had called for, so may well have made off to sea. I had not the least idea what the Navy did to new Sub-Lieutenants who missed their ships as they went off to wartime operations, but could imagine that it would be something pretty drastic.

Harry made the point that if she had sailed altogether, there was nothing I could do in a hurry, so it might be worth wasting time on a hunch of his. Some weeks ago, a cruiser had been in and there had been a similar scare. She had merely made off towards the Bocas and laid up in one of the many bays guarded by small islands in that direction. There was enough deep water for *Indomitable* so she may have done the same.

So, on the off-chance, I took a taxi down the coast looking in all the bays. The relief to find her tucked into one was terrific. Then I found a local fisherman with a motor-boat to take me off. Horror of horrors, as we set off I could see the hoses playing down her navel pipes – sure sign that she was already weighing anchor. As we got out to her, she was just under way, but my shouts to the Quarterdeck got me recognised and the Quarterdeck brow was lowered again so that I could jump across and regain my ship. Sydney-Turner, the 827 Squadron Commander, had somehow got himself there in time to greet me. I was to retire to my cabin until sent for and in no way was I to inculpate Len Williams by suggesting that he had granted overnight leave, which had been outside his powers.

An hour or two went by; I imagined court-martial for desertion and all sorts of possibilities – don't forget that in those days to desert 'in the face of the enemy' was a capital offence. Eventually I was called to the Quarter-deck for a walk with the Commander. I told him that I had had permission to make a brief call on local friends and had assumed that, just as in Jamaica or USA, all-night leave could be assumed. Deep apologies etc. etc., for the inconvenience to the ship manoeuvring in close waters whilst I was picked off my fishing boat. 'Did you get the girl?' 'No, sir, I merely stayed the night with her family.' 'Well then, you have wasted everyone's time to no advantage to anyone; I reprimand you and will enter it in the Log.' I have never known whether, had I got the better of Jean Ross, or at least claimed to the Commander that I had done so, I might have avoided this official blot on my escutcheon!

So off we went into the South Atlantic. Quickly we got into a routine – mainly flying anti-submarine patrols ahead of the destroyer screen, but interspersed with navigational, shooting, bombing and depthcharging exercises. Tom Troubridge quickly picked up a short-cut when sending us off for anti-submarine patrol: instead of turning the ship dead into wind to fly off just two Albacores, when he was going to have to do it again ten minutes later to land the two they had relieved, he would send the outgoing patrol off the catapult which did not necessitate a turn right into wind. The catapult take-off was a nasty unnerving acceleration of itself; with four depthcharges and a full fuel load and the ship not into wind it was terrifying. As you left the Flight Deck you seemed to drop like a stone; as the pilot struggled to keep out of the drink, I could look aft; the ship's bow wavecrest seemed higher than us and the ship itself seemed to tower above us. Never, in fact, did I witness an aircraft dropping into the water this way, with the consequent running down by the ship. In the end, we got quite accustomed to it and also made frequent night take-offs from the catapult (better in a way as you could not see the frightening panorama). Always, though, we aircrews took a close look at the loading we were asked to carry if, as sometimes happened, we were asked to go off the catapult in harbour. Then, of course, as the ship lies to the tide, there might be no wind at all against the off-taking plane.

My worst catapult fright was on a pre-dawn take-off. For once, I was to fly with the Senior Pilot, Cocky Reed. He was a bit pissed in the Wardroom the night before, so told me to go to briefing on my own, as it was only an anti-submarine patrol. Pilots of his seniority seemed able to get away with this sort of thing. He would get the fitter to pre-warm the engine and thus climb in himself just before we went.

Catapult drill involved the plane being loaded in a tail-up position on a collapsible carriage on the catapult way. When all were aboard, the pilot would run up his engines and test the two magnetos. After this, the engineer officer in charge on the deck would rotate his signal flag to tell the pilot to rev up for take-off; when he judged that full revs were being held steadily, the engineer would drop his flag and the man on the catapult lever would fire. Not too simple on a dead dark night.

Come this morning, the gunner and I went to briefing and then to the plane on the catapult and climbed aboard. The engine fitter came at the same time and started the engine to warm up. In the course of this, he did actually test magnetos (switching each out in turn) as the pilot would. After a bit the engineer officer, presumably thinking we had a pilot aboard, signalled for run-up for take-off. By coincidence, as I learned after, the fitter opened up the throttle to warm up the engine more. Any second we were going to be shot off with a fitter to fly us, because he was not watching the engineer at all; there was no reason why he should! All I could think of doing was to jump out: a sore business that proved, dropping three feet on to a wet steel deck to be swept away by the slipstream of full propeller revs. At least it saved the day; at first the engineer cursed me for being too frightened to take off, but I explained the lack of qualification of the 'pilot'. End result of all was that in spite of his seniority, Cocky got a tremendous rocket from Commander Flying.

We spent hours and hours on standby in the aircrew room at that time. It was whiled away with a great range of bawdy songs of which I can only remember inconsequential snatches and filthy stories, some of which seemed very funny. The only one I recall now is:

'The Rape of Mrs O'Flaherty'

(This tale depends much on the use of Irish speech, so I fear much of the humour may vanish in my efforts to convey it in type.)

Scene: The Magistrate's Court in Ballyhobgoblin. Mrs O'Flaherty's Lodger is arraigned for raping her. She is in the Witness Box.

Beak: Tell us in your own words, Mrs O'Flaherty, just what took place.
Mrs O'F: Well, your Honour, 'twas like this. As was me wont I took up

his tray of tay in the morning. This day he were laid there on the bed, naked as the day he were born and his member upright as a lamp-post. He was ticklin it with a feather he'd taken from the quilt. He points to a fiver at the bedside and says: 'Mrs O'Flaherty, that fiver says you'd never find a big enough fhart to blow this feather from the end of my prick.'

I have always been of sportive disposition, for a bet, so, says I, 'You're on.' I puts down the trhay and lowers me drawers. I lifts me shkirt and bends to the scene of action as you might say. Jusht as I were searching my bowels for a breath of wind, he ups me, feather and all.

It wasn't the focking I minded, y'r honour, it was the low' down filthy cunning of the bhastard.

I recall some personal sense of achievement when crossing the Line for the first time. Whether it was muted by wartime or because in *Indomitable* most had done it before, I do not know, but we had none of the high jinks with funny 'Neptune' etc. such as is the supposed tradition. This was at Christmas time, so it could be that the main celebratory fervour was being saved for Christmas. I do not remember much about Christmas Day, although it was the first I had spent at sea. After the dawn A/S Patrol, I had a normal Wardroom breakfast; we then tidied into best uniforms and the ship held Divisions on the Deck, a well-supported Christmas Mattins. Then 'Up Spirits' and, following tradition, this was the ratings' day: we officers did much visiting of the mess-decks and the Petty Officers' mess and we helped dish out Christmas lunch in the mess-decks.

Our Wardroom Christmas Lunch came on Boxing Day. Things being quiet operationally in that part of the Atlantic, we relaxed into unheard of numbers of pink gins to prime us for the lunch, which was held with all in a high old state. War, however, has a nasty habit of breaking out when it is least wanted. Just as the pud and mince pies were sliding down, all air crew of 827 and 831, the two torpedo/bomber/reconnaissance Squadrons, were called in emergency to the briefing room.

A German battlecruiser and an armed merchant cruiser were reported loose in our parish; the major unit was thought to be *Gneisenau*. Half of us were to go off and search for them, the other half to stand by with bombs and torpedoes. So, in a high state of Christmas lunch, off we went.

My search pattern was simple: virtually a straight course away from the ship to extreme range, then back to the ship. After I had given him the course, Richard Meakin seemed very quiet, but no-one yelled to and fro through those Gosport tubes just to make conversation. I assumed he was preoccupied in looking out for Krauts just as we were in the back. About ten minutes before we were due to turn for home, I called on Richard for the manoeuvre whereby I could check the wind speed and direction. No answer. There was no way of talking to the pilot in an Albacore other than through the Gosport tube; you cannot prod him because he sits a good yard and a half further forward and the entire intervening fuselage is petrol tank.

I tried putting my Gosport mouthpiece in the slipstream (a cruel way to blast the ears of a pilot who may have gone on to 'auto-pilot' and then nodded off). No effect; his Gosport must be disconnected and his long silence suggested he was asleep as well. What to do? At extreme range, flying away from home with pilot asleep and unproddable. After discussion with Ward, the Air Gunner, I decided that I must go 'out' and waken him. There is a top hatch in the observer's cockpit and just forward of that a little post where the aerial wire from the tail fin was attached. Forward again of that was the pilot's cockpit. Thus I was able to get head and shoulders through my hatch and grasping the aerial post pulled myself on to the top of the fuselage, Ward hopefully hanging on to my heels. From there it was an extreme reach, I could just make a good fist thump on the perspex inches above Richard's head. This I managed 'handsomely', as they say, completely shattering the perspex. He came to with a start. By the time I had got back into the safety of my cockpit and plugged into the Gosport, he was raving into it. Did I normally fly disconnected from the Gosport? Did I not realise we had been hit by something – his cockpit roof had been shattered? It took quite a while to calm him down, explain the happenings and coax him on to a path for home. I still wonder whether the Germans went straight under us and Richard missed them!

During this phase of our commission there was one 'pet' aboard, a Swordfish equipped with drogue-towing equipment. This was quite a clever piece of apparatus. The drogue was a small canvas wind-sock, which was used as a target for ship's guns or other aircraft to practise firing at. It was let out after take-off from the bomb-aiming hatch of the Swordfish and plenty of wire on a reel allowed the drogue to fly at a safe distance from its 'tug'. After the firing exercise, the target operator could reel up the wire by turning a little propeller on the side of the winch into the aircraft's slipstream; this was ample to drive the winch. The plane then flew low up the Flight Deck with the drogue 'close-hauled' and the operator cut the attachment rope at the right moment for the drogue to drop on deck for (hopefully) all the holes to be counted.

Bill Bailey was the keenest and most skilful drogue tower whilst the Swordfish lasted. Unfortunately one day when he was dropping the target, which necessitated watching the ship's 'Island' so as to fly close to it, they had forgotten to lower the ship's aerial masts to the horizontal (sticking out from the ship's side) position. As Bill came down the deck, his port lower mainplane was severed at about the position of the outer struts. It says something for both plane and pilot that Bill was able to bring her round to a safe landing although the port wing braces were trailing in the wind. On an earlier occasion, he distinguished himself with sending the signal to the ship (which was doing a 4.5 inch shoot at the drogue):

'I am pulling this target, not pushing it!' when a misplaced shot had accidentally burst ahead of him.

Without further incident we came up to Table Bay in the early afternoon on New Year's Eve 1941/2. We were lucky, mooring alongside in Cape Town docks; our destroyers had to go on round to Simonstown. We were thus the better placed to enjoy Cape Town's very considerable hospitality for the New Year celebration.

Chapter 11

Far Eastern Fleet

MUCH HAS BEEN WRITTEN about South African hospitality to the British during World War II. It must be remembered to their credit that this was not just a matter of one or two bonanzas offered to the odd passing convoy. For years there was a continual stream of ships passing the Cape – the RN going to cover the Indian Ocean and Far East, troop convoys first to India and the Far East, then for East Africa and the Western Desert. When we read to-day of the miracle of sending the paltry little force which re-took the Falklands so far from home, we seem to have forgotten that we sustained the whole of the Eighth Army via the Cape Route and that meant crossing the U-Boat infested North and South Atlantic Oceans. All these ships, after some three weeks at sea – at their generally low speeds and the devious routes to avoid U-Boats as far as possible – called either at the Cape or into Durban. Both cities kept up their hospitality over the years without flagging.

Security being what it was, the voluntary organisations ashore would not have been aware that *Indomitable* was coming in until we were tying up at about tea-time on New Year's Eve. As we had had Christmas at sea, three parts of Watches were allowed ashore and, as this was possibly the last civilised place we would see for a bit, all took the leave. As each officer or man reached the Dockyard gate, he received his invitation to a family New Year Party. This was not just a triumph of hospitality but a triumph of its organisation, for three parts of our Watches represented about 1,600 chaps. All fixed in about two and a half hours.

Richard Meakin and I were 'taken on' by a delightful family. They lived some way out of the town but I cannot for the life of me remember in which direction – annoying, because in Metal Box days, I became familiar with the whole area. We had drinks at their home to meet the family which contained several in our age bracket. Then on to one of their magnificent country clubs to join up with several other families for the dinner and Ball which saw in 1942. When it all broke up, our hosts were taking us back to the ship, but offered to drop us off if we wished at a good out-of-town night club. Richard being him and me being me, we opted for the latter. There again we had a tremendous reception although they must have been totally used to a transient British services population. There we danced and jollied until the sky was lightening.

It was only when we set forth that we discovered that taxis had stopped in those outlying areas hours before and that we were some six miles from the dockyard. We had done about the first mile when we were overhauled by a street-sweeping machine, driven by an affable coloured gentleman. When he learned our plight, he immediately offered to take us. His machine, one of those things with a little kerbside cab, a large rotating brush under-neath and a tank for the brushings behind, was slow, but a lot faster than walking so we climbed aboard the tank and earned a small applause from the Quarterdeck as we were dropped from this conveyance right at the bottom of the brow. Not many minutes later, Richard and I were outshone in choice of returning vehicle. In those days the dockyard was miles long, running round quite a sector of the bay, and was served by a complex of railroad lines and sidings. Just after our arrival, with clouds of smoke and steam there arrived at the bottom of the brow one of South Africa Railway's largest freight engines. There it stopped and whilst its safety valve blew off to a deafening roar, Bill Bailey and Bob Illingworth (an Engineer Lieutenant who was a pilot in 800 Squadron) dismounted and came aboard. They were quickly followed by an irate and short of breath engine driver, arriving to complain and reclaim his charge. Apparently, discovering that their cab had dropped them at the wrong gate to the dockyard and with two more miles to go, they happened upon this loco fully steamed, but whose crew had gone off for an early morning cuppa – stealing of locos was not, after all, common in those days. Bob had enough engineer knowledge to drive and quickly showed Bill how to switch the hand-operated dockyard points.

I have only two other memories of that visit to Cape Town. I will tell the non-discreditable one first. Someone in the Squadron managed to buy there the Inkspots' record of 'I don't want to set the world on fire' with 'I like coffee, I like tea' on the back. Insignificant, you may say, but it meant a lot to us in future months. These Inkspots renderings were the most favourite and frequently played records at the Glass Bucket in Spanish Town, Jamaica, when the band was resting. They were almost our signature tune and a great solace and reminder of better times when, a few months hence, we lay bored to death at anchor in Addu Attol lagoon.

I do not remember its name, but in central Cape Town there stood a club which was the direct equivalent of the Carlton in London. I imagine it still exists, but I have not seen it in Metal Box days – it would be too far up in the world for mere manufacturers, however far up in their world they might be. In line with standards of Cape hospitality, this closed society opened its doors to give honorary membership to all visiting British naval officers. My first visit to it was with a group of 827 chaps and we had 'primed' ourselves elsewhere rather generously. At the turn of the very grand stairway by which one entered stood a full-sized statue of a very busty Queen Victoria, in somewhat decolleté attire. What overcame me, I know not, perhaps it was just the realism of the piece. As I passed, I reverently put my face into her bosom and then bobbled it from side to side with appropriate sounds of delight. By the time we reached the head of the stairway, there stood a vast dignitary, some ten feet high and apparently 110 years of age. He turned out to be the Secretary; funnily enough he seemed very Afrikaans for such a post in the Cape, but they are very, very puritanical:

'Having witnessed the gross insult offered to your own late Queen, I cannot admit you to this Club.'

I think it was George Measures who quickly apologised if he was af-fronted and explained that I was from a very wild part of Scotland where the greeting I had offered was the one traditional for older ladies whom one held in high respect, such as one's mother or grandmother. Whilst obviously crude in origin, this greeting was the most reverent I could make as I had been brought up, and quite the reverse of an insult. Surely, one would hardly expect the British Navy to offer other than respect to the Great Queen? He let us pass into the Club; whether because he was taken in, or because Cape hospitality overcame his better feelings, I do not know.

All too quickly, our forty-eight hours in the harbour came to an end and we headed out of the Bay once more. I am always confused by compass orientation in Table Bay; it faces north – i.e., you head north to get out of it. When you do geography at school, you expect from its position that it faces south, but in fact the Cape itself is some dozen miles further south. The illusion of facing south is also strengthened for us northern hemisphere dwellers; you look out of the Bay towards the midday sun and thus tend to think you are looking south; it comes hard to remember that for half the world the midday sun is to the north.

It was not long before we were headed east, anyway, now a unit of the

Far Eastern Fleet. Our three escorts came out of Simonstown to meet us off the Cape and we headed away for, initially, we knew not where. It was the beginning of what was perhaps the most depressing six months of the War for the Allies. Things were going badly in the Mediterranean but were unmitigated disaster in the Pacific, China Sea and Malaya. In the Navy we were soon to grieve for the loss of Singapore, which we took as another ineptitude by the British and Australian armies. We already felt deeply the loss of *Repulse* and *Prince of Wales*, two of the finest ships afloat, to the little yellow men who were beginning to look a lot less of a joke than they had seemed to begin with. Worse still, if we had been there with them, instead of tangling with non-aggressive Jamaica, our fighters could probably have saved them, as said earlier.

It seemed that we could be stuck with our present lot in the East for years if no-one sank us. To people like me, who still liked home, this did not seem a line of thought to latch on to too strongly. It was better to take life day by day as it arrived and be thankful for it. What never occurred to me at the time and only comes as a realisation now that I am recalling these times, is the incredible fortitude of our immediate seniors (in years). Only after a taste of married and family life can one realise it. Our married men had left their families on a basis that letters each way could take three months and that was the only communication. Like us, they faced this separation continuing into the indefinite future. There was no special leave or relief to take home leave after so many years in this theatre. I cannot imagine what it was like for them, but they never bleated about it. There was, for instance, Terry Blank, a pilot in 827. He had been a Merchant Navy officer, sunk in mid-Atlantic. He had done sixty-three days in a lifeboat in the tropics virtually without food or water for the second half. The boat was crammed with some fifty-odd people at the start. When it eventually drifted into a small Caribbean island, it contained three unconscious men, one of them him. Terry thus got home to his wife and child and then transferred to the Fleet Air Arm. Now he had left them again, with another Blank on the way. Not surprising that he was the 'quiet' (but never complaining) man of the Squadron.

We had been only a day or two steaming East when Tom Troubridge announced that new orders had come. We were to go to Aden and disembark the two Albacore Squadrons temporarily to leave space in the ship to embark RAF fighters which were to be ferried from the Western Desert to help the defence of Singapore. Thus, we only had about ten days at sea before flying ashore to the RAF base at Khormaksa outside Aden. The ship only came into port for a few hours for us to board and collect kit. Then, sadly, we watched her sail. It is a funny feeling to see your home, for that is what she had become, going away to leave you! Anyway, watched from ashore, she was a fine spectacle as she cleared Steamer Point and made off to Port Sudan to find her Hurricanes. We returned to Khormaksa for the novel experience of learning what life was like in a peacetime style RAF base. The answer was 'lousy' for the Royal Navy. I imagine that it may be a little worse now as a front line Russian airbase, but not much!

Chapter 12

Bloody, Bloody RAF

BEFORE THE WAR, the British reckoned virtually to control the Arabian peninsula. A variety of methods were combined to achieve this. One could bribe the various local leaders to co-operate; one could remind them that we had quite a lot of nasty things we could do with our armed forces; one could indulge in the very foundation of the Pax Britannica, the principle of 'Divide and Rule', whereby one stirred up enough chiefs to niggle at each other to keep them too busy to unite against us. A main weapon for retribution of the disobedient was the RAF; with planes, our chaps could live in comparative comfort and not have to make uncomfortable journeys to take matters up with the recalcitrants, as the Army had previously had to do.

A disobedient village, or more likely a tribe living in tents, would be flown over and told by loudspeakers to get out and after a pause their homes and possessions would be bombed to smithereens. Because we gave them time to get themselves out (just), ours was a relatively benevolent rule. In comparison, the Italians in Eritrea and Abyssinia were evil because they just got on with the bombing and sometimes used poison gas. I am not sure that we always remembered to carry out the first exercise with loudspeakers. Anyway, all that is to explain why the British had made themselves the owners of a pretty well-built and equipped air base at Aden, long before the War.

It had a very grand Officers' mess, with rooms for bachelor officers in two wings running off it. On arrival, we were told that these quarters were full, so we must live in the 'Other Ranks' married quarters the other side of the site, some half mile through the sand and extreme heat. An inconvenience and an irritating one, because it came out later that there was some room in the wings, but the RAF was keeping it 'in case we have more drafts of personnel sent to us'. We suggested that at least they should move out their most junior officers from the wings to let in our senior officers. No dice.

They saw our arrival, some fifty officers, as a Heaven-sent opportunity to whack up their mess funds. The day before we arrived, their mess committee just about doubled the messing rates, telling the RAF locals that there was a financial crisis but the doubled rates would only need to apply for about two months – the expected duration of our visit – to clear it. Our wise and artful seniors told us to make no complaint about this; they would 'see us right'. On messbill day, our senior officer, mess bill in hand, went to the Group Captain in charge, but with a copy of a recent Admiralty Fleet Order in the other hand. This stated that whilst their Lordships did not wish to interfere with mess arrangements for officers, it had to be fixed that junior officers in wartime (Lt. Commanders and below) were not to be charged more than £x per month. £x was only a little above the previous Khormaksa rate. End of mess financial crisis; everyone's bill back to the old rate.

For their intrepid work of bombing unarmed Arab ladies, the two RAF Squadrons at Khormaksa had Vickers Bombay bombers, vintage but sound twin-engined bi-planes. However the Vichy French were still in control in Djibuti and Allied policy was that it would be easier to sea-blockade them to stop supplies than to invade and winkle them out. Sea blockade was relatively easy – air patrols, with a couple of Aden-based destroyers to call up if anything was found making in a Djibuti direction. So our RAF friends had been given a job of work to do with their Bombays. As soon as we arrived, the gallant Group Captain invited us to take on a share of the patrolling, which we happily accepted.

We were less happy when we discovered that the share of patrolling allocated to us was one hundred per cent. The Group Captain explained that this was fair as we had planes which had been designed to go over the sea. We felt that planes do not really know whether they are over the land or the sea and made for good measure the point that RAF's Coastal Command did many more hours than us flying over the sea in planes designed originally for 'flying over the land'. However, we got the last laugh. We found a coaster making for Djibuti (Richard Meakin and I did, actually) so the destroyers brought her into Aden. The Officer in Charge there took from her a vast barrel of 'Biddy' (French army issue wine) and sent it up to 827 Squadron as a prize. With great generosity, 827 decided to share it with all the other aircrews currently involved in the patrolling.

The RAF had several grounds for being none too pleased with their Fleet Air Arm visitors. We caused a comfortably half-full mess to become rather uncomfortably overcrowded, particularly in respect of recreational facilities, e.g. tennis courts and 'The Yacht'. In relation to the last item we completely blacked our name. It was a 35-foot dhow hull which had been ingeniously Bermuda-rigged. She had had to be 'stiffened' with a great deal of scrap iron ballast, so that all who used her had to be warned that if partially capsized to let in much water, she would sink like a stone. Not only would an irreplaceable boat be lost, but probably also the crew, because off Steamer Point it was said that there lurked the hungriest pack of man-eating sharks in the world. We could book in advance to borrow her for half a day at a time and enormous fun she was. Bill Bailey, who had been coaching me in sailing in the ship's whalers, cutters and dinghy (we had an International 14 ft. in the hangar deckhead) took me off in the dhow a few times and we had some terrific sails. Then one day it happened; one of our FAA parties took her out and getting a bit too sporty on a beat, put her over. She went down like a stone; they saw no sharks so had the shame of returning to the mess to confess.

I think the problem really was that the RAF were a bunch of career regulars who had been a year or two in their concentrated community. They had not suffered the large dilutions of the un-pukka 'hostilities only' which units of all three services were used to in the European theatre. It jarred that we, substantially HO (hostilities only) people, were in a much more operational mob than they; it jarred that we had our rather alcoholic and carefree ways in 'their' mess. Either way round, little love was lost. They indulged in inordinate worship of aircrew; we gave higher priority to looking after our men on the deck.

We achieved close alliance with the RAF for one operation. Here the enemy was the local Army garrison. One morning a hospital ship, a converted liner, called on her way up the Red Sea, empty of patients but full of nurses to collect Anzac casualties from 8th Army and take them back to Oz. A shipload of healthy Aussie nurses who have been cooped up idle at sea for four weeks is a powder keg well worth the broaching. Our RAF mess Secretary was despatched to the ship to invite them all to a dance in Khormaksa mess. He was just ten minutes behind the Army's ambassador on just the same mission. The latter had been accepted, so our invitation was turned down as the ship was going up to Port Sudan next day. At least he had the wit to find out what time the ladies were bid to the 'Brown Jobs' ' ball.

All Khormaksa's transport was lined up outside the dock gates just in advance of the due hour, occupying all parking space nearest to the gates. The Army thus had to park further down the road. It was easy work in the dark to call out to the ladies (?) emerging from the gates : 'Transports for the dance' and fill up our vehicles. By the time they had gone all the way to Khormaksa and emerged into the light of the RAF mess to realise their mistake, it was rather too late to go back and anyway they found us all too gorgeous to be wanting to. Talk about a Ball!

Another evening's entertainment was a purely FAA affair. A few miles up the road from Khormaksa – away from Aden – there was an Arab small town called Sheik Othman. The RAF had put it out of bounds to all personnel, regarding it as dangerous for those off-duty because it was reputed to be full of 'disaffected elements'. They were unamused at our query as to why they had not bombed it flat instead of putting it out of bounds. To a bunch of us in 827 who had never seen an Arab town and had visions of the casbah seen in *Beau Geste* films, this was too much of a challenge. We argued to ourselves that the gallant Group Captain might put a ban on RAF personnel, but surely he had no authority to keep the Navy out?

After dark, therefore, about half a dozen of us headed off to foot it to Sheik Othman. As we approached, it appeared ominous in the moonlight but very dull – rows and rows of flat-roofed mud-brick buildings lining narrow streets. The 'streets' were bare sand. Because of its reputation with the RAF, we grew a little nervous wandering these streets; we had no side arms and would have been helpless if ambushed, but there was absolutely no-one about at all: no dirty postcard vendors or dusky maids in doorways such as the lucky Beau Geste and his chums encountered without fail in such places. We had just concluded that we had made a long dusty march for nothing and the more faint-hearted amongst us (which included me) were wanting to depart as quickly as possible when a tall Arab appeared walking amongst us as if by magic. Not blessed with fluent English he had difficulty in conveying that he would show us the way. Where to?

The majority felt we had better fall in with him to avoid trouble. I and the rest of the faint-hearted were sure we were being lured into a trap. The debate was conducted on the move and before the motion was put to the vote we were ushered into a dim courtyard with paraffin lamps and given chairs (these had to be fetched). Then our guide and his friends put before us cups of what he called 'char', which we, of course, understood. It was quite incredibly strong and very, very, bitter (?drugged, wondered the faint hearts). Then began the dreadful caterwauling of Arab music on a hand-wound gramophone. In came a bonny lass looking about seven months pregnant and performed what we took to be a belly dance. The girl was so far gone and her dancing so far short of Sadlers Wells' standards, it was excruciating. At the end we applauded with gusto, fear of offending by now overwhelming our honesty.

Next appeared a string of little girls, about ten years old, naked except for a sort of G-string. It took time for the message to come through to us that we were in fact in a 'knock shop' and here were les girls! (What would Beau Geste have thought?!) We kept stolidly on at our tea sipping – you will realise that it was the kind that invites being made to last. Our lack of immediate interest in the 'ladies' was starting to cause concern. One of them was brought up to us and up-ended. The G string and something unmentionable else was pulled aside and for the first time we heard the catch phrase of the East uttered seriously:

'See, sirs, pink inside just like Queen Victoria.'

Led by our most courageous, we passed round a hat to collect all the local currency we could muster and passed it over. Consternation at what was taken to be quite unknown payment in advance, and many times over the going rate, allowed us to get up and flee before resentment set in. We went back to the gates of Khormaksa at a pace which the Light Infantry would have been proud of. This is a silly venture to recount; it was amazing though, at the time, what fun it all seemed – after we were safely home!

Our only other (and legitimate) resorts if escaping the mess – it hurt in that last paragraph to call it 'home' – were the Aden Officers' Club, the Steamer Point Hotel and a beach reserved for officers to bathe. The Officers' Club was no more than a bar, snack bar and billiard table. Quite chummy atmosphere, but really rather dull. The only 'funny' I ever witnessed there concerned Bill Bailey. Seated on the bar at closing time one evening, he was haranguing us about something or other when accosted by a Paymaster-Commander from the local naval base:

'Have you been round both Capes, Lieutenant?' says the Paymaster-Commander (an attempted tick-off: tradition says that only those who have been round Horn and Good Hope are entitled to sit on the bar).

With absolute truth, Bill replies: 'Yes sir, under sail.'

Collapse of stout party; Bill had in fact served an apprenticeship in the Merchant Marine which involved a return trip to Australia in one of the last grain ships under sail. The Steamer Point Hotel was a sleazy sub-Trust

House Forte level oriental hotel; its use was that you could eat there – quite dreadfully – in between drinking sessions at the Officers' Club. The beach was a bore; what is the point of a beach with all male officers and no bikinis?! Shopping in Steamer Point amounted to no more than stocking up with tropical uniforms: the Indian tailors were good and very quick; there was also a funny little shop which made Egyptian cigarettes of high quality. It was a little off-putting to see the filthy little proprietor making them; his few teeth were black and he kept spitting disgusting gobs on to the floor in between licking the seams of the cigarettes one was purchasing. One or two visited the local whore, an aged and very dark lady who hung around one of the hotel bars.

All in all, Aden was a great bore and an anti-climax just as we had thought ourselves to have become a fully fledged part of the Eastern Fleet. I suppose in fact we were not there much over four weeks, but it was a great thrill to get our twenty-four hours' notice (security being what it was) to pack and fly back aboard. We packed all we had got and succeeded in getting the remains of our barrel of Biddy back to *Indomitable*. The joke with this had rather misfired in that we had found it almost undrinkable; back aboard, however, we discovered how to use it palatably, disposing of two unpopular items in the booze stocks: one part of Cape brandy to two of Biddy made quite a good poor man's port. Whilst most of the stuff went back to the ship by truck, we took our airfield equipment in traditional style, bicycles, bomb trolleys etc, tied to wing struts or slung underneath; we had all the appearance of a gang of flying tinkers.

It was great to be back aboard. Only one change really; the Wardroom committee had sacked the messman. Probably the system has been dropped by the Navy years ago so one might record here what a messman was. He was a civilian hired directly by the Committee of a Wardroom (usually only capital ships and the largest cruisers); in no way was he an Admiralty employee. He was usually British but quite often Maltese or Chinese were hired on those stations. He made a contract to provide food and drink to the mess to a standard the Committee laid down for an agreed figure per month. He got no salary; he was expected to use his expertise in buying in all sorts of places to make his own money in the profit at which he sold to the Wardroom. Usually they gave a very good service; usually too, in a big ship, they were very, very rich. Ours had sought too often to put up his rates to the Wardroom, pleading wartime inflation. The Committee thought they could do better themselves. In time did we learn that busy officer committee members directing chief cook and chief steward, neither of whom know local markets, cost a lot more than the expert giving the job full-time, even if he does take a massive profit.

With great relief we sailed, but yet again headed north-west. All Squadrons left a few planes at Khormaksa (flown ashore, with other planes fetching the crews back aboard). We were to do another ferry run, for RAF Spitfires this time.

Chapter 13

In which, at last,
we join the Fleet Proper

FROM ADEN, we headed up the Red Sea to Port Sudan, in order to embark our new RAF 'friends' or 'Crabs'. The Navy referred to the RAF by this term because of the colour of their uniform. The standard naval treatment for the affliction of crabs, caught by some naughty sailors ashore, was an unpleasant ointment of a bluey battleship grey colour, generally known as 'crab fat'. In fact, being operational men from the desert, they proved to be a far superior type to what we had encountered at Khormaksa. On the previous ferry trip, we had all been left ashore to make room in the ship's hangars for standard Hurricanes, which took up a lot of hangar space per aircraft. This time we used two new ideas to get more of the RAF fighters stowed without having to leave as many of our own complement ashore.

First, one of *Indomitable*'s engineer officers had the idea of 'Outriggers'. These were bits of channel section steel pivoted to the edge of the Flight Deck by a vertical pin and stayed from swinging fore or aft by ropes. When at right angles to the deck side, the tail wheel of a fighter could be run out along the channel until the main wheels of the plane were right at the edge of the deck; thus, only the engine and propeller were obtruding into the Flight Deck area. By this means, planes could be parked all along the side of the ship, virtually on the Flight Deck but not inhibiting flying operations.

Second, it was thought that if we took a few RAF airframe riggers with us, they would be able to teach our naval aircraft riggers *en route* the details of how to fit the wings on to Spitfires. So all the Spits parked in our hangars had had their wings taken off and stored elsewhere on board and quite a few could be got into the limited space.

Luckily we managed to get them all embarked at Port Sudan in little over twenty-four hours in port. It was hell whilst we were there; the whole of the ship's ventilator systems had broken down. In a temperate climate this would be bad news in a ship overcrowded with a wartime extra complement of people; in the Red Sea it was really hell. The cabin I shared with Colonel Brown, Jock Smith and Prangle Pike had been designed for two junior officers and was immediately under the Flight Deck. This deck was a naked steel surface, capable of attaining some fierce temperatures in sunny climes. As an example, the latest fashion in footwear, brought in by our guests, was 'desert boots' – suede uppers on crepe rubber soles. It was quickly discovered that if you wore them on the Flight Deck, they went all sticky; if you stood still for a few seconds, they melted on the deck and you were stuck to it. Some wag broke an egg on to the Flight Deck and it was cooked in minutes. Our cabin was uninhabitable whilst the ventilation was off, as you may imagine. This was, of course, long before the days of air-conditioning, so I would not be too sure that we could have stayed in the cabin long with ventilation running. We had to bed down on the Wardroom sofas.

We lay alongside the wharf for this embarkation with other ships ahead and astern of us and thus needed to move sideways to get out when we were ready to go. By then, of course, a local tug strike had begun. I believe we were the first carrier to think up the way out of this situation; we lined up all the aircraft we could accommodate on the Flight Deck with their tails pointing at the quay. Lashed down and chocked, they then ran up their engines to full throttle; the thrust from them all was enough to move *Indomitable* sideways out from her berth.

After four or five days at sea came the big thrill; at last we joined up with the Eastern Fleet, of which we had been nominally part for quite some weeks. This was bigger, I suppose, in terms of men and numbers of big ships, than the entire British (and probably EC) Navy of today. It was a magnificent sight at sea. Our Flagship was *Warspite*, a battleship of the Queen Elizabeth class. These ships had been among the most modern battleships to serve in World War I, so were some twenty-five years old but that is, after all, no older than *Hermes* is now (1970s). Some of them had been virtually rebuilt (*Queen Elizabeth* and *Warspite*) with new engines to give them over 20 knots and secondary armament – sixteen 4-inch guns, if I remember right – mounted in turrets instead of batteries. The main armament was eight 12-inch guns. Then we had four of the old R class battleships, also with eight 12-inch guns, but not rebuilt since Jutland: *Ramilles*, *Royal Sovereign*, *Revenge* and *Resolution*. Our sister ship *Formidable* joined a little later and we had the old carrier *Hermes*. I cannot remember how many cruisers we had: three or more with 8-inch guns and half a dozen with 6-inch. Several Tribal class destroyers, the largest class in this category and very beautiful looking ships with a turn of speed around 35 knots. Dozens of other smaller destroyers.

They kept company with us until we were well round Ceylon, when we parted again, taking an Australian pair of destroyers and an English one as escorts, and made towards Java. Then our flying was steadily reduced for twenty-four hours whilst our ground crews worked round the clock putting wings on the hangar-stowed Spitfires. As they were completed, these planes were ranged on the Deck. Their pilots, a pleasant bunch, were getting steadily more apprehensive. They had had some days to watch our flying and it seemed beyond their comprehension that we could get airborne from such a short 'runway'. They did not seem able to believe that a ship's speed of say 20 knots (it would probably be 30 for them) in a wind of say 15 means that the plane has 35 knots towards take off speed before it has begun rolling. They would not be required to land on again; indeed, without any arrestor hooks, they could not do so in theory. Maybe their apprehension was because their wings were being put on by sailors who had never handled Spitfires!

In the outcome, the Japs were closing in on Singapore and things got urgent, so instead of going to Java, they were to go to Sumatra, which was nearer. They all got off OK as might have been expected; one in fact had engine failure after getting off and we landed him on again by dint of steaming full speed into wind and having no barrier up, so doubling the normal length of the landing run. This plane we kept in the ship and rigged on it an arrestor hook taken from a Sea Hurricane. Flown by Dicky Cork, it proved its worth in the later convoy to Malta.

We withdrew from the Sumatra coast to rejoin the Fleet. At this time, Richard Meakin was very seedy with dysentery and when we were within range of Colombo he was flown off to hospital and I lost my regular pilot. My first 'driver' after losing Richard was a very inexperienced chap who had come in as a replacement – a New Zealander. The fact that I am alive results from the naval practice that the Observer, not the pilot, is Captain in a naval aircraft (or was in those days). First time out with this clot we were some forty-five minutes away from the ship when the rear cockpit filled with smoke. I asked Morrell what was up. He then noticed that he had very low oil pressure – another Taurus engine packing up. As we were up at about ten thousand feet he said he felt we must jump for it.

'Not on your Nelly!', says I.

We had a strict radio silence, so in no way could we put out a distress call and have a hope of being found, if we jumped. The thing to do was to get as near to the ship as we could; then we might meet other planes who would watch us; we might even get back on board. So I persuaded him to ease off the throttle into the shallowest glide he could keep and 'steer' for home. When we were nearly down to the sea, the smoke had reduced, so we opened throttle enough just to climb and continued to do so until the smoke was again too thick. After two repetitions of this manoeuvre, the ship was distantly in sight and, bless her, seeing our smoke, she put on full speed toward us and then turned into wind – so we got down with dry feet. It turned out that one of our lower cylinders had cracked and leaking oil had made the smoke. It was amazing that it had kept going – a better Taurus than some of them; at least the sharks had had to look elsewhere for their tea.

For quite a while now I had no pilot – in fact it was not until July, after being loaned to 800 Squadron, that I got back to a regular 827 pilot – John (Prangle) Pike. I think I only got him because Colonel Brown, his regular, had by then refused to have any more to do with him – but more of that in the right place.

So then we made the long passage back to Aden to pick up the few planes we had left behind. This was our first experience of keeping sea for weeks on end. It involved some novel seamanship for those days – we being refuelled from a tanker who came out to meet us and we from time to time refuelling our destroyer escorts. To-day's Navy has drilled and drilled at such games; we were pioneering them, which was perhaps more fun. We certainly felt a sense of achievement when we flew off planes and landed on whilst the tanker attended to our needs on the starboard side.

The other memory of long spells at sea is how dull the diet got. I recall that in those pre-instant potato powder days, spuds had to be kept in ventilated storage of which there was not much; in less than a week we were out of spud; in under a fortnight we were bored with rice. I do not think we had freezers, only refrigerator 'chill' stores, so after about a month, fresh meat and vegetables had disappeared. I recall lunching with Colonel Brown at such a period and grumbling at the nosh. The Paymaster-Commander who happened to be sitting opposite was stirred (as Chairman of the mess Committee which had sacked the messman, he was, perhaps, a little sensitive):

'Do you realise, young men, that when Lord Nelson had been at sea for half this time, all he would have had to eat was hard tack and perhaps occasional maggoty salt pork? What was good enough for him should, I would have thought, be good enough for you!'

'Really, sir,' replies the Colonel, quick as a flash, 'You know, I wouldn't have touched Lady Hamilton with a bargepole.'

It was a straight turn-round in Aden and back to the Fleet in Trincomalee. This was a lovely harbour and for the day or two we were in I had great sailing with Bill Bailey, one trip in a cutter with some of our 'ground' crew and one in a whaler on our own. As we came back from the last, *Indomitable* was signalling the recall of all her boats. The entire Fleet was putting to sea on an emergency basis, which could only mean that there were Japs about. Whilst Singapore had fallen, the Japanese Navy had up to then been too busy with the Yanks to come into the Indian Ocean.

Incidentally we heard in Trincomalee that all the Spitfires we had carried to Sumatra had been lost the next day. The silly clots had left them parked in a line in front of their hangars; it did not take more than one or two runs for Jap fighters to bag them all on the ground. One felt that intrepid airmen from the Western Desert might have done a mite better. So 28 March found our fleet at sea, but not all together. By this time we were at our new Fleet base, Addu Atoll. Colombo and Trincomalee, which had been our supposed homes, were now regarded as too insecure for re-fuelling, re-fitting and re-victualling. They found us an anchorage in a coral atoll lagoon called Addu Atoll. It was ten miles south of the equator at the tail end of the Maldive chain. There was nothing there but coral; auxiliaries came there to bring us replenishments. All you could do was admire the sight of a big Fleet at anchor and swim from the shore. The latter was a risk too; the coral grazed you easily and caused a virulent sepsis. Some cruisers were in Colombo. *Hermes* had been delayed leaving Trinco; the rest of us fairly quickly split into two groups, so that the four R class who could not keep up could be left astern at sea. I seem to remember that 10 knots was their limit, such was the state they were in by then.

There followed a very sad few days for the RN. Somewhere around 31 March, Colombo suffered a major air strike, indicating that the Japs had moved in in some force. Later I was to learn that they had wounded Richard Meakin. We were to rendezvous successively with two big cruisers coming out of Colombo: *Dorsetshire* and *Cornwall*. In both cases our aircraft looking for them only found flotsam and a few survivors in the water. Leaving a few destroyers to help them, we moved towards a meeting with *Hermes*: again the same story. Also sunk had been the corvette *Holyhead* and two Fleet Auxiliaries. The second week of April was spent in searching for the Japanese Fleet and eventually they were found by 827; I do not remember who was the pilot involved but I think it was Robin Grant-Sturges. The Observer was 'Hutch' Hutchinson. They found at about maximum range and broke radio silence to report virtually all Vice-Admiral Nagumo's Fleet: five carriers, four battleships and two big cruisers. The critical factor was their air strength; following American practice, they had unarmoured carriers which could carry a lot of aircraft – over three hundred in this fleet. *Indomitable* and *Formidable* were armoured, which made them less vulnerable, but at sacrifice of the number of planes they carried, some seventy between them.

Admiral Syfret was Commander in Chief flying his flag in *Warspite* and Vice-Admiral Dennis Boyd, Admiral i/c Carriers, flying his in *Indomitable*. Boyd had joined us in Aden. Syfret was responsible for all strategic decisions. He decided the only hope for a British success would be by a night strike; we could use cover of darkness to get through their formidable fighter screens and maybe get a few hits. At the same time we must avoid them getting in a daylight strike as they had enough planes to swamp our thin fighter screen. As soon as Hutch's signal was received, our Fleet turned back on its tracks to get as far as we could beyond Jap aircraft range until dusk. Hutch was given no signal of this; it would be better to lose his crew than risk betraying our position by using radio. Thus, by the time he was back, we were some sixty miles from where he expected to find us. Luckily he guessed what we had done and found us with about one pisspot of petrol left. They had had a poor time; a Nip fighter had jumped them before they got into cloud; the air-gunner was hit and also the petrol tank. Hutch had to attend to the latter if they were to get back, so the gunner had lost a lot of blood on the hour and a half run home. You will remember that the fuel tank occupied the entire fuselage between Observer and pilot; luckily it had not been hit by explosive or incendiary ammunition, so he had no fire and a fairly clean hole to plug. He did this by hand using a rag; this cost him quite a lot of skin – human skin does not take kindly to being soaked in petrol for an hour and more.

No attempt was made to send planes to shadow the Japs; it risked giving away our presence and losing much needed planes for our forthcoming night strike. *Formidable*, being more recently out from home, had four Albacores equipped with the latest gadget which we called ASV (Aircraft/Surface Vessel) – a primitive radar which, with luck at a good height, could pick up a sizeable ship at forty or so miles. Thus, it was calculated, if these four fanned out at dusk with this range of 'visibility', they must find the Japs whatever courses they had taken since Hutch had fixed them. The rest of our Albacores were ranged on deck and armed, a few with flares and armour-piercing bombs, the rest with torpedoes to be sighted by the light of the flares. A torpedo attack involved diving to the surface about five miles off the target and skipping the wave tops until under a mile off, then dropping the 'fish' and dodging out of gunnery range as quickly as possible. Once they were aware of us (they were known to have radar), they could fire starshell to illuminate us and pick us off with their guns. I cannot even remember which pilot I was crewed with that night; I presume he was as frightened as me!

After briefing, as the wait would be quite long, we were allowed to sit in our gear in the Wardroom. At least, when *Formidable*'s four searchers went, we knew there would not be much over an hour to go in all probability. I cannot say that our mood was of itching to get at them; it was more a matter of keeping wanting to go to the loo. They may have been funny little yellow men a few months back; now they were cruel, skilful, well-armed supermen who had sunk a lot of American and British Navy as well as taking Malaya, Singapore and half the Pacific in what seemed like a few short weeks.

I remember the fury of the Squadron at Sydney-Turner, our CO, who tried to take the mickey out of me. It had already been noted that he was a funk; for weeks he never went out of sight of the ship on his assignments; minutes after taking off he would be back with supposed engine trouble (always a real possibility, after all, with the Taurus). He asked me as we waited how I felt.

'Frightened silly, sir,' I said.

He then called the attention of the boys to the fact that they had a self-confessed coward in their midst. I was relieved that they gave him the contempt he deserved, all implying that they too were frightened but that was not the same as being yellow.

His subsequent history was sad and it becomes obvious that he was a man who had been pushed for too long on operations up to the point of mental collapse. He was sent home before the end of *Indomitable*'s commission and eventually the news came back to us that he had drawn his revolver on the Portsmouth/Gosport ferry and shot himself. One of us speculated why he should go and do that.

'Because,' asserted Colonel Brown, 'He always wanted to die at sea.'

Our wait was a very long one; we heard the four *Formidable* planes come back and were then stood down. The ASV in the two planes at the centre of the 'fan', the most likely ones to find the enemy, had gone on the blink, so they found nothing. After the War I read that Nagumo was short of fuel and stores and he had made off once he had been spotted; that night must have been the last chance we had of jumping him. I often wonder whether, if those ASVs had worked, I would have participated in the first British victory over the Japanese Navy. This action did however earn me a medal – at the end of the War they awarded campaign stars for all the major campaigns of the War, besides the 39/45 Service Medal (with a rosette for those in before 1941) and the Victory Medal. In my case I had the Atlantic, North Africa and Burma Stars and the 39/40 rosette. For the Navy the Burma Star qualification was to have been operational north of Lat. 10° North and West of 80° East. Nagumo led us just into that area so we all qualified but I have never been anywhere near Burma!

To think that a few months previously I had felt some sense of achievement in crossing 'The Line'; now, having been catapulted off for A/S patrol if we were in harbour, or flown off if at sea, we crossed the line four or five times a day!

We had one quick dive into Colombo in *Indomitable* in this period. I spent it at the hospital, where Richard Meakin had gravitated. He had recovered from his dysentery some weeks before and was waiting at China Bay (Trincomalee Fleet Air Arm Base) for the opportunity to get back to us when the alarm of the impending Japanese raids went up. Richard and a few others in the same predicament were put into the few Swordfish at China Bay and told to fly to Colombo, where they could pick up a torpedo each and set forth to sink the Japs. Whoever had this idea either did not know the size of the Japanese force, or was lining up the boys for posthumous VCs! They had the luck to arrive over Colombo city at the height of the Japanese raid. After an encounter with one bunch of fighters, Richard realised there was no hope of keeping his Swordfish in the air with so many of the Japs attacking, so he landed on the beach. He and his crew were making for the cover of palm trees when a Jap strafed them; his crew were killed and Richard had a leg shot off. So that was goodbye to him from *Indomitable*. He was very low then but much more cheerful when I met him years later in Rosyth; he had just discovered that his aluminium calf would nicely accommodate a bottle of Johnny Walker, so every time he visited ships in harbour, he could smuggle ashore a bottle of duty-free. Most of 827 went to his wedding.

We seemed to be ages based in the boredom of Addu Attol for a couple of days and then patrolling at sea for a few weeks. I cannot however say that I regretted that the Japanese were not livening things up for us. At this time I got to know George Measures much better; he was another Observer in 827 who had been on the same course in Trinidad. He had been studying music in Paris before the War and had many a tale to tell about the Rive Gauche life. He claimed to have known Mistinguette well and also Piaf: old enough respectively to have been his mum and his granny, I would think. He was trying to get a symphony he had composed published and performed. He loved Gregorian chant and spent hours drilling me at it. Every day we had to chant our way through Ship's Daily Orders, which ran to about two pages of foolscap, until we had got it up to a standard he could accept. It passed the time and I have loved Gregorian chant ever since. There was one great compensation: a supply ship brought that very rare commodity, mail from home.

Like all good things, our servitude at Addu Atoll came to an end and the whole Fleet sailed up to Bombay. Why, I do not know, because I cannot see what threat to either Germany or Japan we could present from that part of the ocean. What they did need to know was where we were; there could be no easier way for them to find out if we lay in the roads off Bombay in full view of the city. Perhaps kind powers that be had decided it was time for Jolly Jack to have a nice jolly ashore.

It was a nice place to go, but the only problem was that the ships moored several miles from the Gateway to India, where our libertymen had to be landed, and all ships had only their own boats for ferrying. No overnight leave; all ships' last boats off at midnight. Jolly Jack takes no boat but the last one in these circumstances, so the result was that around midnight you had eight to ten thousand drunk Jacks around the modest sized Gateway steps awaiting boats. There were always too many for each ship's last boat, so it had to make another trip (maybe another after that too). Boats could take over an hour to make the return trip, so by two or three in the morning you had a lot of very bored and bloody-minded, besides drunk, matelots. Every night the Patrol had one hell of a job keeping order.

The Patrol was the equivalent of the Military Police, of which in those days we had no equivalent in the sense that the Patrols were not full timers on service police work. The Duty Ship provided the Patrol from its ordinary crew, sometimes supplementing it with ratings from other ships. They were gunnery ratings on duty under the command, in a big place like Bombay, of the Duty Ship's Gunnery Officer, resplendent in his shiny black gaiters and assisted by several tough gunner's mates, and, of course, the Master at Arms. The shore patrol were armed with batons, longer and thinner than a policeman's truncheon.

In circumstances like this the more liberal ships officers' boats would fill up, when they had room, with some of their ratings. One night a boat from one of the stuffier battleships refused this; it was their Guns who was officer of the Patrol. Bravely, with his patrol lined on either side of him, he shouted to all to keep back; this was an officers' boat. Inexorably the mob of tired ratings slowly crept forward from pressure at the back. Thump, thump went the Patrol's batons; still the pressure was there; Guns' heels were over the edge of the harbour wall and he was tum-to-tum with a bunch of stokers; thump, thump, thump . . . splash; Guns was in the 'Oggin.

We had some pleasant times in Bombay, though, before the nightly wait for boats. The first event of the typical run ashore was the Thé Dansant at the Taj Mahal Hotel. (I had some fun in 1972 making a complaint to the management . . . 'I have been using this hotel for forty years . . .!') It was a very stately do, strictly officers only. The ladies were local British and Indian of the upper bracket; many very young and beautiful, but you were not allowed more than three dances with the same one. However, all seemed willing to dance without first being introduced! We were made honorary members of the Royal Bombay Yacht Club, the Bombay Gymkhana and the Willingdon, so did not lack clubs to go to. The only problem was that all bars shut at nine p.m. It seemed worse than Scotland! We experimented with a way round this. Taking a couple of horse gharries at nine one night we asked the drivers to take us where we could get a drink. Our ignorance of Bombay was such that we saw no significance in the name as we turned into Grant Road. For years it has been known for its range of brothels from the caged girls standard up to the five star hotel touch. Our gharries stopped at one of the latter. It was very comfortable inside; the girls were quite stunning, mostly Anglo-Indians and by no means pushing to get on with the business. So we were able to meet our objective of some more to drink and enjoy some pleasant female conversation at the same time. The girls at one of these places were very proud of the fact that the film star Merle

Oberon, later Lady Korda, had been one of their sorority until a few years back. After the third round, Madame would get a bit restive that business was not proceeding and it was usually after the fourth that it was get upstairs or out. You could find difficulty in getting in again on another night, but there were always more establishments down the road. Thus 827 were able to claim that we had been thrown out of more Bombay brothels than most in the Navy!

Chapter 14

Eastern Fleet in the Indian Ocean

B OMBAY HAD BEEN A pleasant 'civilised' stop-off after so long at sea or in places like Addu Attol; like all pleasant things, it was not allowed to last too long. I supposed that we were not there for more than a few days, although memory prompts the notion that we were there long enough to become pretty familiar with it. It was astonishingly small, of course, compared with the great metropolis which I visited frequently in the 1970s.

Our departure resolved a mystery which had existed during our stay. Whilst moored in the roads, we had seen a ship some way down the line of moorings looking very much like a King George V class battleship. It would have been encouraging to have such powerful support join our Fleet; we were not told which ship she was, merely that her presence was secret. We never encountered her ship's company ashore as we did the crews of our fellow Fleet members. As we sailed, we went down the line of moorings right past her and 'all was revealed'. She was in fact an old hulk whose upper works had been done up in wood and canvas, like a film set, to resemble a modern battleship. Whether she was capable of going to sea we never heard, but I would certainly think she would have fooled any enemy agents ashore watching with telescopes. There were some personnel aboard, whom I presume were required to show some signs of activity, like sending signals on her signal lamps. What interests me is that she seemed a good hoax but I have never read anywhere in war histories that we built hoaxes on this sort of scale.

Another hoax was discovered after sailing which was a very distinct annoyance and yet another reminder of the imprudence of sacking the Wardroom messman. News had reached us before we got to Bombay of one of the war's great disasters. During the bombing of Plymouth, the famous Coates distillery had been obliterated. Their product, 'Plymouth Gin', was the foundation of every naval officer's (except Dicky Dyke's) diet, the Pink

Gin. We had virtually run out of this nectar, so our Wines Officer (so appointed after the messman went) felt that he was planting the first feather in his cap when he met ashore an Indian gentleman who could offer limitless quantities of Plymouth. On our behalf he invested heavily and just managed to get it aboard before we lifted the hook. The first evening out, the good news having spread, we gathered in the Wardroom for the first case to be broached. The bottles bore authentic labels; their content was the colour of *vin rosé*! The good purveyor had even been well enough briefed to know that the Navy drank 'Pink Plymouth'. Needless to say, the flavour was that of diesel fuel.

We sailed westwards from Bombay as a Fleet, all rather feeling that we were running away from the Japanese. At the same time, I was not the only one who felt none too keen on having a go at them before we had resources more equal to theirs in the air. Our first port of call was the Seychelles, where we lay for forty-eight hours. There was no shore leave there; rumour had it that these islands were so riddled with venereal disease that it would have been a disaster to let Jack get there. Gosh, we felt, it must be bad to be that much worse than Portsmouth!

At this time, I was put on loan to 800 Squadron. I suppose I was chosen because I had lost my regular pilot in my own Squadron. 800 were the Fulmar Squadron of two-seater 'fighters'. The Navy had only just come around to the idea that by using radar and radio telephony (as we quaintly called it) fighter direction officers in the ship could navigate fighters around the sky out of sight of their ships – hence our Hurricane Squadron. Prior to that realisation all fighter Squadrons carried navigators or Gunners and all signals were by wireless telegraphy (W/T), or morse code.

The man in the back of the two flight leaders was an Observer to navigate the formation back to the ship after their encounters. The men in the back of all the other planes were telegraphist Air Gunners. All still used W/T; the accent was on telegraphist rather than Air Gunner because they had no rear guns! In fact we had been issued recently with infantry Tommy guns for rear defence; so useless was the 'fire from the hip' concept in air combat that no-one even bothered to give any instruction in how to use the weapon.

Actions in the Mediterranean had shown up the limitations of Fulmars as fighters and their need for rear defence; even Junkers 88 bombers were catching them up and attacking from astern, they were so slow. I heard that our tommy guns had been issued as a result of one such encounter. With nothing else to use, a desperate Fulmar Telegraphist Air Gunner had drawn his Very Pistol and fired a smoke puff. By luck this had burst under the 88's wing and the crew, impressed by the size of the burst, had promptly bailed out of their undamaged machine!

Because the outrigger idea, already mentioned, provided the accommodation, *Indomitable* had picked up a half Squadron of Grumman Martlets at this time, the first good American Navy machines to be given to the Fleet Air Arm. This formed 806 Squadron. It was thus decided that we should try to use 800's Fulmars more as high speed (relatively to the Albacore!) reconnaissance aircraft, so they needed to borrow a few more Observers to do their navigation. I loathed it; there was hardly room to move and the pilots still thought of themselves as fighter men and would complete an assignment with a flash of rolls, loops and spins which left me vomiting in all directions, scared out of my wits and with all my navigating instruments scattered in the entrails of the machine, leading to an hour or two's hunt for them after landing.

These redispositions of our fighter strength were in preparation for our next operation, the invasion of Madagascar. Looking back on that, it was an operation not dissimilar in military requirements and scale from the recent Falklands invasion. This time, the enemy were the Vichy French. We had much greater naval strength (in numbers of ships, but not in weapons) than in the Falklands; the Army units were about similar in numbers but were from ordinary line regiments, not crack units. Similarly, they had come all the way from UK to do their stuff.

827's role was to bomb the French airfield on the eve of the invasion and drop lots of leaflets on the town of Diego Suarez explaining the peaceful nature of our mission if they would only surrender and let us garrison the place to ensure the Japanese U-Boats could not use it as a base. I still have one of those leaflets. In 800, we had a more mundane role; we had to maintain a standing patrol at about 9,000 feet circling the French harbour to report any movements of their Navy. This we did in two-hour stints. By the second day one realised that the time was kept for us by the French. They were so short of ammunition that the AA Battery could only fire one salvo an hour, which timing they maintained meticulously. Their aim was equally consistent: always half a mile astern of us! Why they should think a Fulmar slower than it really was passed comprehension.

There was little to watch: *Illustrious*'s Albacores (she had come out with the Army convoy) and the cruisers had seen to the French naval units the first night (5 May). The armed merchant cruiser *Bougainville* was sunk; and the submarine *Beveziers* too. The sloop *D'Entrecasteaux* had to be beached. Again, on the 6th, *Illustrious* sank another submarine, the *Heros.*

It had been expected that after a little show for the sake of *l'honneur*, the French would pack it in. Not so; still bitter from the British attack on Dakar, they were determined to give as good as they got. The objective of the operation was merely to capture the northern tip of Madagascar including the big harbour of Diego Suarez to the eastern side of the northern cape, Cap Amber. The Fleet stood to the west and the Army were put ashore on the west coast, expected to fight through to capture Diego Suarez on 5 May. We suspected that the Army was none too clever as well as the French showing more than the expected aggro; the latter got out their 75s and the Army were still at it on the west coast on 7 May. Meanwhile 827 did some close support bombing for the Army but in 800 all we did was bog round and round above the harbour. 880's Hurricanes ranged about individually, to strafe any French army they could see. Hugh Popham had an interesting encounter; all he was able to find was a French officer with trousers lowered enjoying his morning constipational with his back against a large rock. Turning in on him, Hugh found the Frog too spritely for him; even with breeches round his ankles, he was behind the rock before Hugh could bring his guns to bear. He made quite a few runs before deciding that the Frog would always be too quick. Rocking his wings in salute to a successful enemy, Hugh left him to get on with his business, if indeed there were more to be concluded. On his way back to the ship, poetic justice was done: Hugh caught a spent and luckily dead (i.e. it did not explode) 20 mm shell in his bottom, so his flesh wound was our first casualty of the operation.

More were to follow. Saddest were Prangle Pike, Colonel Brown and Leading Airman Rough. Their engine failed half a mile offshore, so they had to ditch. Not finding them before dusk, they had to be written off as missing. I had my first experience of having to pack up a comrade's kit for sending back to his next of kin, once we reached port. But, it's an ill wind . . .; with Pike and Brown gone, there was much more room in the cabin and I could sleep in a bunk instead of on a camp bed on the deck.

The next day, the Navy decided to finish the operation. Several destroyers came round the capital ships of the Fleet, collecting their entire Royal Marine detachments. That night, under cover of dark, they ran straight into Diego Suarez harbour and discharged the Royals into the town. The French, thus taken in their rear, decided to pack it in. By next morning, we were able to steam in as victors. Not without one alarm though; I still have the photograph of the torpedo track which was the last effort of a surviving French submarine to get us. By a rapid turn towards the track, we avoided being hit but they had been quite close.

We were all sent ashore to a French barracks (I have some pictures of this, too) to loot a revolver each with ammunition. The Admiralty did not issue these to aircrew and it was seen by the Captain as a good opportunity to rectify this omission. You never know, it was felt, when you might find yourself ditched in unfriendly territory where a side-arm would add to confidence or possibly prove useful.

Otherwise, we were quickly back to work. Submarine patrols had to be flown and we had the horrid business of having to catapult off with full depth-charge load in harbour and likewise land on. For the latter, the barriers normally used across the Deck were not used, so we had twice the normal landing run and, more important, the option to open the throttle and go off again if we had failed to catch an arrestor wire. A ship lies at her anchors to the tide rather than to the wind and sometimes the wind was too much across the deck to be able to land. So then we would have to go to the French airfield. Based there were now a Squadron of twin engined Beauforts of the South African Air Force.

We asked them to take on the anti-submarine patrols so that we did not have the risky job of flying off in harbour. They declined because, they said, their engines were very unreliable. They admitted that they could keep up on one engine, but felt flying over the sea too dangerous. Their engines were Taurus! So we had to continue with our one Taurus efforts.

By the end of the month we were off to sea again and I went back on loan to 800. We made a fairly quick passage to Mombasa, where the glad tidings were announced that *Indomitable* needed three weeks to clean down her boilers and do some engine-room refitting. Aircrews would each be allowed ten days' local leave. While one half were away, the other half would be based at RAF Kilindini. I was to be in the second batch for leave.

If you go to Mombasa today, you will find a picturesque little old Arab port at one end of a highly developed 'old town' virtually covering the island (like so many British outposts, the harbour is in the strait behind the island on which the town was built, as in Singapore, Bombay, Cochin, Lagos, Mombasa). Beyond the Arab port for miles up the coast is a chain of magnificent tourist hotels. In those days it consisted of what could be built along two roads bisecting the island at right angles to each other. The

4. Group of aircrew officers from Indomitable *in French barracks at Diego Suarez, Madagascar 'liberating' personal sidearms. Jock Smith is furthest left, I am the bearded one, centre.*

principal of these ran from the Kilindini (British port) landing steps to the Arab port. There was little in the way of wharves, so ships lay at moorings in the channel, served by lighters. Now there is a full port installation. The town supported just three 'European' bars.

When the Fleet came in, having been at sea some time, three parts of the Watches were allowed ashore. It is said that the bars were drunk dry in forty minutes flat. This caused a disaster because it caused Jolly Jack to search out other alcohols of a more indigenous nature. Most were ill for days; some were said to have been blinded for life. Urgently, the dockyard godown stocks and rushed supplies from Nairobi had to be provided. Thereafter only one Watch was allowed ashore at a time (half instead of three-quarters of each ship's company).

The aircrews going on leave first had only about three days in Nairobi when all were recalled; an emergency required the Fleet to put to sea. We never heard what it was all about; after a couple of days, *Indomitable* was detached to return to Mombasa and get on with doing up her engine room. Just after we got back, there was a bad fight in the town one night. We still had the two Aussie destroyers as escorts; a unit of Aussie Army in transit were also ashore. The rumours of the conduct of their Army in the last days of Singapore had reached us. Encountering them caused our Aussie sailors to pitch into them for shaming the fair name of Oz. The rumours had indicated that in the last days of Singapore, the Australian Army had largely deserted their posts and streamed down into the port. There, claiming an urgent need to get back to Oz to defend it, they had tried to drive off the women and children given priority to catch the last ships out, and sail themselves instead. I never heard whether there was a grain of truth in this. In those grisly days, anything seemed credible.

It was decided shortly after arrival that the Fleet must 'Show the Flag' a little. A parade of the massed bands of the Royal Marines was arranged, with the Governor sent down from Nairobi to take the salute. I suppose there were nine to a dozen ships in the Fleet carrying bands, so they made quite a show when massed together to beat Retreat. Whilst they had never rehearsed together before, such was their capability in playing and drill you would think they had worked together several times a week for months. The finale of their show was the bands marching towards the saluting base in files of about twenty abreast. Without an order, just as they arrived, they crashed to a halt and the music ceased, supposedly to complete silence. This was too much for Marine Shacklady, playing a trombone in the centre of the front rank. Crash, halt. Half a bar of silence then 'Whaaaaoooooo . . .', up and down the slide with his trombone went Shacklady. Thus followed his next stint of cells.

'Well worth it, sir; I like to take the mickey when the bullshit's thick!'

We lived up at the RAF place with our planes whilst the first batch were on leave. It was very pleasant; we did a few flying exercises but most afternoons, Bill Bailey and I went back to the ship and took away a whaler for an afternoon's sail. Other days we played rugger; we still had most of *Indomitable*'s first team around. Having beaten all the local teams, we got too ambitious and challenged Nairobi, which was virtually the Kenya team. We had to do the match as a day trip so we crammed our team into four Albacores to get up there. Little had we recognised the need to have a few days getting used to the altitude (it is some 6,000 feet above sea level). By half time we were already totally exhausted and duly receiving a thrashing. Albacores get tired at that height too; with the necessary full fuel tanks and four men and their gear up, it was a nearer squeak taking off for the home run than we had bargained for.

One day when Bill and I were sailing down the line of the ships' moorings a destroyer coming in stopped almost alongside us and began to turn rapidly. Her side caught us as she swung; we locked against her just below her bridge. We were being moved sideways with such pressure that our gunwale was bending inwards and splintering; we were almost capsizing. Bill screamed up at her bridge:

'Get out of our way, you bloody power boat; don't you know you should give way to sail?'

Eventually their immaculately clad Captain (a Lt. Commander, half a ring up on Bill), looked down upon us.

'Go away, little man,' he said, 'It's your fault for trying to push us in the wrong direction; you'll never do it!'

And we didn't! Once she had stopped swinging, we could get clear and returned to *Indomitable* with Bill swearing to himself (and he was an expert) all the way.

The RAF Station was very pleasant and relaxed; they were not proper RAF, just local Kenya settlers with civilian pilot's licences put into Reserve uniform for the War. This presented one difficulty for us as short term guests; they insisted (in proper Kenya style), that the mess servants could only be spoken to in Swahili – they must not become the ones who became bi-lingual. Each meal, therefore, one had to try to memorise the words for the more common necessities for that meal. Around the third day I confidently demanded that one of the Totos brought me hot milk to put on my porridge. He stared at me in blank amazement. Like all English in a communication difficulty, I bawled my message to make it more intelligible. All the Totos were so convulsed with laughter they had to withdraw.

'Do you really want that?' asked a local, 'If so, I am sure we can get it for you.'

I explained my need in English, which he then interpreted for me – it sounded quite similar but far from exactly what I had said.

'What you were asking for was hot woman's milk!'

The loos there were unlike anything I have ever seen. The hole beneath the seat seemed to go direct and indefinitely into the bowels of the earth. It was about five minutes, seemingly, after releasing that you heard the smack of it actually arriving at the bottom. The illusion that they had dug too far into the earth's mantle was strengthened by the fact that as you sat there, thick blue smoke came up between your legs, quite pleasant smelling: a slightly sulphurous incense. Apparently the system used a very deep pit trench long enough to put a whole range of loos above; these were a permanent structure, because in theory the pit digested its contents at much the same rate as it arrived. The smoke was a chemical digester, or the result of it, which was fed in daily. The seats had to be left shut when not in use to preserve the digestive action. Very interesting!

Eventually our turn came to take leave. Immediately, we took the overnight train for Nairobi. It was, and I believe still is, a wonderful trip. However, in those days the once daily train was a sort of mobile club for those outlying stations at which it called before too late at night. The locals would climb aboard for a 'peg' and a chat to hear the world's news, so far as the passengers had any picture. It was a narrow gauge railway but by dint of much lateral overhang the carriages were of normal size, with very comfortable diner/club cars and sleepers. To face the considerable climb, (6,000 feet over 250 miles) the train was hauled by Garrett locomotives. It left Mombasa at about 5 p.m. and got into Nairobi after breakfast at a comfortable hour. The train was very long and at one point along the route the line went round a complete loop and bridged over itself in order to gain height. If you sat at the front, you had the unusual experience of seeing the back of your own train disappearing beneath you under the bridge.

On arrival, we booked in at the Norfolk Hotel which was and still is the traditional hotel, unchanged in atmosphere since the foundation of Nairobi, like Raffles in Singapore. Wonderful comfort, wonderful food and drink and lots of super girls about. Just then, after a series of society scandals, Nairobi had the reputation of being the cess-pit of British high society immorality: wife swapping, the lot. It seemed to deserve it, but the great disadvantage was that to be in the life needed funds. What we had available to last for ten days would not have lasted for two. Thus, on the third day, having been careful, George Measures and I accepted the invitation of a coffee farmer to stay on his farm for the rest of our leave. This was near Nyeri in the Aberdare Hills. George and I had a marvellous time on the farm; it is a shameful thing to have had such perfect hosts for a week and be totally unable to remember their name. It was large country house style living, but with great informality of dress except for dinner. There was wonderful hill country and a busy farm, all the workings of which were explained to us. They were mainly in coffee but were experimenting with the new farmer's fashion, pyrethrum. They also fattened beef. They employed hordes of Kikuyu and it seemed such a happy community. I wonder how it survived Mau-mau, indeed whether our host and hostess survived at all. Polo had stopped for the War and they had a string of polo ponies needing exercise so most days George and I took long rides. Learning that Bishop Walter Carey was visiting his son in Kenya at the time, my host drove miles away to fetch him and Fanny, his wife, over for a day or two when I remarked that he had been our chaplain at school whom I much admired, and who later, in 1945, christened our first son in the school Chapel.

One day George and I inadvertently completely let the side down. To make a change for us, our hosts lent us their golf clubs and dropped us at the smart Nyeri Golf Club. There two little black Totos were appointed to caddy for us. Neither of us had any idea how to play, so we made slow progress round the course, averaging about thirty strokes a hole. Luckily being mid-week, there was no-one there to witness it. Even so, by the time we were approaching home we and the Totos were so bored that we tried a variant. George and I carried the clubs and bet on which of our Totos would win the last holes. Considering that they were only small boys and the clubs full adult size and that presumably they never had opportunity to play, they were terrific and we went along in fine style. As we came up the eighteenth fairway towards the club house, a furiously angry Secretary came down to meet us. Who the devil did we think we were to so abuse the hospitality of the club by behaving so familiarly with club servants and letting them mimic their masters and actually play on the course? Would we please get off the club premises as quickly as possible; the Totos, who should know better, would be disciplined in due course. So, we had to await our hostess, who had been coming to lunch with us at the club, at the gates and apologise there for how we must have embarrassed her, as our sponsor to the club.

She quite understood that our crime was innocently committed. In the context of the farm, all natives were treated rather like children within the family, so how were we to know that you could not have a laugh with any of them anywhere, even at the club? She found it hard to explain the difference. We felt genuinely sorry – after all, it was their country, and we had caused embarrassment. I do not think in the Kenya of today you would see whites caddying for black people, but it would at least not be a cause of social affront.

All lovely things come to an end and thus did this, one of the best holidays of my bachelor life. Back to Nairobi and farewell to the hosts at the station.

On the morning of the third day of our leave, the train had brought up from Mombasa passengers who caused the biggest lunchtime celebration of all time. Colonel Brown and Prangle Pike had returned from the dead! They were very emaciated but otherwise fit – but they later reported with great disappointment that in spite of Nairobi's opportunities, a month on a diet of only coconuts had removed all sexual capability! They were thin as matchsticks and burned black. At first we didn't even recognise them. All they wanted to do was eat and drink, which they did on a gargantuan scale. There is a full account of their time marooned on a desert island in Adrian Vicary : *HMS Cromer – The Story of the Town's Namesake Ships in the Royal Navy*. (1989, ISBN 0 9514654 06.)

When their plane had come down, Pike, Brown and Rough had happily launched the dinghy without much care because they seemed so near the shore. The lack of care cost them the rations of food and water always packed in the inflatable dinghy. No matter, they would be ashore in a few minutes! In they got to paddle for the shore, only to discover that the combination of wind and tide carried them out to sea no matter how hard they paddled. By dusk, they were out of sight of land; a little later, they could see the silhouette of *Indomitable* stealing past in the night but were unable to attract attention. After drifting for three days they were about done for and semi-conscious when they grounded on a coral-reef, the outer reef of a little island in the Isles Glorieuses group. When they had dragged themselves ashore, they found an abandoned coconut plantation with, what saved their lives, a rain water tank still full. Over the days they recovered on a diet of coconuts and water, and also found that there were some chickens left running wild, but for a time they were too weak to catch any. Eventually they got one, but could not make a fire and found they did not fancy it raw. After a couple of weeks without seeing ship or plane, they decided they must make use of a boat they had found. They patched it up and rigged a mast and made sails out of hessian sacks using drawn threads for sewing. They stocked it with water and coconuts and decided to try to sail to the Comores or Africa. This all took days of effort, and they had to drag the craft a long way before they could eventually launch off the main outer reef. Once launched and drifting away, Prangle Pike lost their only paddle, so the trip had to be abandoned. It took them hours of effort against the wind to regain the reef and the island. It was at this moment that the Colonel swore that he would never again let himself in for cooperative efforts with Prangle, which is how Prangle became my pilot! John Pike was a marvellous pilot, kept to the course without having to be checked constantly, never did a frightening deck landing, and never went to sleep with his Gosport tubes unplugged!

Getting on for a week after this, they heard aircraft engines. They rushed to the sandy beach and wrote SOS in the sand as large as they could and stood by waving everything white they had. A South African Beaufort (at last risking flying out to sea on two Taurus engines!) circled and saw them. It dropped some food and matches, so they were able to cook their chicken at last. Two days later the minesweeper *Cromer* arrived and picked them up. It was their luck that there had been a scare that Jap submarines were lying up in remote islands, so the South Africans had been sent out to search for them.

Coming back from Nairobi, the train seemed full of returning *Indomitable*. One of the fighter pilots had a gorgeous girl with him; she explained that she was coming back to Nairobi next night, but, having enjoyed him in every possible way all the week, she thought she would like to enjoy him on a train! *Indomitable*'s engineers had done the necessary to the engine room and were justifiably jealous of our leave, but as soon as we were back we sailed.

Chapter 15

Farewell to the Eastern Fleet

FROM MOMBASA we made our way back to the rest of the Fleet at Addu Atoll, much expecting our boring life of patrols and exercises to continue from there for ages. In fact, we were not there for long.

I suppose we were in Mombasa during June 1942, and we were already on the move from Addu Attol by July. I had had the good luck to be back flying with 827 again; it must have been somewhere around this time that 800 Squadron started to receive Hurricanes as replacement aircraft instead of more Fulmars, so they were able to start thinking more of a fighter role again, instead of being the reconnaissance unit. I note from my flying log that at around this time I went up with the assistant 'Bats' (Deck Landing Control Officer) for one of his 'keep your hand in' flights. He and his boss did the signalled guidance of all landing planes and were also in charge of ranging planes for take off and getting them parked and stowed after landing. Every now and again they would borrow a Squadron Albacore and do an A/S patrol, just by way of getting flying practice and being allowed to continue the extra pay we got for flying – I seem to remember that that was five shillings a day, or it may have been per week. The only point of mentioning that flight was to mention his rather unusual name, which always tickled me: Peter Bodham-Whetham.

To our surprise, we left Addu going westward, arriving in due course in Durban. Again, apart from her destroyer escorts, *Indomitable* was detached from the Fleet. I was very cross about Durban, which the boys reported to be even more hospitable than Cape Town. I was on my back, not allowed out of bed, with a septic shin; this was a souvenir of Addu Attol coral on which I had lightly grazed my leg when swimming. Being infected on the bone, there was some cause for concern; remember we had no penicillin in those days. I was treated with what was all the rage with the medicos of that age – the new sulpha drugs. They were quite an advance but had the side effect of making you very depressed; that side effect came my way, but may have arisen from not being allowed ashore at Durban.

Surprise turned to optimism about a return home when our next port turned out to be Cape Town. We were not there for more than a forty-eight hour store ship and then west again for the mid South Atlantic, beyond the normal course of Cape convoys, to minimise the chances of being sighted by U-Boats. When we were well at sea, Tom Troubridge gave us the first hint of what was afoot. We had been given the 806 Martlets and 800 Hurricanes to strengthen our hitting power for a special operation in home waters, after which we would return to Eastern Fleet. Besides more fighters, we had also picked up an admiral; we had become the Flagship of Rear Admiral, Aircraft Carriers, Dennis Boyd. You do not usually have a flagship steering about the oceans on her own; obviously we were to join an aircraft carrier force of some size.

Dennis Boyd was a nice guy and a great chum of Tom Troubridge's; he had been in command of *Illustrious* as a Captain, at the time she took such a pasting from the Luftwaffe at Malta. They were great rivals in the deck hockey league.

Our next port, for fuel, was Freetown. We had only time for a short walk ashore; it seemed a very unsophisticated little place, even in comparison with places such as Mombasa, and the climate very hot and steamy. For the first time in my life I saw quite large ships, still coal-burners, coaling ship, for our anchorage was alongside the coaling station. Up nets from the bulwarks to the coal lighters, swarmed coolies, the crew – indeed everyone available – carrying coal sacks which were emptied into the holes in the decks over the chutes to the bunkers. A black cloud misted the operation; African and European had become the same colour: all this labour with the temperature in the hundreds and very high humidity. It made one thankful that oil had come in for the Navy during the last three decades.

Once we had left Freetown, Tom Troubridge felt that he could tell us about the operation we were sailing towards without security risk. The last convoy to supply Malta had not got through sufficient supplies to see the Island through until the 8th Army had advanced along the Libyan coast far enough to allow convoys to Malta to go from Egypt. From the Gibraltar end, the narrows between Sardinia and the Tunisian coast and then those between Sicily and Pantelleria and Tunisia funnelled convoys and their escorts into sitting ducks for U-Boats and E-Boats and the large number of bomber Squadrons guarding these narrows. Malta must be saved, not only because of our debt to the inhabitants who had endured much but because it was a vital base from which to snipe at the Afrika Korps' supply

5. Hurricanes, Martlets and Albacores on Indomitable's *Flight Deck in harbour. This photo is believed to be in Freetown, Sierra Leone harbour; note the aerial masts in upright (non-flying) position, also the crane used for lifting boats, planes and stores aboard. In the bottom left hand corner the 'crash barrier' is coiled on the deck, with its Y-shape support, starboard side, visible in the lowered position.*

convoys. At the highest level, therefore, it had been decided to risk one last major effort; the merchant ships would be picked for speed – none below 15 knots, which was fast for freighters in those days, the escort the strongest ever sent with a convoy. The heavy part of the escort would not go into Malta; once the local RAF had taken over the air cover, around the Pantelleria narrows, we would turn back. It would be about six days fighting out to that point and then back to Gibraltar. *Indomitable*'s orders were to rendezvous with a Fleet oiler west of the straits of Gibraltar after dark and out of sight of land and top up with fuel and get through the straits under cover of dark to meet the convoy inside the Mediterranean. Obviously, the further the convoy got to eastward of Gibraltar without being spotted, the better.

I believe it was the night of 8 August when we met the tanker. It was pitch dark and running half a gale. It was decided in these circumstances that the tanker would stream a line astern, which we would pick up; using that, we would first take in a hawser and then the fuel pipe, ringed along a second hawser. The point was that the first hawser would keep a constant distance between the two ships, so the fuel line should stay slack. In theory, the tanker would be slightly towing *Indomitable*. For a proper towing condition in such seas, a very long hawser would be used, to have enough 'spring' to take up the movements of the ships in the considerable sea. We had to use a limited length hawser because of the amount of fuel line piping available.

I went up to the fo'c'sle to watch and a frightening operation it became. You will appreciate that if a hawser that size parts, the snaking end will cut a man in half. *Indomitable*'s speed and heading had to be adjusted all the time to keep the right tension. This was done by the Navigating Officer 'conning' over the telephone to the bridge from the fo'c'sle. It was so dark, he could not see the tanker half the time. Every now and then the hawser would start groaning under strain; the order would come from the Commander, who had taken personal charge, 'Clear the fo'c'sle,' and everyone would rush for between decks safety. Twice the hawser parted which meant the weary business of taking another line in the dark. Several times, after clearing the deck, the strain on the wire eased so that the fo'c'sle party could return to their duty. We got the fuel line in and took fuel but had lost so much time we had to abandon taking all our ration in favour of being through the strait before dawn and out of sight of land.

Memory says the following day was a Sunday and that in the forenoon we only had one Watch closed up; this left half the ship's company available for divisions. I think we were all gripped by the service, and 'For those in peril on the sea' was sung with much sincerity. The God to whom we prayed gave less immediate signs of support than the Lords of the Admiralty had caused to meet together during the night. *Victorious*, who had sailed back to home waters after Madagascar, was there together with the carriers of older vintage, *Eagle* and *Furious*, also the USS *Wasp*.

In fact, *Furious* and *Wasp* were not there as operational carriers in the normal sense; they were carrying RAF fighters to Malta in the same way as we had carried them to the defence of Singapore. They still looked good though to us, and hopefully they would impress the enemy even more. The Spitfires were launched halfway once they were in reach of Malta, and USS *Wasp* returned on her own. *Nelson* and *Rodney* were there, the most powerful battleships we had ever built (main armament nine 16-inch guns); cruisers galore of the more modern classes, *Kenya* and *Belfast*; special anti-aircraft light cruisers; destroyers spreading as far as the eye could see. The fourteen merchantmen were ranged in the middle, all very modern businesslike ships and carrying more than the normal wartime complement of anti-aircraft guns.

From this day we stood by for eventualities at any minute but all seemed quiet initially. Then the radar picked up a strange aircraft closing the convoy and *Indomitable* scrambled a Hurricane to intercept; I seem to remember it was Dicky Cork who went. It was, I repeat, desperately important to us that an enemy seeing our great force should not be allowed to survive to raise the alarm. Unfortunately the enemy 'invader' was a Vichy French civilian airliner flying from France to North Africa; she had seen us and was certain to report it if left alone, so she had to pay the price. During the afternoon, Prangle Pike and I, now teamed up together on a regular basis, made one of the few Albacore take-offs during this operation. Our first duty, with minimum use of radio, was to tune our set in the air to *Nelson*'s spotting frequency; should the Italian come out to challenge us, we would fly to report her fall of shot for *Nelson*. We also took a large bagful of papers and orders across to *Eagle*; in the event, this made us the last TBR aircraft (Torpedo/Bomber/Reconnaissance) to take off from *Eagle*.

By evening, it was obvious that the enemy had appreciated that we were making a major effort which they must stop. There were several Italian torpedo aircraft attacks and a flurry of U-Boat fired torpedoes and U-Boat contacts by our destroyer screen. We were encouraged by the fact that no hits were made on us and more, perhaps, by the incredible visual and audio impression of what the convoy as a whole could throw up into the sky in the way of flak. I suppose, between us, we mounted some 150 or more 4.5-inch A/A guns; against low-flying torpedo bombers, many of the cruisers could bring their 6-inch main armament to bear as well; I think the Bofors, Vickers 2-pounders etc. must have amounted to some five hundred or more guns. At dusk, all this going off, even without the enemy tumbling out of the sky, was a great confidence booster.

By the following dawn we were all called to action stations; here we seemed to remain except for short individual breaks for the next few days. I think I mentioned in an earlier chapter that my action station was in charge of a pair of Oerlikon (20 mm) gun mountings on the starboard side aft, just below Flight Deck level. It was a good position from which to get a view of what was going on in general and, of course, of the comings and goings of *Indomitable*'s fighters in particular. Steadily mounting in intensity

6. Albacore taking off from Indomitable *during the early stages of Operation Pedestal. HMS* Eagle *can be seen astern of* Indomitable. *The Albacore is carrying no bombs or depth charges, so either going up on test or carrying papers to another ship (?* Eagle*) – as Pike and HCBM did just before* Eagle *was hit. This picture was taken from the island on HMS* Victorious.

through the day, raids came in; off went our fighters; up went the many tons of flak. We seemed to be winning through; the fighters claimed successes against the attackers; not too many bombs seemed to come all that close to the convoy. The nearest merchantman to us in the formation was loaded with ammunition; I cannot remember her name, perhaps just as well for the pride of her crew. She suffered a near miss around her bridge which started a fire. When an ammunition ship has a major fire, it is very prudent to get off her quickly; understandably her skipper ordered: 'Abandon Ship!'. This was not a normal operation; immediately his crew were away in their boats, two destroyers put men aboard her and fairly quickly extinguished the fires. They then called on the merchant crew to re-board and take the ship on. After what they had been through, one could understand their reluctance. We were subsequently delighted to hear that she fought her way, sustaining more damage as she went, all the way into Malta.

All day long, we plodded on, shortening the distances the enemy planes had to come from Sardinia and Sicily to get at us and thus receiving steadily intensifying attacks. However, I do not recall our side sustaining anything significant in the way of hits. Thus whilst fatigue grew because of long periods at action stations, so did confidence that the hitting power of our convoy was going to allow us to survive these waters, which had seen so much disaster for others. Still the sky was covered over with the bursts of flak we threw; the noise of it being fired and then bursting was tremendous, and, I suppose, fatiguing, but it was most reassuring.

The night did not quieten things that much; U-Boats and E-Boats kept our escorts busy as well as all of us at action stations. The Italians launched some phenomenally brave aircraft torpedo attacks; still, thank God, they had no success.

Come 11 August, we were in the thick of it and attack seemed to follow attack in a continuous action, rather than in the bursts of activity which had characterised the previous days. Each of us was allowed a half-hour away from his station to wash and get food. For officers, there were sandwiches and coffee available at one end of the Wardroom anteroom. The rest of this space had become a standby extension for the medical aid facilities. Anyway, one could eat sufficient there and relax with coffee – or something stronger at the right time of day – for one's half hour. On my way back to station, I called into my cabin to get my Leica. Whilst I was there a colossal explosion went off astern of us; I dashed up on deck to see *Eagle* already lying almost on her side; she had been torpedoed by a U-Boat. (see Plate 7.)

Casualties of other kinds were also now hitting us as our fighters met stiffer opposition. Whilst most of our losses were sustained out of our sight, some were all too much right amongst us. Johnson, Commanding Officer of 806, having made a few kills, was himself hit and wounded as well as having a damaged plane. We broke convoy lines to get into wind to give him an emergency landing. He got down well, but with neither undercarriage nor arrestor hook, skidded along the deck and over the port side. His plane floated briefly there alongside but out of reach; he was too wounded to get out unaided; all we could do was acknowledge his farewell wave as he sank in his machine. Shortly after, Judd, the terror Commanding Officer of 880, was himself shot down whilst protecting the tail of one of his junior pilots. It became more and more evident that we were not on a picnic; we had not got to the easiest bit for the enemy yet, either.

So it continued on the 12th: more and more intensive attacks, but most

7. HMS Eagle *sinking, August 1942. Horrified, we watched her little matchstick men getting over the side, avoiding the planes also sliding over; remorselessly she went further and further over until completely turned turtle; her bow then raised slightly and in clouds of smoke or steam she slid below. I had never seen a big ship go; I do not think it matters which side the ship is on – somehow it is a very terrible sight.*

encouraging reports of shooting down attackers by our boys. I cannot remember what was reported, but post-War analysis credited *Indomitable*'s fighters with some thirty to forty kills during operation Pedestal. This is at least more than the number of fighters we started with, and bear in mind that with intensive flying over several days, the number of our own planes declined fairly fast owing to deck landing strains and engine problems, without any enemy action. However, we had had a bit of a top-up with planes. When *Eagle* went down, she had quite a few in the air, who had to land on us. We got so congested with too many planes that speed of operation was threatened, so there followed at dusk a most extraordinary operation. The Air Engineer Officer and Commander Flying walked the crowded Deck and each plane's condition had to be reported on. If there were any fault more serious than, say, a tyre puncture, the plane was condemned and the whole machine tipped unceremoniously over the stern. This went on until we were down to numbers which gave space to operate efficiently.

That dusk, we had a tragedy which affected us all deeply. 'Bats', Lt. Commander Pares, the pilot responsible for signalling down all the landing aircraft, was a very popular man. Not only was he very highly respected for his professionalism by both aircrew and the Flight Deck ratings he commanded, he was loved by all as a very nice guy. Whilst he was on his job, batting down the dusk landers from his position on the port quarter, another raid was coming in, so our guns were firing. There were two turrets just ahead of his batting position; one of them fired a 'premature' and he was cut to pieces and died within the hour. (A 'premature' is a shell where the fuse to explode the shell at the right altitude for the enemy aircraft is faulty and explodes the shell as it leaves the barrel.)

The 12th, we felt, must be auspicious, because it heralded the start of grouse shooting. It rather turned out to be so for us. Intensive attacks all day and it seemed that the enemy was starting to give priority now to knocking out the escorts just as much as the merchantmen carrying the vital stores. Both seemed to receive hits more and more as the day wore on. There was a most unusual incident as I returned to my station from my morning half-hour break: as I walked down the port side, a U-Boat came to the surface right alongside us; she was so close to us that we had no gun which could depress enough to bear on her. As she dropped astern, we still could not fire for fear of hitting our destroyer escort, who were quickly bearing down on her. About a cable astern of us, the destroyer *Ithuriel* rammed her; it was an almighty crash which about split her in half – it also made a nasty mess of *Ithuriel*'s bow, but she had sunk the U-Boat. We later heard that it had been an Italian called *Cobalto*. She had been badly damaged by depth charges from our forward screen and thus forced to surface. Some of the crew managed to scramble out and were picked up by *Ithuriel*. In his book *Pedestal*, Peter C. Smith (publ. William Kinher 1970, ISBN 0–7183–0632–5) claims that *Ithuriel* picked up 3 officers and 38 ratings from *Cobalto*; his version of her demise, which I saw with my own eyes, is entirely

8. *Italian U-Boat abandoning ship, taken from destroyer* Ithuriel *which had just rammed her (Note the survivors and debris in the water, and that the submarine's forward aqua-planes seem to be set for full dive; the calmness of the sea which prevailed throughout Pedestal – otherwise I don't think* Ohio *would ever have made it into Malta.*

incorrect. *Cobalto* never submerged after surfacing alongside *Indomitable* until she sank. I guess those picked up would have been a good half of her total complement. I believe we brought the *Cobalto* survivors back to UK in *Indomitable*'s double bottom. I know we loaded some POWs in Gibraltar and were told by ship's officers (truthfully or not, I do not know) that they were in the bottom.

You might well ask how I came to be seeing things on the port side, when my action station was on the starboard. It happened that, in a lull, I had gone across the Flight Deck to chat with Colonel Brown, who had the port equivalent to my station. During one of these chats, as the next raid threatened, he came up with one of his more quotable remarks:

'You pray for us, Hector. You, as a public schoolboy, will have more influence.'

Late in the afternoon, very large forces were seen flying in ahead on the radar – we were now within easy reach of Pantelleria – and almost every fighter we and *Victorious* had was sent up there. Naturally, all eyes tended to look in that direction. Too late, several of us on *Indomitable*'s stern saw simultaneously that we had been taken in by the oldest trick in the book. A major force draws off the defenders down sun whilst a hitting force dives out of the sun during the diversion. There, already diving at us in perfect formation of two Vee's, were six Junkers 87s. They were very brave men; I have already said we could throw a lot of flak and whilst it came on to them in a rather panicky eleventh hour aim, they held their course straight down at us. At around 500 feet, we could see the bombs drop away; whilst they hit home, the Stukas pulled out of their dive at sea level and flew up the lines of the ships, in confidence that they would not be fired at for fear of hitting one's own ships. The merchantmen alongside us had no such inhibitions, I may say, but I don't think they caused us any casualties.

I met one of those Stuka pilots after the War and am not surprised that they thought they had sunk us; the photographs taken from elsewhere in the convoy make it look that grim for us too. All I can recall is a dreamlike hour or so from the moment I saw the Stukas dive. You could say I was scared quite out of my wits and convinced that 'the end was nigh'. Whilst the explosions rocked the ship there was considerable pain, in the ears and in the backside (I was half seated on a rail), from the whiplash effect aft of the bombs striking forward. For ten minutes or so one expected us to sink or blow up; also, in spite of all these simultaneous sensations, there was a feeling of thinking quite clearly and calmly.

We had taken a big bomb through the Flight Deck forward and another similarly aft. Another had struck the portside tearing a hole about thirty feet in diameter, mostly above the waterline. Two more had burst below waterline near the portside and had blown large holes. Fire seemed to be everywhere. Most particularly, the Martlet parked by our Oerlikon position was fully fuelled and ammunitioned for action and blazing merrily above us. I went with one of the ratings to see if we could get a hose from the portside foam generator to bear on it. The deck was such a mess and the list of the ship so steep, it was not easy to get there. Smoke made it hard to see where one was going; flames leaped from the great holes fore and aft in the Flight Deck. By some error the Captain's Tannoy mike had come on and from the bridge, entirely lost in smoke, came his voice to Boyd:

'Christ, Dennis, I believe they've buggered us.'

The ship, steering jammed, had swung round in a wild circle during these first chaotic minutes. Incredibly, order began to set in very quickly.

One by one, the major fires were brought under control. Calmly, damage control orders were passed; the wounded were steadily brought into the various dressing stations; the sickening list stopped increasing and then reduced as spaces on the starboard side were flooded to compensate; then, astonishingly, the screws started again and we moved forward with new-found steering control. Tom Troubridge announced that with the forward aircraft lift blown two feet above deck level and jammed and the after one jammed at the bottom, the operation of aircraft was impossible and in any event we were within five miles of the point where the operational plan would have turned us back for Gibraltar, thus we would make for Gibraltar, accompanied by the heavy units of the escort. It was nice to have them with us! I suppose the most effective benefit was having *Victorious*'s fighters and some of our fighters now aboard her. Having seen them firing, *Nelson*'s and *Rodney*'s main armament were spectacular morale boosters to have in company. I believe that this was the first time battleships had fired main armament at aeroplanes; they had loosed off high explosive shells at the low-flying enemy torpedo bombers. Our fighter pilots reported that even though thousands of feet above these shell bursts, they were lifted about 500 feet if over one when it burst. A 16-inch shell is no hand grenade!

It was not an easy time for morale; a principle of naval warfare is to damage major capital units to slow them and their accompanying defenders, so as to pick them off at leisure. The major expectation, damaged as we were on the enemy's doorstep, was for some concentrated raids to follow to finish us off. To our great relief, these never materialised in the event. This cannot have been entirely because those who had attacked us had had a severe mauling. It is probable that they thought us sunk, not damaged, and concentrated on continuing to attack the convoy which was inching nearer and nearer to Malta, albeit with reduced numbers. Their major objective, after all, was to stop supplies reaching the island.

Because of the casualties we had suffered, our duties were re-allocated. I was given the least favourite job at that time of expectation of attack – hangar officer. The tendency in carriers was for the blast of bombs coming through the Flight Deck to decimate everyone in the hangar; even so, someone had to be there to be ready to put out fires promptly if, luckily, they had not been killed. In the circumstances, I was not fond of being anywhere at all between decks and I spent a very anxious Watch trying to encourage the party of ratings who had been condemned with me. Every half hour that went by without attack seemed a gift from heaven, to clock

9. Indomitable, *minutes after being stuck during Operation Pedestal, gets under way again, still listing and on fire. Note the curtain of flak in the sky. The cruiser steering the opposite way is either* Nigeria *or* Kenya

right through the Watch scot free a total answer to a public schoolboy's prayer; perhaps the Colonel had been right.

Encouragingly, during this Watch, one was conscious from time to time of increases of engine revs – a sign that our engineers were overcoming their difficulties. Speed actually picked up from five knots to something just over ten. Before dark, *Nelson* had flashed to us:

'You set the pace, but do buck up.'

At dawn she was flashing: 'Any more of this and I will not be able to keep up.'

By then we were doing over twelve knots; not bad with all those holes and the port propeller shaft (there were only three) completely useless.

Emerging from this Watch below, one started to get news of what had really happened and who had been casualties. The burst on the portside had blasted through the Wardroom and taken out all those officers who had been taking their break at the time. Sadly, one of these had been George Measures. I name George as my closest friend, but there were many other friends killed too. The worst carnage had been caused by the hit forward; it had taken out the entire turret crews of the two portside twin 4.5-inch gun turrets. The stink of death was everywhere – for some reason, although not the most terrible thing we had to put up with, it is one of the most enduring memories of the awful aspects. I spent some time in particular looking for 827 Squadron friends; on the whole, we had been lucky, only one or two others killed and their names escape me. Many other friends from other Squadrons and the ship's complement had gone though.

In the temporary sick-bay rigged in the Aircrew Ready room in the Island, I found Colonel Brown. He had a piece of shrapnel through his foot from the bomb landing on the port quarter. Not a serious wound, luckily. Blast and fire damage had taken their toll of our cabin flats aft and we had lost a great deal of our kit. In that funny way in which one frets about the unimportant in adversity, I recall being furious that the collection of photographs I had built up during our cruise was ruined. The only personal document to survive (it still does) was a somewhat waterstained flying log. All of us not at action stations were put to clearing wreckage and getting things as nearly back to normal as possible and it was incredible how much was achieved. Within days, we were back in our cabin on camp beds, albeit using bedding with that tackiness of dried-off seawater. Our ratings again had habitable messdecks, some grossly overcrowded because of some crew space having been lost. We had the Wardroom anteroom back to serve as Wardroom and anteroom, with some surviving items of furniture. There was one gruesome mark; the panelling lining the ship's side of the anteroom had a punctured hole. Here had been found George Measures's head, blown from his body the far side of the mess.

During the forenoon of the thirteenth, we put our dead over the side. It was a moving service, with as many as could be spared from gun stations attending. The ships in company flew their battle ensigns at half-mast until the bodies had gone. I cannot remember how many there were, all laid out on the Flight Deck in their shrouds. I recall being vaguely surprised that we carried a large enough stock of White Ensigns to cover them. It looked an awful lot. Whilst most were the shape you would expect of a sewn-up corpse, some were no more than two foot or more cube-shaped parcels, the assembly of odd pieces which had been found. I do not know why, really, but we all felt better when that was over.

We were lucky to be granted an unimpeded run back to Gibraltar and as the Rock hove into sight, in the setting sun, a few days later, we were all very thankful. Already we started to wonder where we would be sent for repairs. UK would be marvellous, but so many carrier repairs were done by the Americans, we were very afraid we would be sent there. However, it would obviously be a long job so the Squadrons could not stay with her in the USA, and might thus still get back to the UK. Then it started to dawn on us that even if *Indomitable* went to a British yard, the length of the repair job must mean that the happy community we had become was inevitably going to be broken up.

In darkness we crept into the harbour, straight into the graving dock for inspection and patching of our wounds. What had been achieved? As it turned out, Malta had been saved but by the narrowest of margins; of the fourteen merchantmen, nine had been lost. The Navy had lost a carrier, two cruisers, three destroyers and a submarine (I say this from memory and thin references). Also a major carrier and two cruisers were so badly damaged that they would be unserviceable for a very long time. *Indomitable*'s fighters had downed some thirty or forty enemy planes, for losses of about a dozen of ours. The convoy had been fought through narrow seas beside which 540 operational planes were ranged in bases sometimes only eighty miles from our track. What you might call running the gauntlet!

Addendum to Chapter 15

The following list indicates the major units of the Royal Navy involved in Operation Pedestal in August 1942. It does not include units such as salvage tugs which were in the convoy, or submarines which co-operated with it.

Battleships:

| *Nelson* | (34,000 tons, nine 16-inch guns, twelve 6-inch guns, and many other A/A) |
| *Rodney* | (34,000 tons, nine 16-inch guns, twelve 6-inch guns, and many other A/A) |

Carriers:

* *Indomitable*	(23,000 tons, sixteen 4.5-inch guns + A/A, 18 Hurricanes, 6 Fulmars, 8 Martlets, and 24 Albacores)
Victorious	(23,000 tons, same arms, 12 Fulmars, 24 Albacores)
+ *Eagle*	(22,000 tons, nine 6-inch guns, five 4-inch guns + A/A, 15 Fulmars, 12 Swordfish)
Furious	(22,400 tons, ten 5.5-inch guns, six 4-inch guns + A/A, 38 Spitfires, being ferried for Malta RAF)

Cruisers:

+ *Manchester* (9,400 tons, twelve 6-inch guns)

* *Nigeria*   (8,000 tons, twelve 6-inch guns and eight 4-inch guns)

* *Kenya*   (8,000 tons, twelve 6-inch guns and eight 4-inch guns)

+ *Cairo*   (4,000 tons, eight 4-inch guns)

Phoebe   (5,450 tons, ten 5.25-inch guns, A/A & six 21-inch torpedoes)

Sirius   (5,450 tons, similarly armed)

Charybdis   (5,450 tons similarly armed)

Destroyers: (19th Flotilla)

Laforey   (over 1,800 tons with six 4.7-inch guns, 4-inch A/A guns)

another identical

another identical

another identical

another identical

another identical

another identical

8 older destroyers

(6th Flotilla)

Ashanti   (over 1,800 tons and six 4.7-inch guns and two 4-inch A/A)

some ten others

(+ = lost; * = seriously damaged)

Chapter 16

Patching Up

I T TOOK QUITE A WHILE in Gibraltar to patch us up sufficiently for the main passage to wherever the final refitting would be done. For the first week or so we lay in the graving dock. This had its inconveniences, such as water rationing and the obvious necessity of having to go ashore to some very scruffy dockyard loos to answer the calls of nature.

I took the first opportunity I could to walk the bottom of the dock. It was most impressive to have a fish-eye view of *Indomitable*; from underneath she looked even more enormous than when seen afloat. The huge holes below the waterline left one wondering how on earth she had kept floating so well.

There was little for aircrew to do during this phase; about half a dozen Albacores were disembarked and taken by lorry to the airfield so that we could keep our hands in with occasional exercises or be available in the event of (unlikely) emergency. I do not recall flying from there personally at all. We spent much time shopping and browsing round the quite pleasant town. One great bargain was sherry; wartime had left the producers with a shortage of bottles, so if you brought your own, you could get them filled very cheaply. I seem to remember getting a dozen squash bottles filled with 'La Ina' for about ten shillings and then going back the next day, on behalf of Colonel Brown, and getting an even better bargain. There were also things unavailable in wartime England which could be picked up with a view to returning home with prized gifts, such as silk stockings. We were still the best part of ten years short of the nylon age! There were many good restaurants and bars; it was a good place if only you had money; they even had WRNS in the shore base.

In respect of the last mentioned, we had a typical Tom Troubridge incident shortly after arrival. A party of young officers shore-bound and perhaps hoping to meet some WRNS, met him coming aboard with a crowd of them: 'Sorry, lads, I think I've got the lot. They're coming to see my ship.'

Money was the difficult thing to spin out, as we were all imbued with the optimism that said we would be going to UK and wanted to shop accordingly. I had my first lesson in credit-worthiness from Hamish Muir-Mackenzie, a pilot in 800 Squadron. He said we could cash UK cheques at the local Gieves. Gieves were the most celebrated of naval and military tailors. No overseas bank branch was able to do this because of currency control. So we went to Gieves.

'Sorry gentlemen, but we cannot extend peacetime services of that kind these days, there are so very many officers now.'

Hamish was a Regular Navy chap.

'Nonsense', says Hamish, 'I have a standing account in Bond Street and must owe them over £120; if they are happy with that, surely you can trust me with a cheque?'

'But how can we tell whether that is the case?'

'There was a time when Gieves trusted the word of their customers. Never mind, cable Bond Street and deduct the cost from the amount of the cheque.'

They agreed to do this and an hour later Hamish cashed a cheque large enough for his needs and mine. It should be noted that £120 was no mean sum for a junior, or almost any, officer to be owing. It was being trusted by Bond Street Gieves which did it; another chap whose account was in minor credit there was refused! But Hamish was a bit of a *burra sahib*; in similar circumstances in Mombasa, he announced that he would fly down to Tanga and sell one of the family godowns there. Back he came in his Fulmar at lunchtime; the lawyers insisted that the cabled agreement of his sister be obtained from England and cabling from Tanga was too slow, so he did it from Mombasa, refuelled, flew back to Tanga after lunch and was back before dusk with a bag of cash big enough to allow him to cash cheques for us all for a week!

I had two experiences in Gib which have not occurred before or since; a bar fight picked by the party I was with and a cruise in an operational submarine.

The first happened in a little bar cabaret that 827 frequented because we all adored the lead singer. Arriving early as a group one evening, we found a bunch of Army officers in our favourite bar stools. The place was still quiet and unbusy. Charles Gordon, who could really be the supercilious Wyckhamist when he wanted and had a penetrating voice, glared armywards from the other end of the bar:

'I say, you chaps, look at the brown job at that end; he's so dim that even the others have noticed.'

We seemed to win rather easily, probably because, being longer term residents in Gib than us, they felt less able to risk the outcome of a major dust-up between officers. Our victory had a marvellous reaction from our adored singer, who had to that date taken singularly little notice of our regular attendance. Now she was all over us; she knew the best beach to bathe next day; would we come? (silly question!) She wore a swimsuit rare in those days and disturbing too for those who had been at sea for a time – when wet it was as good as transparent.

The submarine patrol was a locally organised exchange of experience. We could go out with them for a short run; they would come up for a flight with us. Bear in mind that that unless you were in one of the flying services, going up in a plane was not a much more common experience that going out in a submarine. I cannot remember how long my trip was, either a long day or about forty-eight hours I would think, and I went with John Pike. It was a 'T' Class boat, just about the biggest the Navy had. Several were based at Gib, mainly for ferrying urgently needed small cargoes to Malta, but they also did short operational patrols from their base. It was pretty claustrophobic but that was not the main impression. That was what a tremendous crew spirit there was and how remarkably happily they accepted their very cramped and difficult living conditions. A visitor like me could not help feeling in the way all the time, because there really wasn't room for more than their own complement. When we were at the limit of the patrol, the officer of the Watch sighted 'unknown suspected enemy vessel'; the Captain, a Lieutenant, took over the periscope. In due course he identified two Italian destroyers; before he could get into position to attack they got us on their ASDIC and charged: crash dive.

'Stand by for depth charge attack!'

Dive further. Lie still. Eerie sound of propellers churning above us. Just as I was thinking I would burst if I could not get to the heads instead of staying where I had been told, they all started grinning. There was enough experience on board to distinguish the sound of an old merchantman or fishing boat tramping along from destroyers at full speed. Things returned to normal.

'One of the skipper's games,' someone explained.

When I complained to him about putting on an act just to scare me, he swore it was not so; he used every opportunity to exercise his crew, he claimed, without them knowing in the early stages whether it was action or him 'kidding'. I just don't know which it really was; I did know now that in no way was the submariner's life for me. They are very brave men. Even so, they did not come on the reciprocal trip; they claimed that they were far too scared to go up in an Albacore, having heard about their engines!

The worst experience in Gib was when *Kenya* went into the smaller graving dock alongside ours. When she had been hit, she had had to shut all hatches in the affected areas to contain the flooding despite thus sealing considerable numbers of her crew to their deaths. They had been there for some days in the August climate by the time she was dry-docked, and the hatches opened up. The stench was quite dreadful; the town was complaining and you may imagine what it was like in the adjacent dock. Luckily our bulkheads around the damaged areas were fairly quickly repaired and shored up with steel, timber and concrete. We were thus enabled to leave drydock and moor at the breakwater to await the others completing patching up, so that we could make up a force strong enough for mutual support to go on to wherever we were to be sent for full refitting with minimal escorting commitment.

Coming back on board one evening, I was astonished to see two naval launches in the dark patrolling round the harbour dropping small charges (hand grenades). These made quite sizeable disturbances of the quiet. I later heard that the Italians had made a successful one-man submarine attack on Libyan ports and had got *Valiant* (a Queen Elizabeth Class battleship) by sticking magnetic delayed-action charges to her bottom. Now, Mediterranean ports arranged these launch patrols in hopes of deterring any more attacks by these brave men. Much later in life, in Metal Box, I was to meet one of their number, Ulisse Pelagatti, Chief Engineer of Superbox, our Italian subsidiary, but he would not talk about this part of his life. I do not know whether he had actually done operations against our Navy.

We had only been a week or so on the mole when at last we got orders for sea. One by one the wounded ships joined formation outside the harbour, with three destroyers as escort. We were still fairly spectacular, our above-water holes covered with timber tingles. The forward aircraft lift was still jammed two feet above Flight Deck level and put us out of commission for operating aircraft. To disguise this from enemy agents as we passed their binoculars, a skirt of bunting was rigged around the lift and it served as a bandstand whilst the Royal Marines played us out to sea. A formal photograph of the ship's company was also taken to hide the damage.

Westwards we went all day, increasing our fears that we were America-bound for our repairs, although all of us really knew by then that a weakened force like ours could not take the shortest route home – we would have to get to mid-Atlantic, beyond reach of the more intense reconnaissance aircraft patrols from France. In the evening, Tom Troubridge came on the Tannoy to say that we were UK bound.

We were almost bored with the passage, which was totally uneventful, and of course we aircrews had no opportunity to exercise our hobby. One of the sights of the passage I recall was *Ithuriel*. You will remember that it was she who had rammed the U-Boat which surfaced alongside *Indomitable* during Operation Pedestal. Her wrecked bow had been cut back from about six feet below the peak for about twenty feet of her length. She thus presented a flat concrete wall to the sea where there had been a knife-edged destroyer bow. As a result, as seen from us as she followed astern, pushing to keep up, she appeared to be nothing but an enormous bow wave and we speculated as to whether her bridge could really see where she was going!

Chapter 17

Homecoming

HAVING TRAVERSED the north coast of Ireland, a dull September day saw us fetching up, having parted from our fellow travellers, off the Formby light to pick up a pilot for the Mersey. We all suffered from an overpowering excitement in the drab dullness of the outer Mersey. Probably, when we had left the Clyde just under a year previously, none of us expected to be back in the UK so soon. Possibly, with quite a few of our number lost on the way, we thanked our lucky stars that we were the returners.

Even in those days, the Scouse docker had a reputation for caring nothing for anything outside his own immediate interests. Certainly we did not expect any reaction from him at our return. By this stage of the War, Liverpool had got used to naval arrivals, in spite of being a merchant port. The threat of the Luftwaffe virtually denied the use of Chatham, Portsmouth and Plymouth to major naval units. Liverpool was about the most southerly port they used. Our course into the King George V Dock brought us past a long line of other wharves along the Bootle and Liverpool waterfronts, which we passed at about a cable's distance. For what seemed miles, as we slowly glided in, all these wharves were crowded with dockers cheering us in. It was a very emotional experience. Such a Scouseland gesture was so unexpected on the one hand. On the other we knew, unlike them, that we had not really achieved anything particularly heroic. Very quickly we had to 'man the side' and return the cheers. I can only think that because the news had been released some weeks previously that Malta had been relieved, the dockers were stirred by us coming in with very visible battle scars. Looking at the post-War performance of Liverpool one might be tempted to think that it was not us they were cheering at all, but the ironmongery in which we were travelling, representing, as it obviously did, many hours of dockland overtime in the weeks to come.

So, once again, we were in dry dock. Leave was granted to the majority immediately. 827's remaining Albacores were lorried to Speke, ready to be flown up to Machrihanish immediately following leave, for that was to be our immediate base. I agreed to stay with the ship a few extra days, in which period Colonel Brown was expected to be recovered enough to go on leave with an escort to help him to his destination. He was by this time hobbling around with a plastered foot and a stout walking stick; his drinking capacity was picking up famously.

In the same way that dockland had greeted us so generously, so too did the Customs men. Going through my stuff, when I declared my silk stockings, the man asked whether they were not artificial silk. No, I said, they were clearly marked real silk.

'Pity, because the duty on artificial is far lower; let's have a look at them. Sorry, son, whilst they're marked as you say, I think you've been cheated at Gib, so I can't charge you more than the artificial rate.'

There was a wine merchant near the docks who would bottle properly our squash-bottled sherry and send it on in cases for almost nothing. I struggled out to him with my dozen on a tray. At the gate I declared it to the Customs man.

'Your're mistaken, son, the labels say Kia Ora; there's no duty on that.'

I explained the history.

'Sorry, son, you've been done; that's fruit squash and all I can do is clear you through.'

Next day, I went on the same mission for Colonel Brown with his sherry. Same Customs man.

'Enough's enough; you can't push your luck with me too far, son.' I explained that this was my wounded friend's supply. He looked again at the bottles. 'I do believe he was taken in the same as you; you take his squash through for him, son.'

Not a penny of duty did I have to pay.

This made an amazing comparison with our return to the same port just over a year previously in a merchant ship from Trinidad. Then the Customs men had gone through us as with a fine-tooth comb. As a rating at that time, I had been able to get myself into the baggage party – as tipped off by one of the ship's crew. Thus, instead of paying duty at the head of the gangway going ashore, one merely stepped into the last cargo net of baggage and had a by-pass lift ashore, courtesy of the craneman.

Colonel Brown's home was in Oxford, so the Navy provided us with transport to Birkenhead station. As we awaited the train, an old girl asked the Colonel about the running of the trains – some were still prone to mistake junior naval officers for railway staff.

'Madam,' he said, 'I am not employed by this railway,' and, pointing to his conspicuously plastered leg, 'Did you perhaps think I had dropped a trunk on my toe?'

Having dropped him back home, on I went to London. I was pleased to have a reporting time four days later than my colleagues who had gone on immediate leave. I could go direct to Macrihanish without flying from Speke; I had had several good dinners at the Adelphi; I had dealt with the sherry without hassle, and seemed to have avoided the rush which all the others had been involved in. Maybe also, I was fond enough of *Indomitable* not to have wanted to leave too precipitately!

At that time, the parental home was still a stately flat at 7 Princes Gate. It must have been around nine at night that I arrived there. Luckily, I ran into Clapp, the Head Porter of the block, in the hall. (Since coming into the Navy and widening my vocabulary, I had come to wonder how he came by this name!) He explained that my mother had been prevailed upon to get out of London and the worst of the bombing, so had taken a place at Laleham, near Staines. So I dumped my heavy baggage and set forth for Waterloo, catching the last train for Staines. No transport from there to Laleham, some five miles away. My suitcase became heavier and heavier. All signposts and placenames were obliterated in those times so I was pilgriming in the faith that the Staines ticket collector's advice on the way was correct. Eventually, at about one in the morning, I saw a sign 'To the Ferry'. I was not a navigator for nothing; Clapp had said that the address was Ferry Cottage. I banged on the door of the nearest house to the ferry staging. Eventually a funny old dame answered it; I had never seen her before, so was astonished when she yelled like a banshee, 'Madam, it's Mr Hector!' Thus began a long and fond friendship with Mrs Davis.

She was to become so much part of the family that no excuse need be made for a diversion here about her. Of north-country origin, she had had a long married life to a major representative of textile firms, who did nearly all his business in South America. This was done by extended visits; his wife and home always remained in UK. They were apparently prosperous but I suppose he worked entirely on commission. In any event, when he suddenly died, his estate was found to be zero and there was no insurance. He had well-to-do relations: a brother was proprietor of the Davis gas cooker firm, who were leaders in their field until after the War. In no way would

Mrs Davis look to them for support. She was a proud woman and not fond of her in-laws. Whilst well educated for a middle-class woman of her generation, she felt qualified for nothing except housework. She duly applied to an agency for a housemaid position. Whilst she could cook, she was ashamed of her talent in this direction and solidly refused to cook in the twenty-odd years she was with my mother.

When my mother went to the agency, Mrs Davis was offered reluctantly as someone without experience or references (so important in those days!) and who was rather too old for hard work, being the wrong side of sixty by an unknown margin. Her age remained a closed secret throughout her service – maybe she was afraid of being retired. Maybe in her desperation to give value for her wages, she did not want inhibitions on the employer's part on how much she was given to do. My mother took her, *faute de mieux*; in those days of direction of labour, domestic servants of normal age were almost non-existent. In no time, they took tremendously to each other. Probably, as widows, they had a common starting point. However, Mrs Davis insisted from the beginning that she be treated as a housemaid rather than as a companion. It was only in the last years of their relationship that Mrs Davis ever sat in the drawing room, and that was only when my mother was alone there, and in order to watch the new wonder of the age, television. Admittedly, unlike a housemaid, she was always 'Mrs Davis' and not 'Davis' or 'Adelaide'. My mother, not I think by choice, was always called and referred to as 'Madam'.

The cheerful courage which Mrs Davis set out on this new life lasted throughout her twenty years' service. She became a little lame with rheumatism in later years but never complained. I do not recall her 'reporting sick' either and at her age there must frequently have been times when she was feeling somewhat off-colour. The two of them were both obstinate, and querulous disagreements were far from rare, although one of the parties never forgot even during these to show the deference she felt was due to the 'boss' and thus battled with one hand tied. There were times when my mother's patience with her would end and then she could be abominably rude to her. Mrs Davis accepted all that as part of the boss's right, and her fondness for the boss would never allow her to take serious umbrage. But the relationship was genuinely founded in deep mutual affection and not feudalism. Sometimes, thinking that my mother had gone too far, a member of the family would creep into the kitchen to comfort the old duck and apologise for Mama. 'There's no need for you to come apologising for

10. My brother Kenneth, Ensign Scots Guards, 1941.

your mother,' she would say, perhaps near to tears, 'She has the right to do and to say as she likes in her own home and she never really means it. She has given me a home and something to do in life and nothing she says when she is upset will stop me being grateful for it.' It was a great comfort to my brothers and me, as we steadily all drifted away into the War and then into marriage, that our mother had such a steadfast and common-sense companion.

To return to the narrative . . . apparently, because my letters from Gibraltar had arrived so much more quickly than previous ones, my mother had started to have hopes that *Indomitable* was perhaps coming back to home waters, so maybe I could be turning up. You will appreciate that my efforts to telephone Princes Gate from Liverpool never got an answer, and I did not have Clapp's number. I had not been unduly worried because public telephones got extremely unreliable in the War. They had both happened to be awake as I approached.

'Mrs Davis!' called out my mother, 'There's someone walking down the lane at this hour . . . they've stopped at our gate; I wonder who it can be?'

'I'm going down,' says Mrs Davis, 'I expect it's Mr Hector.'

So when it was as she had predicted, she called up in matter of fact tones to confirm that, as usual, she was correct.

So my mother rushed down in her dressing gown too, and then began a tremendous welcome home. Out came the scotch bottle and I had downed a couple before remembering that civilians could hardly ever get it and I was just taking for granted what must be a precious saving for a rainy, or very special day. Was I hungry? I had only had a lunchtime sandwich with

Colonel Brown on the train, so definitely I was. Bacon and eggs? Lovely! As I sank the last delicious mouthful, the awful thought occurred. Were rations much easier now with so much bacon and eggs to spare? No; questioning brought out that I had consumed without thinking both their rations for about a fortnight. It was awfully difficult after a year at sea with plenty of such things to eat to have the forethought to realise the shortage of such things for civilians. It was very shame-making even though they were delighted to give it to the 'returning hero'.

The news of my brothers was more or less as expected. Sandy was still at medical school (it was primarily he who had persuaded them to leave London temporarily). Kenneth was doing his officer training at Sandhurst, having been accepted by the Scots Guards. Ian was still at school. Next morning, it was decided that Laleham was no place to spend leave, so the three of us returned to 7 Princes Gate.

Kenneth came up on several weekend passes during the leave. He was tremendously fit as a result of Army training and the Guards had made him grow a full two inches. He was miles taller than me. He was a great enthusiast for 'The Brigade' but unable to stop his humour allowing a continual gentle laugh at their ways. An example:

'Tomorrow we're going to have a live round exercise.'

'What does that involve?'

'We will be advancing, a battalion strong, up a valley; the enemy will be represented by cardboard targets which appear here and there and we shoot at them as they appear. The scores are counted up at the end.'

'Oh, so no-one actually shoots at you then?'

'Yes, if they see us; Guards NCOs are under cover all the way up the valley and they shoot at us if they see us. But their sights are set at the wrong range, so their shots should go over our heads. It is to get us used to being under fire and to indicate when we are not hiding ourselves well enough.'

'Well, if you see a Guards Sergeant behind a bush, can you fire at him?'

'Don't be silly; you are never allowed to see an NCO of the Brigade when he's taking cover.'

There was another little tale which comes to mind. The scene is the Orderly Officer's parade for requestmen and defaulters. A new guardsman, with a stammer, wants compassionate leave for the weekend. By tradition, having been marched in front of the table, turned and saluted, the guardsman must begin with, 'Permission to speak, sir?' On this occasion . . .

'P p pp permissmission t t to s sus sus suspeak ssssir?'

'Yes, man, get on with it.'

'P pup pup please c c ccan . . .'

'Sergeant Major, I can't understand what this man is trying to say.'

'Sir! He says, "I'm a dozy, idle guardsman, sir, and I want three extra drills".'

'Permission granted!'

'Right turn, quick march, left, right, left, right . . .'

Sandy came down from hospital quite a few evenings too; at that time he was a houseman at Dollis Hill. Between us, he, Kenneth and I got up several parties to dine and dance at the various restaurants with dance bands which kept going. They could charge 10s. or so place-money, but the food rationing regulations did not allow them to charge more than 5s. for the meal, and you could still get quite a respectable three course meal for that in London. You needed to be able to on pay of about 17s. 6d. per day.

Leave went by in a flash; at the end of it I got confirmation that I was to rejoin 827 at Macrihanish, so had the long trip to Glasgow and then on the drifter from Wemys Bay to Campbeltown. It looked as though we should be in UK for a bit, working in our casualty replacements, and the thought of a long spell at 'Machri' was depressing.

Chapter 18

With 827 in the UK

MACRIHANISH HAD GONE through big changes during the year we had been away in *Indomitable*. The airfield, moved a mile or two, now had a runway, perimeter track and taxi-ways in best tarmacadam. No longer were officers accommodated and messed in the pleasant little golfing hotel down by the shore. They had cabins in Nissen huts and a Wardroom constructed of king-sized Nissens. It was beautifully planned; some of the officers' cabins (mine, of course) were three-quarters of a mile from the Wardroom. Our Squadron office and workshops, the centre of our aircraft dispersal area and our place of work, was some two miles round the airfield periphery. Being a supposedly carrier-borne Squadron, we had no transport, as had the locally based Squadrons. All we had were the half dozen or so bicycles we took everywhere, tied to our aircraft wingstruts when we were being moved.

Luckily, I only had a day or two to digest Macrihanish's decline in comfort before the order came for 827 to move to Lee-on-Solent. This was good news. Lee, or HMS *Daedalus*, was the Headquarters base of the Fleet Air Arm built upon a peacetime airfield with peacetime standards of comfort for the majority based there. More important still, it was a place from which you could get somewhere interesting at weekends whenever you got a weekend pass.

Thus we settled down happily to gentle exercise programmes in the air and thorough servicing of our aircraft. For me, it was a pleasant initiation into the comforts of living as an officer in a shore-based establishment of peacetime standards. The food was not so good as *Indomitable*'s (except after protracted sea time); on the debit side, drinks were no longer duty free, so one had to return to enjoying beer. I became acquainted with a delightful Wren, June Hedges, but made little progress as everyone else was after her and she was expert at protecting herself by the safety in numbers theory. Then I fell hook, line and sinker for a tall, blonde, radar mechanic, Jane. Funnily enough, although we became virtually engaged, I just cannot remember her surname, so perhaps she did not mean that much to me. Because radar was such a novelty (827 still did not have it), I suppose she must have seemed terribly clever to know about it! I do recall that we were both staying overnight at a mutual friend's flat at Hillhead (near Lee), and I encountered her in the morning on the way to the loo. She invited me to her bed and I was inordinately shocked. To our funny generation, this was not something to be done before the return trip down the aisle by those intending matrimony!

A big event at this time was Richard Meakin's wedding. None of us had seen him since the loss of his leg in Ceylon, so when he invited the whole Squadron, it was like a three-line whip. The wedding was to be at Ascot on a Saturday morning. It was planned that we would all meet at 10.30 a.m. for coffee at Swan & Edgar, Piccadilly, and travel to the church together. I invited Colonel Brown (still at home in plaster), Jock Smith, Prangle Pike, Hutch and one or two others to 7 Princes Gate, on a floor-dossing basis, for the Friday and Saturday nights. Thus, after one night out, some of us were already in good form by the time we got to Swan & Edgar. I doubt that they had ever seen such a morning coffee party. Nearly everyone had a bottle in his pocket and it took little time to empty the cups of coffee so as to use them for a proper party. By the time we were at the church, we might be described as being in top form; never were wedding hymns sung so heartily even if accuracy of pitch or words was lacking here and there.

The reception was at the bride's home, a large Edwardian mansion on one of those roads bordering the racecourse. 827 could be described as having tucked in well on the liquid side. What the bride thought of her new-found spouse's friends, I cannot think, but she put on a brave show of seeming to approve of us. She actually suggested that her sisters join our post-wedding party in London that evening. My memories of the reception are hazy. I am sure this is the passage of time (I do hope so!) but two memories stand out. First, the bride was ages changing to go away, so we were all in the garden a good while. Presumably in the interests of safety, the hosts had stopped refilling glasses before we had come out. Suddenly Jock Smith emerged from the front door with a magnum in each hand:

'Come on, chaps! I've found where they keep it!'

The children present were fooling about with a football. One or two of 827 joined them and this quickly became an 827 football match, played with great vigour. Charles Gordon made a scorching shot at goal and the ball caught the bride's Mum square in the kisser. We all quickly recognised that this was not funny and in that she was ahead of us. As Colonel Brown remarked – always pontifical when pissed –

'The trouble is that Charles went to a soccer school.'

The evening party was something of a riot. We all went to Hatchetts in Piccadilly, where Stefan Grapelli and the remains of the Hot Club de France held sway. Django Reinhardt had remained in France. I suppose they closed at one or two in the morning. Just before we left, there was a nice touch. We had had a table near the band and just before he packed up, Stefan Grapelli came over and asked Colonel Brown why he had not danced. Did he not like the music? The Colonel displayed his plastered foot from under the table.

'Surely you could do a very slow waltz on that with your lady?'

The Colonel thought he might. So the great man announced:

'I am now going to play my latest composition, The Cripple's Waltz!' So the Colonel got his dance.

I believe we were gentlemanly enough to get our partners home or well on the way there before the Princes Gate party all returned. Sandy was staying the night (to support my mother through a difficult event?) and the two of them were up to greet us. To this day I am amazed how calmly she met the situation, considering the state we were in, me particularly. Would we like some nice black coffee? No thanks, but what about a drop of scotch? Round went Sandy with the carefully saved family hoard of whisky, a single bottle at the outside. It took little time for the boys to help themselves and drain the bottle. Give them their due, it was replaced for her at a later date. Tactfully, it was suggested that perhaps the time had come to bed down and to my relief, as well as Mum's and Sandy's, this was accepted.

It was then realised that somewhere along the way we had lost Jock Smith; as a Glaswegian, he was a stranger to London. However, it was decided that he was at least temporarily disposable and before long all was peace apart from a few snores. About an hour later there was an impatient ringing at the front door. My mother got out of bed and was there first. It was Jock, high as a kite and thus at his most courtly:

'Hello, Mrs Mackenzie. Sorry to disturb you by being late, but I just dropped off at the circus for a cheap bang.'

With equal courtliness but not undue warmth, he was led to his bed-place.

I also managed to get into the leave a trip back to Eastbourne College, lodged for the War at Radley, to play for the old boy's team in the annual rugger match. My brother Ian captained the College side; he was also head prefect. The day before, I got Prangle Pike to fly me up there to look for the best landing place, bearing in mind getting on from landing to Radley. In the course of this, we overflew the school and Prangle could not resist giving it a minor beat up. We selected Greenham Common, Newbury in the event, rightly guessing that the USAAF would have plenty of transport rolling their boys past Radley into Oxford on the Saturday.

Before the match, I was walking round Radley with Ian when a small boy came up:

'Sir, were you in that Fleet Air Arm bi-plane which came round here yesterday?'

When I admitted it, he said:

'Well, sir, did you lose your dividers?'

I had missed them on the way back, but often one's small instruments fell around the aircraft deck and were lost until the next good clean out.

'Well, they came just over my head and landed in front of me, so here they are!'

I thanked him profusely – not so much the joy of getting the dividers back as relief that they had not scored a direct hit. The point would have gone some way into his brain.

I had not played rugger since we were in Kenya; the pace of good schools rugger is pretty furious. I do not think it was my best game.

Two weeks after that, a signal came from Admiralty to say that Charles Morgan and I were to be given a week's embarkation leave with immediate effect, before posting on loan to the RAF for overseas service. Charles had been with me on number 44 Observers' Course as well as in 827, so at least we would each seemingly be with someone we knew. On the other hand, on the impression made by the RAF at Khormaksa, this was about the worst news we could have! As usual, no details of what sort of unit we were joining or for what sort of service were given.

We returned to Lee from our leave to be told that we were wanted urgently, so we were to be flown to the RAF units. It was now clear that we should not be in exactly the same unit. We were appointed to different Squadrons in the same wing. The Squadrons were on different airfields in East Anglia. Thus, we loaded all our kit into a De Havilland Rapide transport and off we went without even the time for a farewell party with 827. We got to Charles' airfield first and dumped him plus kit at the foot of the control tower. I was taken on another fifteen miles or so to RAF West Rainham, where I was similarly dumped.

I felt very depressed, although at that stage I had no reason for guessing that the next few days were going to demonstrate an RAF capacity for incivility and boneheadedness which made their boys at Khormaksa look like paragons. That we will deal with in the next chapter!

Chapter 19

Joining the RAF

THE RAPIDE which brought me had more calls to make, so it taxied away and took off as soon as it had dumped me and my kit at the base of the control tower, leaving it to me to report in as to who we were. So I climbed the stairs to the top of the tower to meet the duty officer. He was a Flight Lieutenant, and obviously thought that being control officer at West Rainham was a mighty important job:

'Who are you, just putting in here and then buzzing off without reporting?'

I explained that I had just climbed all his stairs in order to report but had been going to start by wishing him good day.

'I don't know who the hell you people think you are, taking off before you've even reported!'

I made the points that I had not in fact taken off and was reporting and that not being the pilot or the crew of the Rapide, I had no really deep responsibility for their actions. However, I had agreed with the pilot to furnish the necessary details on his behalf. In the Fleet Air Arm, we were pretty busy and it seemed a reasonable time-saver for me to report since I was joining his station.

'Well, at least if that is so, you will get an opportunity to learn a bit about the etiquette of the world of aviation.'

'That is as may be; it may not be too much use to me because in the Navy we stick to essentials and on the air side we do not go in for bull-shit.'

I then explained that I had come to join 114 Squadron, on loan to them as their Liaison Officer.

'I have no notification of your coming and it seems a little odd to me because they are officially an Army Co-operation Squadron.'

The last was news to me, but proved to be true. So, after this cordial greeting he rang up the Squadron to report my arrival. They too had had no notification that they were to have a naval liaison man.

'You had better go over and talk it over with them.'

The Squadron Adjutant was a little more civil but confessed that they were totally nonplussed by my arrival. He took me in to see Wing Commander Bill Molesworth, the Squadron Commanding Officer. He too was quite friendly but started by objecting to my having come into his office with my cap under my arm, instead of wearing it and saluting him once I was in his office. I pointed out that I was following the custom of my service; he felt that I should adopt RAF habits if on their premises. Knowing that I was in the right, I pointed out that when we had RAF officers temporarily in *Indomitable*, they wore their caps between decks and went into senior officers' offices and saluted; in no way did we try to make them adopt the naval custom. He got his adjutant to check which of us was right and the fact that I proved to be made me the less welcome!

'We have had no notification from Wing that you were being appointed, so first we must check with them.'

The result of this was that Wing said that they had no knowledge of it either but ??? Squadron (I cannot remember the number) had just reported that they had had a naval liaison officer drop in from the skies. I explained that he was a chum of mine. So, they had to check with Group . . . They too had no information. I suggested they rang up Assistant to the Second Sea Lord's Department at Admiralty, the department responsible for posting naval officers. It was Saturday afternoon and NA2SL staff had gone home. Much play was made about how the War had to stop for the Navy on Saturday afternoons. I suggested they rang the Air Ministry equivalent and to my everlasting delight, they too had gone off for the weekend!

I was told that I could stay until Monday, when they would get clarification. With such a warm welcome, I offered to return to my previous unit instead. At this they got quite narked.

'I suppose an RAF mess is not good enough for you?'

It was, in fact, a very comfortable mess, built in between the Wars to a very high standard. I was introduced to the Squadron officers and taken under the wing of a junior pilot, Flying Officer Philip Fuller.

He proved a pleasant beer-swilling type and was to become the nearest thing to a friend I made in 114. He was most interested in my career to date and how we did things in the Fleet Air Arm. What astonished them was that as a navigator, I had not been trained to navigate by 'pin-pointing'. By this system, their navigators gave the pilot an approximate course for the right track along the ground and corrected the course by trial and error as they 'pin-pointed' features on the ground against their maps. I pointed out that our system of finding the wind accurately, calculating (and the pilot flying) an accurate course and accurate speed was generally more useful, particularly when you could not see the ground. Our maps of the sea were a plain piece of paper with a compass rose in the corner – not much use for 'pin-pointing'. But, they said, that would never be accurate enough for finding a small target. I replied that it had had to work quite often for finding a small aircraft carrier in dark or foggy weather; odd too that the system seemed so superior to RAF navigation in the Western Desert that Fleet Air Arm Squadrons were being used as pathfinders for RAF heavy bombers. Pathfinders located the target and marked it with flares or incendiary bombs for heavy bombers with fewer navigating skills to come in and plaster with high explosive. This they found impossible to believe and they pointed out that carriers had radio beacons we could home on to. Again they did not believe that almost all the time I was in *Indomitable* there had been radio and radar 'silence'. Thus, I had a fine beginning: it was impossible to convince them that I was quite safe to navigate them around the skies!

Phil Fuller took me in to my first dinner in the mess. As the main course came up, the WAAF waitress put a steak in front of Phil and a mean helping (but too much for my taste!) of steamed fish before me. Assuming a choice, I said please, could I have the steak. They all laughed; aircrew had special rations, which was why Phil got steak. I admitted to deploring the serving of different rations in the same mess and to being in a strange world: the one I came from regarded aircrew as a lowly order, not one to be pampered. In any event, I happened to be aircrew; to this the answer was that I was not, so far as they knew, posted to them as an aircrew member. Even so, if aircrew needed special foods to keep their strength up, surely I should at least be being fattened up for my next posting? They did later reluctantly class me as aircrew in the mess, but I only took the dishes special to aircrew when the dishes offered to the others were things I did not like. This whole practice seemed to me a complete absurdity, and still does. I am sure that RAF psychology, the worship of aircrew, was more behind this than any necessity to have different ration scales. Once we were all overseas, everyone had the same rations.

Over the weekend I had some pleasant evenings in the local pub in Fakenham with Fuller and his mates, usually followed by rather boisterous sessions post-dinner in the mess. These mainly took the form of ragging me good-naturedly – I was picked on for being different. In the course of that I gained a twisted ankle from someone trying to twist my foot off while two others sat on me, which I can still feel today when the weather is cold and damp. It may be the cause of my present trouble, which the physiotherapist ascribes to some long-forgotten injury.

On their recent operational tour, working from West Rainham, 114 had been equipped with Bristol Blenheim bombers and had mainly been used against shipping in harbour and around the enemy coasts. Now they had re-equipped with Bisleys and were intended for strafing enemy Army formations in the field, in support of our own Army. The Bisley looked extremely similar to the Blenheim, out of which it was developed. It was a bit slower and carried slightly less bomb load because it had been fitted with some armour plating to protect the crew against light A/A fire when flying low. It was poorly regarded by those who had grown up in Blenheims.

At this stage, no-one except perhaps Group Captain Sinclair, the Commanding Officer of the Wing, knew where the Wing was going to be sent, merely that we were going overseas. The majority guess was that Burma would be the destination. On the Monday morning, I was paraded before Sinclair who was as puzzled about my arrival as everyone else at West Rainham. He warned that everyone was going on embarkation leave that week and that I would not be able to unless my appointment was confirmed. I was not mug enough to tell him that the Navy had already given me a week, and, thank goodness, Charles Morgan did not let on to his Squadron. Anyway, he called me back later in the day to say that Morgan and my appointments were confirmed, as indeed were those of two other naval officers to the other two Squadrons in the Wing. These later turned out to be chaps from 831 Squadron, our fellow Albacore Squadron in *Indomitable*. The purpose of the appointment was indeed naval liaison; the unexpected need for this in an Army co-operation Squadron would become more apparent once the operation we were to take part in had been announced. So, like all the others, I got a further ten days' leave.

On return from leave, we found that security clamps had come down all around: no leaving the station, no phone calls, all letters specially censored. Special kit was issued to us all, the main items being Army khaki battledress and webbing, pack, knapsack, waterbottle etc.; we also had the latest invention, water purification pills.

'Fill your bottle anywhere; first put in the blue pill, shake and wait five minutes. Then put in the white pill and shake.'

It worked too! The khaki serge reeked of chlorine, being specially impregnated, and the pong lasted all of the four months I wore the uniform. The purpose, again successful, was to stop us picking up lice.

Then we were all called together in a hangar and briefed on the operation. We were not going to Burma (the sarge had told us that!); there was to be an invasion of French North Africa with the objective of taking the Afrika Korps in the rear and gaining control of the entire southern coast of the Mediterranean. The USA would be providing most of the forces; the British would put in the First Army with supporting naval and RAF units. All would be under the command of an as yet unknown US General, Dwight Eisenhower. It was important in the initial stages that the local French should see the operation as an American one. After Dakar and then Madagascar, the French were bitter about the British and this could tempt them to resist longer than they would against the Yanks. So far as 114 was concerned, the planes and aircrew would fly out to the Algiers region once the first wave of the invasion force (British in that area) had secured some local airfields. They would have a refuelling stop at Gibraltar. The ground staff would go by sea in the 'second wave' convoy.

For travel purposes, I was classed as ground staff, not having a regular place in any of the allocated crews. It was at last explained why an Army Co-operation Squadron needed a naval liaison officer. In the first place, the post-mortem on the disastrous Dieppe raid commented that there had been insufficient inter-service liaison. Now they would err on the side of too much! Second, and more direct, it was feared that the Italian Navy might well put to sea to scotch our plans. If so, 114 would be one of the units to strike at them. As they were unable to distinguish between Italian and British ships, the idea was that I should fly in the lead aircraft and do the distinguishing, in the interests of the British and American Navies. Some might say with hindsight that half an hour's training of 114 aircrews in ship recognition would have been a more economical route to the objective. Maybe part of the reason was the impracticability of the RAF's 'pin-pointing' navigation over the ocean!

Next day, we were stuck into a special train in the evening at the local station. We travelled all night, being shunted here and there. We thought we were moving towards Liverpool, from the stations recognised *en route*, but in the early light of dawn we found ourselves de-training, as it was called by the military, in Avonmouth Docks. We boarded a P & O ship converted for trooping. I cannot now remember whether she was *Orontes* or *Oronsay*, but rather I think it was the latter. Our fellow passengers were mainly Army, including a lot of the red tabbed leading lights of some Headquarters of Army Command.

We sailed almost immediately. My only memory of that was the tight squeeze to get the ship out through the tidal lock of the Avonmouth basin. We managed to give the lock walls some most un-P & O-like thumps, but came through with no damage to more than the paintwork. We sailed northwards all day and into the night. By dawn we were in familiar waters to me, the Minches, meeting the rest of the convoy from Liverpool and the Clyde and our naval escort from Loch Ewe.

As officers, accommodation was quite good: at worst, sharing between two what had been pre-War single cabins. For the other ranks, it was the worst I had seen. The holds had been built into troop decks with timber-work and gave most rudimentary resemblance to barrack rooms. Washing facilities were nowhere near sufficient for the numbers. In the main the loos were shelters built on the weather decks with chutes over the side to the sea. As such, there was perhaps nominally enough lavatory accommodation for the numbers carried, but it was situated far too far from their living accommodation. Our chaps, if my memory is correct, had to climb three decks and go about a quarter the length of the ship to find their 'inconvenience'.

Once we were out in the Atlantic, the weather worsened all the time and we were butting into a full storm by the time we were traversing the Bay of Biscay. (Actually we must have been much further out than in the Bay – but were in that latitude.) My fellow Squadron officers were the stores and pay people, the engineers, intelligence officers and general administrative dogsbodies. Quickly they succumbed to seasickness and disappeared to their bunks. So far as I can remember, they had no ship's duties beyond super-vising the welfare of their other ranks. As a naval officer, I was put on Watches as a supervisor of the A/A machine-gun crews from the Army passengers and their official aircraft recognition expert, viz. 'Ours, DONT SHOOT; or Jerry, have a go!'

The 114 officers were in such bad shape that for several days they were quite unable to visit our troop decks, so I had to do much more than my whack of this duty. It needed a very strong stomach too; because they were at sea level over the screws they got the worst of the motion. They were so far from the heads that they were sick around the decks before they could get out; they became too sorry for themselves to clean up the mess. In any event, puke and stink thereof oozed down through the timberwork from the

Army decks above. They appreciated being visited but were impossible to cheer up. It wasn't much good suggesting wrapping up and standing on the weather decks; the tiny patch allocated to our unit was permanently packed. Never have I seen humanity in such a state of depression; never again do I want to experience a wartime troopship. What a comparison with the television shots of the boys in passage to the Falklands more recently; whereas the *QE2* took some 3,000 there, her predecessor, the *Queen Mary*, crammed in some 12,000 for her wartime trans-Atlantic trips and she was not that much bigger.

One of my many visits to the troopdeck provided the only example of mass panic I have ever witnessed and it was horrifying. Extremely luckily, no-one got hurt seriously. In a certain combination of ship's length and distance between waves and speed, particularly with big ships, you can arrive at a situation where having lifted her bow miles out of the water, the ship buries it as it falls right into the middle of an ensuing wave. This makes a fairly spectacular crash which sends a shudder right through the ship. When this happened the first time, some of the RAF chaps screamed 'Torpedo' and rushed for the one ladderway out of the deck. In spite of my shouts and those of a few others who had been at sea before, the entire rabble rushed for the ladder and were jammed on it fighting their mates for priority to get up. What it would have been like with a real hit I dread to think. They would almost certainly have been plunged into darkness for a start, and the show would have begun with a much more terrifying thump.

Another memory is being asked by three desperate 'pongoes', aka 'Brown Jobs' or soldiers, to make a fourth for bridge one evening. When I said I could not play, they said they would teach me. So I agreed to play. No instruction followed, they merely began playing. They were obvious masters of the game and soon got very irritated at my ineptitudes. I got bloody-minded and they got ruder. In the end I left the table, remarking that I had joined what I had always thought to be a game. As it was obviously very serious business, it was no way to spend my relaxation time and never would be. It never has been!

Our great convoy crept up to Gibraltar Straits to receive the good news that the initial American landings at Oran and Dakar and the British one at Algiers had all succeeded and the French were falling over backwards to surrender. The Allies had brought in a great French hero, General Giroux, to put in nominal charge of administration. After two years subjected to Laval Government propaganda, the Algerian French had considerable antipathy to de Gaulle, so this was a canny move by the Allies although it infuriated de Gaulle. Giroux had been locked up by the Germans because he would not co-operate with the Petain/Laval Government at Vichy and had just made a miraculous escape from Colditz.

Unopposed, with only one or two air attack alarms which never developed as far as seeing aircraft, we crept along the coast and into a vast anchorage of shipping off Algiers, where we dropped anchor after dark. All night long we had air-raids and the ship next to us was hit, but fortunately suffered no more than one hold flooded. I later found that Charles Morgan had been in her. The word was that the docks were overloaded so we would have to wait before we could get into a berth. Anyway, so far as possible, the larger ships like *Oronsay* would only be berthed after dark, because of the air-raids; that meant the next night.

At dawn, as I finished with the A/A boys, all the old colonels, brigadiers and generals started coming up on deck to take the air after the disturbed night. There was a full cover of lowish cloud. Suddenly, with a roar, a twin-engined plane broke cloud and came straight towards us. All the old boys scattered for cover (I suppose in fact they were a lot younger than I am now!).

'Don't worry,' I called, as official aircraft recognition expert. 'It's the morning Beaufighter patrol!'

They had just picked themselves up and were starting to brush themselves down when the plane turned and came at us with guns firing. Luckily, a Beaufighter then came through the cloud and chased mine, a Junkers 88, away! Lots of dirty looks and mutterings at breakfast. Why the hell do they rely on a bloody junior naval man to recognise aircraft anyway?

A long day at anchor followed, looking at the remarkably impressive Algiers waterfront. No air-raids. The Allies had established daytime air superiority already. Just after dusk, rumblings in the fo'c'sle told us that our hook was coming up and we were on our way in. Getting in is a suitable break for starting another chapter.

Chapter 20

Arriving in Algeria

JUST AS WE CAME OFF THE SHIP, air-raids broke out again. We were well loaded with kit, like infantry, with all we needed for the first forty-eight hours in our packs and haversacks. We were ordered up to the seaward end of the wharf to await transport and leave room for the Army people to load up, because their transport was already there for them. Not unnaturally, our men whiled away the time with a smoke. This brought squeals of protest from the wharf the other side of the dock basin, where American troops were similarly waiting. All the Americans had come from the USA direct and not from UK bases, so were raw and knew nothing about air-raids. Did we all want to be bombed showing so many cigarettes? Our chaps laughed and called back to ask how on earth a bomber was ever going to see a cigarette being lit. This was received very badly; they opened fire on us and it was only their total lack of ability which prevented any of us being hit. I am glad to say that we went on smoking whilst a senior port officer went round to them to explain the niceties of War and the undesirability of trying to shoot one's allies.

After an hour or two like this, word was given that 114 Squadron's transport was in a ship which had yet to unload, so we would have to march to our first destination, so we 'got fell in' in threes and off we went with an Army officer leading to show the way. We marched some twelve miles, a bit much for RAF types and also for some Fleet Air Arm Observers! At about two in the morning we were shown into empty (apart from cots) barrack rooms in a French barracks. We were wet through because more rain had been falling than bombs, and disappointed to find no blankets or dry covering on a jolly cold night, it being late November. By about three, no-one was asleep, we were all so cold. Suddenly a door burst open and in came Flight Sergeants Ted Sharp and Ken Jones with arm-loads of blankets. They were respectively spare pilot (from New Zealand) and spare Observer (from Australia), and men of considerable initiative when it came to their own comforts. They had gone all round the barracks and eventually found one occupied by Goums (Moroccan troops in the French Army more or less like Gurkhas in ours, with a similar reputation for resilience and toughness). Drawing their revolvers, our two had switched on the lights and roused them, and, without any knowledge of French, indicated that each man must surrender one of his blankets. They were lucky to have got out alive, or maybe everyone knows when those from down under really mean business. Anyway, we then slept until breakfast.

Breakfast brought the first demonstration of Army 'Compo' (abbreviation of 'Composite') rations. In a box, about the size of a case of wine, were packed all the things an infantry platoon might need for a day. Packets of porridge oats and tinned bacon (gloriously greasy) for breakfast. Tinned stews and vegetables for other meals, biscuits, tinned butter and cheese. A few razor blades and two sheets of very scratchy loo paper for each soldier. We felt that the War Office bargained for a lot of constipation or very small arses; the paper was, incidentally, khaki. There was also a bar of chocolate for sharing through the platoon and five cigarettes per man. Later on, when the Army stores bases got themselves organised in the black market, these last two items were always extracted from the cases before they were sent up the line. There were about five different cases so that changes could be rung on menus. They seemed a magnificent concept initially, but after a month or two, Compo bored one to death unless one could get hold of local foods, such as chickens and eggs, as supplements.

These local foods were bartered for with Compo items; we had not much money for shopping. The British authorities were most concerned that our invading forces should not cause local inflation where they went and had accordingly cut back our available cash. To bring us to about the same level of pay as our French equivalents, we were only paid cash at about one third of normal level, the rest being banked in UK and untransferable. In stark contrast, the Americans, whose rates of pay were about twice ours, paid their men at those rates in the local currency and caused roaring inflation wherever they went.

To resume the narrative . . . Mid-morning, 114 Squadron's trucks turned up out of the blue and we lost no time in getting ready for the road. In pouring rain, we loaded up, thankful that at last we were going to ride. We had only just de-trucked at Maison Blanche (Algiers' main airfield) when we were told to remove ourselves to Blida, an Armée de l'Air base, some twenty-five miles from the city, near the pleasant little market town of that name. About mid-afternoon we were dumped out of the trucks at the guard room by the main gates of Blida, wet, hungry and depressed. We then had to lift our kit and tramp halfway round the airfield to our barrack block. I recall the following exchange between two airmen as we rounded the corner of a hangar:

'What the hell do they call this place, mate?'

'Blida.'

'I know that, but what do they really call it?'

And so we settled into what was to be our home for some two or three weeks. The trucks brought all our heavy gear that evening, so there was a chance to get more comfortable. I had lost a kitbag full of my tropical kit, but that was no tragedy in the circumstances. It turned out that to divide losses on the way, our kit had been split between two ships. Quite a lot of ours was lost in the flooded hold of the ship next to us in the Algiers roads which had been hit. At least I had all my warm clothing and the goodies, standard for an infantry officer, with which I had been issued: canvas camp bed, canvas covered palliasse/bed roll and blanket, folding canvas wash basin/hipbath etc. These items became part of our family camping kit for years after the War, except the bedroll, of which more later.

Blida was a good, well-built, base, but was now rather crowded as the British units were put in in addition to the French ones already there. In the invasion, a Fleet Air Arm fighter pilot had distinguished himself by capturing it singlehanded. Arriving to strafe it, he had found no opposition and saw what he thought to be white flags. Somewhat impetuously, perhaps, he landed and was taken to the Commandant who readily signed a surrender of his airfield and forces, which the pilot took back to his ship! Besides the four Squadrons of our Wing, there was a Coastal Command Squadron of Lockheed Lodestars. Strictly speaking, they were Lockheed 'Hudsons'. The Hudson was a small (approximately twenty-five seat) civil aircraft, the Lodestar an adaptation of it for coastal patrol work by the RAF. There was also a Swordfish Squadron (ex *Ark Royal*) from the Fleet Air Arm. In this Fleet Air Arm Squadron I met a school contemporary, rather senior to me, Derek Empson, who had distinguished himself in 1938 by being British Schools champion hurdler. He was now a Lieutenant RNVR, one ring up on me, and a Swordfish pilot. He stayed on in the Navy after the War and finished up as a Vice-Admiral and Chairman of the Council of Eastbourne College.

Derek's Squadron had had a hard time doing A/S patrols for the incoming first wave convoys. They had lost two planes, shot down by American fighters. The Yanks had briefed all their pilots that any bi-planes were sure to be Italian, so Swordfish had become automatic targets. One instance had caused particular bitterness; the 'stringbag' came down in sight of the convoy and all three crew were seen to get safely into their inflatable dinghy. One of the escorts went over to it but all three were dead, shot up in their dinghy by the Americans. One thing we were learning fast: give a Yank a gun, and he sincerely believes it is for using on anything and anyone.

The RAF Lockheed Lodestar Commanding Officer also had an American tale to tell. One of his Lockheed Lodestars had been shot down by an American Airforce Lockheed Lightning, so he went down to Maison Blanche to make sure that the Lightning pilots based there were taught to recognise Lodestars as Allies. At first the American Commanding Officer blustered that it could not be his unit's doing. Then the RAF CO caught him out at being unable to recognise a Lodestar himself and then persuaded him to go through the flight records. This established that they were the guilty party – pretty obvious as they were the only Lightnings within thousands of miles – and profuse apologies were made before lunch was offered. In the mess, the American CO pointed out the officer who had committed the crime, but said:

'Please don't say anything to him; it was his first kill, and he would be mighty upset!'

I was not, as you may have gathered, over-enamoured with my RAF colleagues and as Derek Empson's lot disappeared within days of our arrival, I spent more and more of off-duty hours in the company of the Armée de l'Air. Quickly my school French developed into an easy, if not always correct, fluency. They had a lively mess and naturally knew where all the best restaurants in Blida were. It was amazing to us how large the French civilian population was. I suppose we had imagined in advance that it would be something similar to our picture of the thin sprinkle of the British across India. Algeria was, of course, a department of France, and was similar to most of them in that every sizeable shop, farm, factory or restaurant was French-owned and run and the entire supervisory class was French. A closer parallel would have been the Europeans in South Africa or Rhodesia. Also as in those parts *les indigènes* got a thin time of it.

When the Armée de l'Air warrant officers' mess discovered that my twenty-first birthday was approaching, they insisted on mounting a celebration of it. My! what a party! It began in the mess with aperitifs and the carving of a magnificent cake, decorated with a perfect sugar representation of Fleet Air Arm Observer's wings. Eventually, on we went into town to a super restaurant. Halfway through the meal I asked my neighbour where to go to answer nature's call. I need not have been so delicate; he called the waitress:

'*Monsieur ici veut pisser.*'

She led me out to the back and pointed to a door. Thinking I had followed the point, I entered a completely dark space and could find no light switch. Pressure was at such a pitch, I had to let fly and hope for the best. As I did so there was a tremendous neighing and I felt the wind of a tremendous kick just missing the point where it would have hurt most. I reversed out into the yard to complete the operation. With great relief, I returned to table and related my escape from a fate worse than death. They called the waitress to protest at her silly joke. She protested her innocence; all she had meant to indicate was that the whole of the outside of the stable wall was mine to pee on; how shy were the English if they must go indoors to pee!

There was little risk that someone might take the opportunity to stick a knife into one in such places. The local *indigènes* were too oppressed in those days to dare attack a Frenchman. They were pro-British hoping, perhaps, that we would replace the French. The French themselves were also not hostile; they'd quickly declared themselves pro-Allies or retreated into neutral apathy.

During this phase, I do not recall 114 flying any operations at all; I suppose the Army were consolidating their hold on the French controlled areas. The Germans were quick to react; they occupied all of Vichy controlled France and also Tunisia. The local French view of the Allies then intensified. Whilst not German lovers, they were hopping mad at our interruption of their peaceful sit-about, waiting for the end of the War. Worse, it very much looked as if we were going to drag them back into the War. Certainly there was no sign at all of the much-vaunted valiant aggression of La Résistance about which we have heard so much post-War! What a contrast to the attitude of all the peoples of the British Commonwealth, who overwhelmingly thought it right to support the Allied cause. As the Army came up against the Wehrmacht on the Tunisian frontier, 114 were called to come a little nearer to the action. As usual, the aircrews flew; we lesser mortals travelled along the ground.

Having been trucked into Algiers, we were loaded into a special train; the officers and most of the men were in standard passenger coaches, but some had to go in the goods vans of First World War fame: *Quatorze chevaux: quarante hommes.* The locomotive was tremendous and I was able to cadge the only footplate ride of my life. It was a very modern machine: no shovelling coal for the fireman as in England. A horizontal archimedean screw in the bottom of the tender forced coal through a pulveriser, whence it was blown to the fire. Our start was delayed by the boys playing with the emergency cord until they had driven the French guard bananas. It made little difference, because the state of the track and rolling stock was such that we could only plod along at about 35 miles per hour, so it took all night to reach Setif, our destination.

We stopped there for no more than twenty-four or forty-eight hours and beyond the fact that we lodged at yet another French Air Force base, I remember nothing of it. We seemed to have barely arrived when a convoy of Army trucks and the Wing's own transport arrived to take us to what became our more permanent home. This was Canrobert, a tiny village on the road between Constantine and Souk el Arbha. It was on high ground, the plateau adjoining the foothills of the north-east end of the Atlas mountains. The terrain was desert scrub, a bit like the more desolate areas of causse in mid-France but with less vegetation. Altitude was sufficient to make nights cold and frosty; sometimes we had snow. The road through the village became a main route to the front for the British Army on the left flank (northern) of the front as well as the Americans on the right flank. At that time, the front was some sixty or seventy miles to the east of us.

Dominating the village was a small peak, whose name I forget. The two biggest buildings were Le Préfet's residence and office and, next door, the school. The latter was requisitioned to make our offices and the officers' mess for the whole Wing. On the other side of the road, a large, tented camp was made, officers nearest the mess, then NCOs with a large marquee mess, then other ranks' tents and their mess marquees. I only resided at this camp for a day or two. It was decided that until I got any flying to do, which seemed to depend mainly on the degree of aggressiveness of the Italian fleet, I might as well serve as an assistant to the Squadron Intelligence Officer. This was the misnomer of all time. Ned Sparkes, the man in question, was a dear old fellow (he was in his later thirties!) but lacked any common sense or aptitude for camping and seemed devoid of anything between his ears. His duties involved briefing aircrew before operations and interviewing them on return (de-briefing) to put together the formal report on results. As such, he had to reside on the airfield, presumably to minimise the chance of his pearls being forgotten as the swine travelled to their aircraft, or their forgetting what they had been up to if they had more than the minimum journey from their planes to de-briefing on return. He lived in a mobile caravan/office of the type often depicted in use by Monty in the desert. Each side of this wagon had a button-on tent, in one of which lived Earnshaw, his batman. He was a Yorkshireman and thicker than a pile of planks. He was also devoid of any sort of charm. Sparkes slept on the desk running across one end of the van and I similarly at the other end. Our kit, stores and the 'kitchen' shared the opposite side-tent to Earnshaw's.

How they lived prior to my arrival I modestly cannot think. Neither seemed capable of opening a tin, never mind operating the two Primus stoves with which they were issued. These did become tricky because we ran low on kerosene and I had to find a blend of that and aviation petrol which would burn and not explode. They did not even know of the Eighth Army's standard stove: fill a biscuit tin (or petrol one with the top cut off) with sand, slop in petrol and apply a match. Earnshaw thought this the invention of the century until he started to refuel it without having first put it out. Luckily I was there to put him out. I did help Ned with intelligence, but my main duties became of necessity cook/batman/boy scout for him and Earnshaw. My proudest deed was Christmas lunch for which I obtained a starved little turkey from an Arab, cut into quarters and 'roasted' in an empty petrol tin upturned on my frying pan on an Eighth Army stove. The bread sauce was not very successful, fried biscuit crumbs cooked in milk! I had wondered if I was being taken for a ride by their incompetence, but they had really not managed successfully to open a can or light a Primus until I arrived.

I had one near disaster almost akin to Earnshaw's. In very cold weather I brought the primus stoves into the caravan to cook a meal. One had developed the habit of losing pressure. To find the leak, I took off the burner unit, put my thumb over the pipe and pumped up a little to explore for the leak. Meanwhile, the spuds were boiling on the good stove alongside. *Au moment critique*, Ned asked me something and I turned, polite as always, to answer him; my thumb came off the pipe. Seeing the look of horror in his eyes, I turned back to see a super jet of flame emanating from the pipe and playing on the ceiling of the caravan. Face was saved a little by the calmness with which I speedily released the pressure on both stoves and applied the fire extinguisher. Coolly I reproved him:

'You know, old man, you ought not to interrupt me when I am working on the Primuses. If I had not happened to be handy with the fire extinguishers, we could have had quite a problem then.'

On New Year's Eve, I quite outdid either this episode or Earnshaw's. We had a colossal party in the mess. In the early hours I crawled into my bedroll, battledress over my pyjamas and naval greatcoat over the top of all as an extra blanket. It was very cold. By this means, one could just about get warm enough to get to sleep by the time the customary last night ciggy was finished. In the night, I awoke to a stinging sensation in my thigh, like a burn. I could hardly breathe and Ned was coughing like a drain in his sleep. On with the light: total fog. Sparks coming from my lovely greatcoat. I managed to beat it all out, but what a disaster. A nine-inch square hole in my irreplaceable (in Algeria) greatcoat; ditto through my bedroll canvas and doubled blanket; rather smaller in my pyjama trousers and only a blister on me. This was followed by what I thought a rather unnecessary wigging from Ned on the unwisdom of smoking in bed, particularly when a little pissed. Until I got home and back to Gieves, at least my greatcoat gave the impression that I had seen some action!

Bathing was a problem initially. The portable canvas unit made a pool about two foot square and nine inches deep in which one could sit cross-legged in the Primus-heated water. I used to have an impressive photo of me doing this, surrounded in snow. We bathed outdoors because inevitably, water slopped everywhere. Later arrangements were made with the Moorish baths in the local town, Souk el Arbha, for us to attend once a week. This was lovely. We all sat about in a very hot room with a stone floor, each with a bucket of water and a bar of soap. When you had finished soaping and lolling about in the heat, you called over one of the Arab women serving the place. She would then set about your back with much vigour with an RAF-issue floor scrubbing brush. Just as you could bear it no more, she would dive to the well in the middle of the floor, fetch a bucket of ice-cold water and dump it on you. Once a week was quite enough really.

I got into the bad books of the Squadron around this time. The first counter-attack by the Hun sent the Americans scattering and the Germans were flooding through the gap between the British, who had held, and the runaway Yanks. Expecting them our way, our gallant Group Captain ordered preparations for defending ourselves. The idea was to take all arms and the bomb stores to the top of the hill behind the village, which would become our last redoubt. The bombs would be fused and as a last resort dropped down the cliffs on the attacking enemy. This, of course, assumed that he would co-operate and stand at the bottom of the cliffs for us.

In any event, all the men laboured hard all day at the task of shifting the stuff. They were still hard at it when I left the airfield to attend a mess party for someone's birthday. To my astonishment, all officers were at the mess. Never in the Navy would you have the men working extra hours and not a single officer with them. I sneaked off from the party and joined the men. Late at night I took a truck to the cookhouse and got them some tea and food which they would have otherwise missed. They and the Flight Sergeant in charge were very appreciative. Unfortunately, next day he mentioned this appreciation to his commanding officer.

I was sent for by Molesworth, our Squadron Commanding Officer. What the hell had I been interfering for? I was not aiming to interfere; I had noticed there was no officer with them, so had just filled in to be helpful. RAF personnel may not require as much supervision as RN and that must be judged by those in charge. It was pointless for an officer of another service to stick his nose in. I had not seen my presence as a supervisory need; just that if the men had dirty work to do late at night, it seemed proper for an officer to be seen to be sharing it. Well, that was even worse. It amounted to an effort to curry favour with the men and show up their RAF officers which was unbecoming in the extreme from a junior officer from another service. I apologised. I had instinctively taken action I thought correct without thought of 'currying favour' or 'showing up' anyone. 'I will enter my displeasure on your records!'

I keep referring to the airfield, but it was only a home-made landing strip in the scrub. Two steam-rollers had been commandeered and had rolled and rolled a strip we watered with the drinking water bowsers to make a fairly flat and hard runway surface. It was not very satisfactory. The planes all too often got punctured tyres during take-off or landing. As often as not, this then crashed the undercarriage legs up into the wing, puncturing the fuel tanks. The exhaust flash as the engines cut then started a fire and the plane would burn out. The crews were adept at the necessary quick dash to the fire to salvage any useful equipment, such as radio receivers, before the fire had too strong a hold. Any bombs aboard the plane would cook off in the fire, blowing the plane to pieces, sharp pieces, all too often, so that more punctures were caused and the vicious circle was complete.

In due course it became Ned's and my turn to have a salvaged radio receiver. They were very popular because if you got them set up well, you could get the BBC news. Just as I got ours on to the BBC, I heard what I thought was a familiar voice. It was a chap talking about being stuck on a desert island . . . Colonel Brown. When I told those present that this was an episode from my last Squadron, they would not believe it.

Around this time, Charles Morgan and I were informed that our immediately senior officer in the Navy, a Commander Pearson RN in Naval Liaison at Allied HQ, wanted to see us. This meant going all the way back to Algiers. With naval efficiency, however, he arranged for an Air France plane to call into Canrobert to pick us up. It was a peculiar little twin engined machine called a Goeland and go along was about its maximum achievement. There were two crew, of venerable age, and they navigated by a totally French system. This seemed to involve one of them pointing in the direction he thought we should steer; the other would then similarly indicate his idea. Then would follow an intense debate and one feared that it would come to blows. Inevitably, they finished up steering halfway between the two suggestions. As a system, it seemed to work exceedingly well, even if a trial of the passengers' nerves. Our first hop was to Telergma, across the mountains and on the northern fringe of the Sahara. One of the debates about course was in full progress as we flew on automatic pilot straight at the vertical side of a mountain. Charles and I were just about to force them to do something about the mountain when they saw it, opened the throttles and pulled back the stick. The poor old Goeland shuddered and creaked but miraculously did not stall and just cleared the ridge but, as Charles said afterwards, you could have reached out and made yourself a snowball. From Telergma, we had a calmer ride to Maison Blanche.

Our boss's office was at Allied Headquarters, a beautiful great building overlooking the city with intense American security, but he had provided all the necessary passes. He was a nice guy and most sympathetic to our complaint that we had not enough to do to justify our presence in the rough of Algeria and our request for transfer back to an active Fleet Air Arm unit. He felt rather similarly as a naval liaison man to the US Forces, which was a part of his duties. Like everyone there, he was particularly impressed by Eisenhower and charmed by him. Although Commander-in-Chief, one of his foibles was always to stop his car at the gate, where all were about to present arms, get out and walk up to the sentry proffering his pass and saying, 'My name is Eisenhower.' It was thought that he quite sincerely believed that they could not be expected to know.

However Pearson had suffered one tragedy at the hands of his American guardians at Allied HQ. A few days before our visit, his Royal Marine driver had arrived for him, as usual around 'quitting time', and stopped by the pathway to the nearest door to Pearson's office. An aggressive US sentry came up to him:

'You can't park there, Limey.'

'I am just waiting for my officer.'

The argument which ensued had reached full pitch by the time Pearson turned up. He gave them both a dressing-down for being childish and giving a particularly bad example of Anglo–American cooperation to the numerous French about, whom we were trying to impress with our total cohesion. The Royal Marines driver saluted and returned to his car door. The US Army sentry, in a complete loss of temper, then came up with his tommy-gun and shot the Royal Marine dead on the spot. Pearson, fearful for his own life, managed to get him arrested.

In the evening, we had a pleasant meal at a good restaurant, Algiers seemingly having reverted to an almost peacetime atmosphere. After dinner we took a walk up through the Kasbah, but there was no sign of Charles Boyer or Hedy Lamarr. Next day we caught our Goeland back to base, hopeful that before long our desire for a posting, now having been expressed, would receive attention. Meanwhile, all we could do was wait at Canrobert, seeking opportunities to be useful and finding what diversions we could.

Chapter 21

Diversions in Algeria

SHORTLY AFTER OUR RETURN, the Wing took part in its first daylight operation. Because of the limited performance of the Bisley, it had been thought best to confine it to night operations. However, when a major tank build-up by the Germans was spotted, it was decided to give the Bisleys a heavy escort of fighters and send them in to bomb in daytime, when they could see what they were doing. Thus, bright and early one morning, 114 and the other Squadron selected set off. They came back to report that the fighter escort had not shown up at all. Even so, they had carried out the attack on the tanks with some success. Luckily, they had caught the Germans by surprise, so our Bisleys had escaped the attentions of enemy fighters.

This success seemed to go to the head of our gallant Group Captain. He ordered the other two Squadrons into a follow-up attack on the target, not even bothering to request fighter escort. Poor devils, they learned that whilst you might be lucky enough to take the German by surprise once, you just cannot expect to do it twice. One of the Squadrons was almost totally wiped out and the other had very heavy casualties. One of our naval Observers flew with them – in one Squadron in the Wing, the commanding officer knew enough to be able to accept Fleet Air Arm navigation as adequate! He had been shot down, but had baled out over Allied territory, so got back. He said that they had run straight into bank after bank of fighters and there was no escape from them. We all felt very sorry and that it was a stupid loss incurred by our Commanding Officer's quite unnecessary thirst for glory.

Months later, when I was back with the Fleet Air Arm, I heard that the Commanding Officer of the Squadron which had been shot down had been awarded the VC. The citation was in terms of a desperate need for support by the Army and how the Squadron had been led through overwhelming fighters in a desperate effort to gain the target at all costs. This compares with my Fleet Air Arm colleague who said that they had been jumped by fighters and try as they did, they had no hope of escape in a crate like the Bisley. I have no desire to detract from the undoubted bravery of the RAF's crews, but I have been left ever afterwards with the impression that it is possible for a stupid Commanding Officer to escape the consequences of his folly by sending in citations of the valour of his men, supposedly acting on their own initiative, to cover up his own impetuosity. Shades of the Charge of the Light Brigade!

The fighters had not turned up, incidentally, because their large base at Souk el Arbha had been plastered by heavy bombing with heavy casualties to both aircraft and men. The bombers? – the United States Army Airforce, a matter of an error of navigation. They did apologise.

During the latter part of my stay, weekend leaves were allowed when operations permitted. On some, we got fairly far afield. The distance record was held by Flight Sgts. Sharp and Jones, from New Zealand and Australia, previously mentioned as blanket purveyors. Strictly against orders, they hitch-hiked by air to Gibraltar, thence to London for one night and back, all in a long weekend. Incidentally, they had made themselves very comfortable in camp at Canrobert, a large French double bed in their tent and an Arab servant. Most of us went back to Constantine for weekends. It is a lovely city built round the junction of two ravines, with spectacular bridges. We had a very pleasant Officers' Club there and there was a good Casino where one could drink and dance as well as playing the tables, but the star attraction was a super barmaid called Suzi. She had started with zero English, but picked up fast from her customers, though unable to distinguish between good English and the more vernacular variety of servicemen. Thus when a General Hospital was eventually set up in Constantine and snooty officer nursing sisters started to come to the bar, they were a little taken aback at such remarks as, 'Get your fucking elbows off the bar while I wipe it,' or 'Can't you bloody buggers make your minds up what you want to fucking drink?' There was a similar linguistic problem outside, where an Arab lad sold the evening newspapers. 'Duff Gen,' was his proud call, in the belief that that was English for 'Newspaper'.

My first stay at the Officers' Club nearly saw the end of me. My room was on the same floor as the front door. Arriving back very merry, I had barely lain down when a major call of nature arose, a frequent problem in those parts, in spite of our wonder water sterilising pills. Unable to find the loo, in my desperation I sat across the balcony rail, my legs curled around the struts. Then, shamefully, I tottered off to bed. First thing in the morning, I crept out to see how dreadful was the evidence and what chances there were of removing it unobserved. To my horror I found that the building was against the side of the ravine, the rear having storeys below the entrance level set on pillars to the valley bottom. The balustrade on which I had perched was at the equivalent of the sixth floor level. At least my misdemeanour was invisible from the Club!

One Sunday morning, a large group of us were taking aperitifs in the big and crowded hall of the Casino. It was *Jour pour les Soldats*, a day for collecting for French Army charities. Thus, the orchestra struck up with the Marseillaise. Barely had we sat down from that before they played the American anthem. Then the British and on and on in turn through all the Allies, Belgium, Norway, Greece, Yugoslavia, Russia etc. etc. We were standing up and sitting down like Jacks-in-the-Box. Finally a pause and then they struck up with 'Little Grey Home in the West'. As a man, our party cracked to attention. We had the whole hall standing in respect to this little ditty!

A less diverting activity was being Airfield Duty Officer. The main responsibility was security. The most frequent breach of it was Arab raiders thieving petrol from the fuel dump alongside the airfield. Believe it or not, all the aircraft and vehicle fuel came in four-gallon throwaway tins. As you can imagine, it took time to fuel up a plane. It also made fuel as easy as possible for Arabs to steal. They crept through the wire fence with donkeys and they could get a lot of tins on to a donkey. We had patrols out but there were so many Arabs it was very hard to catch them. One night when I was on, two were brought in. Following our Standing Orders, I explained to them in my best French that they would be handed over to the French Prefect for punishment. I was astonished at their reaction to this, whining, crawling, trying to kiss my boots for mercy. I thought they had misunderstood my French and explained very slowly that they would go to the Prefect and it was to him they must beg for mercy. I regretted my understanding of them and my slavish following of my orders when my patrol got back from the Prefecture. A note for me explained that the great man was busy entertaining a lady, but he had made arrangements for the miscreants to be flogged at intervals through the night and he would see them to fix punishment in the morning.

On a long weekend, a group of us set forth in a three-ton truck to travel south to see Timgad, a Roman colonial city on the north side of the Sahara. Very impressive it is. It has remained uninhabited since its destruction by earthquake in about AD165. We stayed in a nice little hotel in the nearby French garrison town. Opposite the hotel were the barracks of a Spahi regiment, based there to watch out for any effort by the Germans to work round the desert flank. Thus, they sent several officers in to investigate us. As we had a month's spirit ration with us, they were soon enjoying our company. *'Notre Colonel a dit que l'alcoool tue, mais un Spahi doit toujours regarder la morte en face.'*

Next night we were entertained to dinner in their mess, which was a very super meal. We learned that the married officers had their wives with them, so we asked them all to dine at the hotel with us the next night. They also asked any of us who could ride to come out on patrol with them next day. I was the only one to accept and it was great fun. Lovely Arab steed, and it all seemed so very *Beau Geste* riding with the Spahis in the desert! That night I got my come-uppance. The spirits flowed fast before dinner and it had a very poor effect on my far from perfect French. At dinner, I had the luck to be placed next to quite the prettiest of the wives. I launched into my most charming conversational gambits. She was as polite as she was cool. By the time the entrée arrived, she suddenly said: 'Why don't you speak English? I should understand you so much better. I happen to be English. You don't have to be French to marry a Spahi, you know.' I could have hit her.

The most unusual weekend was one spent by three of us, tired of news bulletins that seemed everlastingly to say that action at the front ' . . . was limited to patrol activity.' We got permission to spend twenty-four hours with the Army in the front line to learn what they actually did do. We were lent a 15 cwt truck to get to the units to which we were allocated. We had to start in the middle of the night and soon learned the difficulties of navigating busy military roads through the mountains without lights. We had seen the amazing difference between the American night convoys and the British ones through Canrobert. The Yanks, who had been so nervous of our smoking in Algiers docks, were flashing headlights all the time. The British drove without lights – just a white painted circle on each truck's rear differential and a pea-lamp bulb shining on it.

Quite a way behind the line, we frequently started to see Arab corpses by the roadside and wondered how they had been killed. We learned later from our Army hosts that on American supply routes this was common. They used Arabs for target practice on the way to the front.

It was evening by the time I had dropped my pals at other units and I was very weary when I arrived at my hosts, the Coldstream Guards. They had also had some attached Grenadiers to make up numbers because of heavy casualties they had suffered a fortnight previously. They were living in dug-outs at the edge of flat ground facing a high peak about a mile away on which Jerry was ensconced. This peak, called Longstop Hill by the Army, earned fame as it was much fought for, and changed hands several times over the months. Even Spike Milligan fought there, as can be read from his memoirs of the War. In all probability, the artillery ammunition involved in my little episode was left behind by him!

I was first taken to the Colonel in HQ which was an office at the back of the wrecked railway station. He invited me to go out with a patrol they were planning for that night. It was to go towards the far side of no-man's-land at the foot of Longstop and search an abandoned hamlet to ensure that no German patrols were nested in it. Then to stand guard to cover a party of artillery men who were coming to recover ammunition they had had to abandon in a hurry when the American unit then holding the front had retreated. We would all be back for breakfast. A company Sergeant Major would come on the patrol to stay at my elbow and guide me what to do if there were trouble – what care the Guards take!

When it was good and dark, we set off into a relatively silent night. When we got to the hamlet, it seemed positively spooky, such was the quiet. Then we moved over to take our guard position and wait for the Gunners to do their work, expected to take some two hours. That is where I went wrong. A thump on my arm and the CSM hissing in my ear, 'Wake up, sir, you are snoring awful and it will give us away.' Unfortunately it had. Down came a stonk of mortar bombs, luckily not close as they only had the sound of my snuffles to aim at! The Lieutenant in charge of the patrol apologised afterwards for the fact that he was bound to report the episode in his patrol report. After breakfast the Colonel asked to see me. He was frigidly polite, even inviting me to sit down for our conversation. 'Do you chaps go to sleep when on Watch on your ships? Were you in your school OTC? Didn't you learn there that one does not sleep on night patrols? Last night's patrol was a success and there were no casualties. Wasn't that luck? How would you have felt if the mortars had got the patrol?' were the sort of questions with which I had to contend. Without any angry word or really any direct reproof, and by total politeness, he left me as full of shame as I have ever been. At the end he said he recognised well that I had gone out very tired and had had no operational responsibility on the patrol to keep me on my toes and the matter was then totally forgotten – by him.

Whilst I was with him, an ensign (Guards nomenclature for a second Lieutenant) arrived. He had a blood-soaked bandage round his neck and looked exceedingly ill.

'Good God, Archie,' said the Colonel, 'What are you doing here? I've only just had a signal saying you are seriously wounded and arrived in Base Hospital in Algiers with a view to return to the UK.'

'Well, sir,' said Archie, 'If you remember, the Battalion was in a bad way when I was hit, so as soon as I felt fit enough I escaped from hospital and hitched back to see if I could lend a hand.'

Archie had been shot through the throat on the assault on Longstop. Their spirit was so tremendous, it only added to my shame. Apparently they had attacked the formidable Longstop Hill a fortnight previously. Continuously for forty-eight hours they had attacked and had received fifty per cent casualties. They took it and the next day hung on to it in the face of fierce counter-attacking, before being relieved by a fresh American battalion. The Coldstream adjutant attended the American briefing as they took over. They had had to march half a mile from their trucks, up the hill track. He was genuinely amused that when at the end their Colonel said, 'Any questions, men?' a sergeant answered 'Shucks, Colonel, I am tired.' After all their effort the Guards seemed only amused that the Americans had surrendered the hill at the first counter-attack. This obviously meant that within the next week or two they were going to have to assault it all over again.

It was a most educational visit for me, emphasising the relative comfort in which the Navy could fight its war. How men could keep up their spirits so, living in holes in the naked earth for weeks on end, interspersed with such bloody fighting, completely staggered me.

On return to 114, I had further trouble from those in charge. Bill Molesworth sent for me. Why had I reported to authorities that I did not feel I had enough to do to justify my presence, rather than to tell him in the first place? Because, I said truthfully, they had asked me the question and he never had. I added that I felt that within 114 this message might have risked them feeling that I was complaining about them, which was not the case. 'That,' he said, 'is just how we do take it.'

The outcome was that I had to make another trip to see Pearson in Algiers, this time hitching back to Maison Blanche with the USAAF in a

Dakota, then known as a C–47. Pearson was very nice and said Morgan's and my posting was being arranged. We should pack and be ready to move at short notice to catch a ship. He was in low spirits about the American who had shot his driver. As the only witness, he had expected to be called to the American Court Martial. The day before he had been informed that only in special circumstances were aliens admitted to US field courts martial. Such circumstances were deemed not to exist in this case, so he would not be called. The man had put in a strong story about extreme provocation and got off with a reprimand.

A week or so later, Charles Morgan and I got our sailing orders. This time, with all our heavy gear to take, we were trucked to Constantine, where we were to stay one night at the club and catch the morning train to Algiers. What a merry time we had in Suzi's bar at the Casino that night! I think we were the first two Allied officers for whom she leaped over her bar and embraced in farewell. It's funny to think that she is probably a dreadful old granny now. I wonder if her English is still bespattered with four-letter words!

Charles Morgan was about my age, dark, big nose, big coarse mouth, great personality and sense of humour. From a more humble background than most of the 827 colleagues, his claim to fame was that he was a cousin of a national star crooner, female and glamorous (and post-War film star), Alma Cogan. I never saw him again after we got home and I do not know if he survived the War. He was a very good pal and colleague in RAF misery.

Chapter 22

Homebound from Algeria

AFTER A NIGHT AT THE OFFICERS' CLUB, Charles and I caught the ordinary civilian 'express' train for Algiers from Constantine. Express was the French euphemism for a train scheduled to take some thirty-five hours to cover the two-hundred mile journey. About an hour after we had been chugging through the countryside, I discovered that I had left my small haversack at the Officers' Club. This was annoying because it contained most of my small treasures and, most importantly, my identity documents and Flying Log, which were classified documents to be guarded with one's life.

As Charles did not mind, we agreed that I should dismount at the next stop, leaving all my other gear with him, and try to hitchhike back to Constantine. I would then find the quickest way I could to Algiers and meet him there to reclaim my kit and sail home with him. It was a rather stupid arrangement in fact. Neither of us was to know whether or not he would be put straight aboard ship on arrival at Algiers. Our next stop was at a signal on a stretch of track alongside the main east/west road, so I dismounted. Disregarding the guard who started screaming at me, I nipped down the embankment and had thumbed down an eastbound army truck within the minute. It got me back to Constantine in a good deal less time that the train had taken in the opposite direction.

Having recovered my haversack, it had all seemed so easy that I thought I might as well try even more. I had left my binoculars in the caravan/tent at Canrobert and could not bear the idea of Ned Sparkes 'coming into' them. So I decided to walk out of town on the Canrobert road and try for a lift if I could get one within the hour. It should not be too difficult as the road was a main supply route to the front, although most of the traffic was at night to gain air-cover. My luck was in and I dropped off at the Officers' mess in Canrobert just in time for the evening drink. After that I went down to the airfield and called in on Ned and disappointed him by collecting the binoculars. Having resigned from cooking for him and his batman, I left them to eat and went back up to the mess to cadge a meal.

Molesworth, the 114 Squadron Commanding Officer, was naturally astonished to see me but seemed most amused at my pertinacity in collecting my carelessly forgotten bits and pieces. I pointed out that my luck might not hold out further. Morgan and all my kit might have sailed before I could hit Algiers. 'My God!' he said, ' You really have hit the jackpot. I have got to send a Bisley down to Maison Blanche tomorrow morning for some urgently wanted spares. Want a lift?' I said I would be most grateful, particularly if he could arrange a takeoff without a puncture.

Thus, after a good meal and a comfortable night in the mess, I reported to Sgt. Pilot Basarich, an American who had found his way into the RAF, climbed up beside him and off we set for Maison Blanche. All I remember of that trip was the nausea caused by the quite disgusting cigars Basarich smoked all the way. You try a 5-cent cigar secondhand in a four cubic foot box! Anyway, it only took us about two and a half hours.

It was easy to get a lift into Algiers and give Pearson a ring. The news was good. Berths were booked for us in a ship sailing in a couple of days, and a room in a hotel in central Algiers. I went there and checked in. They were a little curious about my lack of baggage. I then had just nice time to go down to the station to meet Charles Morgan on the train from Constantine! He got quite a shock to see me there and this was tinged with a little annoyance. He, too, had left something – I can't remember what – behind at Canrobert and would have asked me to get it if he had realised that I was going to be mad enough to go all the way back there.

Algiers had changed a good bit since we had last resided in the area. It seemed just like a peacetime city, apart from the inevitably large amount of khaki about, a natural result of Allied Headquarters still being situated there. So Charles and I had a pleasant forty-eight hours eating and drinking well and 'researching' the Kasbah nightspots.

It's a funny thing. I have really very clear memories of the various ships I sailed in during the War except for the one which brought us back from Algeria. I cannot remember her name or what company owned her, whether she was a freighter or a passenger ship, what she looked like or what sort of size she was. I rather think she was a modest sized mixed passenger and freight ship. I remember little of the passage except that hardly anyone was travelling in our direction, so Charles and I each had our own cabin. For once, for the only passage in all the War, we had no ship's duties to perform and spent our time in bibulous idleness. There were some old newspapers and books borrowed from others around. We played cards (poker) and liar dice, but there were no films or newsreels.

So safe had the western Mediterranean become that our ship travelled alone, not in convoy or escorted, as far as Gibraltar. We were there for less than a day and not allowed ashore, before joining up with a homeward bound convoy. That followed the usual form, travelling west far out into the Atlantic before turning north, and must have taken us about ten days to fetch up in the Clyde. There we were surprised to be able to get on to a special train standing on Gourock Pier, which took us overnight to London's Olympia station, of all places, virtually non-stop, the easiest journey I can ever have had from the Clyde to home in London.

One could do no more than call at home before reporting to the Fleet Air Arm Headquarters at Lee-on-Solent. There it was a quick turn-round. We were told to go on leave until being posted to a unit. I went to see Jane, the Wren with whom I had taken up before going to the RAF, and the turn-round was quicker still. She had taken up with Charles Gordon of 827 within a fortnight of my departure. At the time, I had no realisation how lucky this was for me; it just seemed a gloomy beginning to my leave.

At home, all my brothers were around to some extent. Sandy was on his first houseman job before becoming fully qualified and going off to the RAMC. Kenneth, a Scots Guard ensign, was in town on 'Household Duties' (Buckingham Palace and St James's Palace guards). Ian had left school and was, or was just about to be, a rifleman in the 60th Rifles. Kenneth was very smart and very amusing trying to encourage brother Ian to behave more *comme il faut* in London – no hands in pockets, eating sweeties etc! It rather annoyed me that when trying to flag a taxi at night, they ignored me like everyone else but Kenneth, in his colourful cap, had only to twitch his swagger cane and they would glide up to him. On the whole, a good leave, and a quiet one. It would have been a sad one if I had known that it would be the last time I should see Kenneth.

After I had been home a week, I suddenly bumped into Bill Bailey from 827 Squadron on the pavement. He had succeeded to the command of the Squadron, who were still in England, at Speke near Liverpool. The news of them was, however, awful. They had been the first Albacore Squadron to be put into the latest Fleet Air Arm torpedo-bomber, the Fairey Barracuda. This was a high-wing monoplane of extraordinary Admiralty design, supposedly just the job for dive-bombing because of the excellent view the pilot had. The only problem with the early models was that quite often they proved impossible to pull out of the dive. Without any operations, the Squadron had killed more than half their aircrew during my short absence (September to April). Bill immediately invited me to rejoin the Squadron, if the appointments people in Admiralty would allow it. Naturally I said yes, and he went straight round to Queen Anne's Mansions to see the NA2SL people, whose offices were in this requisitioned apartment block.

NA2SL means Naval Assistant to the 2nd Sea Lord; his department was responsible for personnel and appointments and they proved true to their normal form. Becoming aware that an officer wanted a particular appointment for which he was suited, and that the unit in question wanted the particular officer, they sent him somewhere else! Probably just as well. Shortly after this, Bill lost his command and it was his position that was the main attraction for me to go back to 827. Also, at the rate that 827 were going, unwittingly, NA2SL probably made a major contribution to my survival of the War! Bill, incidentally, lost his command by taking the mickey with the Admiralty over the Barracuda, their pride and joy. At Speke, he received a signal ordering the Squadron to Machrihanish, (about an hour and a half's flight), on a day when two more of them had gone down. He sent back 'Your . . . received. Request road transport for 10 Barracudas.'

I, too, received a signal at this time appointing me as an Observer in 819 Squadron, telling me to go to Machrihanish for joining instructions. This, I assumed, correctly as it turned out, meant that they were embarked in a carrier currently in the Clyde.

Chapter 23

Joining 819 Squadron

ARRIVING OFF THE TRAIN IN GLASGOW, I fortunately decided to call at the naval staff offices in St Enoch's Station to find out what the current best way of getting down to Machrihanish would be. Lying at the tip of the Mull of Kintyre, on the opposite side to Campbeltown, there were various ways of getting to it. Best, if a plane was going, was a half hour ride from Abbotsinch or Renfrew (now enormously developed into Glasgow Airport), the main Fleet Air Arm and RAF airfields for Glasgow. Next best, the train down to Greenock or Wemyss Bay and catch the next stores drifter for Campbeltown. The drifters were wartime requisitioned fishing drifters for service as Fleet supply ships in the Clyde and up the Minches. There was an alternative, the civilian Clyde 'puffers', which did a sort of freight tramping business up and down the Clyde. Or again, one could get across on the ferry to Dunoon and hope to catch a stores lorry for Campbeltown or Machrihanish. This was a long haul, going northwards first over the Rest and Be Thankful Pass, then down the entire length of the Mull. Last, and worst of the lot, was a stores lorry all the way from Glasgow.

It was just as well I inquired. 819 had been temporarily disembarked to the RAF station at Ballykelly in Northern Ireland. That morning a Walrus was going down to them with stores from Abbotsinch, so off I went on one of the very few Walrus flights I ever made. The previous one had been in Trinidad as a trainee.

Ballykelly was a large base of Coastal Command's, a much more friendly and co-operative sort of RAF than I had encountered to date. 819 were there in great secrecy to learn how to fit and operate the very latest anti U-Boat weapon, the 3-inch rocket. This was not immediately available, so the Squadron was to learn all about it so that when they could get it, the stuff had only to be brought aboard *Archer* and we could carry on from there. HMS *Archer* was the Escort Carrier in which 819, a Swordfish Squadron, were normally embarked.

They were a nice bunch of chaps, most of them with less experience of operations than myself. However, I was still very much a new boy to the unit and a learner in the more modern techniques of anti U-Boat warfare which had evolved since 827 had been equipped for *Indomitable*. First, all planes were equipped with 'ASV'. This was a rudimentary radar which presented on its screen a straight vertical line if there were no ship on the surface straight ahead. A 'blip' or deviation of the line would appear if something were detected. The nearer the top of the screen, the further away the object, and the line had an approximate scale in miles, up to about 40. The bottom line, representing the nearest five miles, was usually very muzzy with 'grass', ground or sea echo. The size of the blip at any distance was to some extent in ratio to the size of the object picked up. So far as I remember, in average conditions you would do well to pick up a hull-down (not much more than conning tower above water) U-Boat at 15 to 20 miles. That, of course, was a lot better than would be possible with eyes and binoculars most of the time in the winter Atlantic.

The next new trick for me to learn was 'RT', or radio telephony. Up to then, when radio was allowed to be used, all I had had was 'WT' or wireless telegraphy, i.e. Morse code. It took a bit of study and practice to learn the operating techniques of the set and the considerable procedure and jargonised language in which one communicated. This had been standard in fighter Squadrons so that a ground or carrier based controller, watching them on radar, could navigate them about the sky and direct them on to targets. The Admiralty had never seen the need for Torpedo/Bomber/Reconnaissance squadrons, with an Observer in each plane to navigate, to be bothered with such toys. Now, however, new tactics for fighting U-Boats had become necessary. The Germans had at last learned that the Swordfish was so slow that when it came in at low level to attack with bombs or depth-charges, it was none too difficult to shoot it down and that this was therefore worth trying, rather than panic diving which all too often could not be achieved in time to escape well-aimed depthcharges. As a result, what frequently happened was that the U-Boat got hit, but also brought down the Swordfish before it sank or dived. There was little joy for Swordfish crews swimming in the winter Atlantic with their victims; it was not an environment conducive to warm social exchanges.

The new British tactic, in advance of rockets becoming available, had been to pair a fighter with a Swordfish for the attack. The fighter would hang around above cloud (when available) until called in by the Swordfish on this marvellous RT. As the U-Boat gun-crews stood by to blast the 'stringbag' out of the sky, the much faster fighter would dive upon them, all guns blazing. Then, whilst they were wetting their pants over that, in would trundle the Swordfish and hopefully administer the lethal dose. Certainly with RT and a fair amount of practice, very well co-ordinated attacks could be made. The beauty of the new rockets was that they could be shot from a pretty fair range without need for the Swordfish to fly over the U-Boat. They virtually eliminated the need for the fighter's help.

The main U-Boat tactic was to hunt in groups, widely strung out in line abreast on the surface all day, which facilitated the interception of Allied convoys. On sighting, they would shadow at a distance at conning-tower depth (using their diesel propulsion and conserving their battery power for submerged attack) and work round the convoy flanks to get ahead of it by dark, or, preferably, call up other U-Boats already ahead on their VHF radios, if any were there. Then the 'wolf-pack' would strike after dark. This strategy become less operable the more the ground was covered by air patrols which would see the surfaced and semi-surfaced U-Boats. This the Allies could achieve with shore-based patrols for some 900-odd miles from either the American or the British seaboard. A lot more ocean too could have been covered if the Irish had let us have bases, but I suppose we have to be understanding about their inability to see anything particularly wrong with Nazism. Naturally, therefore, the gap in the middle of the Atlantic was the U-Boats' happiest hunting ground. To fill this, the Allies put together a Fleet of mini-aircraft carriers made by converting merchantmen in the course of building, because there were nowhere near enough Fleet carriers which could be spared. It was more essential to fly lots of patrols in the 'gap' to keep the U-Boats submerged than to sink them. Their visibility range through periscopes and their speed was very much less than when surface cruising. That is not, of course, to say that one did not take every possible opportunity of sinking them when one could. This was the business in which 819 were engaged, embarked in one of the earliest built escort carriers, HMS *Archer*. The slow and robust Swordfish, which had become obsolescent with the main fleets, was an ideal plane for the purpose, because it was possible to land them on these little carriers, terribly pitching in bad weather, without breaking too many. Our pilots were no better than the US Navy's, but in one particular week of winter storm we still had five serviceable planes left out of twelve when an American equivalent ship a few hundred miles from us had been through all their much more modern Grumman Avengers.

To return from all this tactical lecture to the narrative: I had a very happy first week in Ballykelly. At work, the rockets seemed a truly super weapon in spite of the primitive stage of their development at that date. All they consisted of was a three-foot length of standard three-inch steel gas piping, filled with cordite. At the tail end, four stabilising fins, each six-inch squares of sheet steel, were fitted and an electric firing connection. At the other, business, end, there was screwed on by means of an adaptor ring a 4.5-inch artillery shell. In these early days, the 'shell' contained no explosive. It was in fact a solid steel lump shaped with an armour-piercing pointed nose. Primitive as it may sound, this weapon was found to be capable of being fired into the water twenty yards short of a U-Boat but still able to penetrate the pressure hull, pass through it and penetrate out again the other side. Thus, a salvo of eight of these, which a 'Stringbag' could carry, was more than enough for a kill. To be given an appreciation of what their arrival would look like in the U-Boat, we were put into a bunker on the firing range and rockets were fired hundreds of yards beyond us. Many of us had been under a variety of forms of heavy attack but I think were unanimous that this was about the most terrifying thing we had seen. On the one plane available with the gear, we all had turns at target firing. Much enthusiasm was engendered all round.

It was not a weapon capable of precision aim like a gun, but it was more than adequate for our purpose. The height, keel to topside, of a U-Boat would be about twenty-five feet. If the rockets struck the water short, say thirty or forty feet, the underwater trajectory would still take them through part of the hull. If they struck at the waterline, it would still be a kill so that was a big margin for error and aiming was well within it. The rocket invariably went in the direction of the aircraft. The travel time of the rockets was too small for any need to aim off for the U-Boat's motion.

Life 'ashore' was mainly intensely alcoholic but involved a fair amount of travel. The village of Ballykelly had no pub. This must have been rectified post-War, because I noted in the press recently that the IRA had bombed the Ballykelly pub, so Ballykelly must be back to square one! Thus we had either to travel into Londonderry on the bus or to walk the several miles to Limavady, the nearest town. We rather resented the bus to Derry because of the fare structure. The 'evening return' was cheaper than the single fare and we felt that it was a little unjust for us to ride to and fro on the cheap just because the bus company was able to con their simple locals into the more expensive single fare if they were only going in to Derry.

When we walked to Limavady, we had to drink fast because the pubs shut at nine, but after that one could try one's hand at the local Roman Catholic Church Dance, which came up once a week. That was nominally a dry affair, but the locals quickly appraised us of Dan Henry's local industry and how to tackle it. Two people were required. The first had to engage the local worthy of the RUC in conversation whilst the other slipped into Dan Henry's door without being observed. Within was a grubby and seemingly totally empty little shop, with a single small tap in the wall behind the counter, the one link to the distilling apparatus he had behind the wall. Transactions went something like this:

'Good evening to you, Mr Henry, do you have any whisky tonight? My friend is keeping the constable busy talking.'

'Aye, I can let you have a couple of bottles but they'll be fifteen shillings apiece.'

'Yes, please, I'll take the pair.' Dan takes two old wine bottles from behind the counter and fills them from the tap. He bangs in corks with an old mallet.

'Was it Scotch or Irish you were wanting, sir?'

'I think one of each would be nice.'

'Very well,' he says, and rummages in a drawer, to find an old Johnny Walker label and a Black Bushmills one. These are carefully glued to the bottles and Dan Henry, after receiving payment, puts his head round the door and gives the OK that it is safe to depart. Powerful stuff it was; there seemed no possibility of walking back to Ballykelly on it, so we had to resort to Mr Doherty, the local taxi operator.

Somewhere around our last night before return to *Archer* there was a huge hubbub at the Doherty house when we called for a cab. A party to beat all parties was in hand. The drunken crowd within passed us in for introduction to Mrs Doherty, who had reached a stage of glazed near speechlessness. It emerged that they had buried Doherty that day and we were welcome to join the wake. When we declined, she offered to drive us back personally. This too we refused, as not fitting on such a day, thinking our wobbly walking would be a little safer. How we got over those miles I do not know. As a party we were certainly straggled over a mile or so by half way. I have one abiding memory of the journey. Ahead was the sound of happy singing and much splashing. Coming up to its source we found it to be a stone roadside horse trough, generously decorated with green algae. Within was Paul Weekes, one of our pilots, in his best uniform. Singing away, as he dabbed his armpits, he explained that as he had set off faster than us, he had put on rather a sweat, so was just taking a bath before getting back to the mess. This was in early April, and I can assure you that public horse troughs in County Derry do not have running hot water. So much for the powers of Dan Henry's elixir of life – plenty of octane!

The pilot with whom I was teamed was a little senior to me in the same elevated rank of Sub-Lieutenant. He had come from an *Ark Royal* Swordfish Squadron which had been disembarked into the Western Desert to do duty as pathfinders for the RAF (and one American) night bomber Squadrons who had difficulty in navigating to desert targets in the dark. He had broken quite a few planes by bad landings and had been suspected of night blindness. He thought it better to go along with this explanation rather than admit to his own inner suspicion that in part it was because these operations scared him silly. 'Not funny, old boy, to be cruising up and down at 1,500 feet through the flak dropping flares and incendiaries and then have showers of 1,000 lb bombs whizzing past dropping out of Liberators sitting safely another 10,000 feet above.'

In the event, his Squadron commander heard from the RAF that they were setting up a new night vision tester, so he arranged for Co-Co to be given a run on it. Charles Atherton-Brown was called Co-Co because his stepmother was a partner in the Coconut Grove, one of the better wild night clubs in London, which made Co-Co a useful chum when in London. But he was a great character, a very good pilot and wonderful friend quite apart from that. I never heard of him after *Archer*, and several attempts to trace him have drawn blank; maybe he didn't survive the War.

His night vision test was fairly typical, in his own telling. He had to report at a Cairo RAF hospital at 10.30 a.m. which entailed his getting to the city the night before. After some months under canvas in the desert, he had cut loose for the night and Co-Co knew how to cut very loose. Even so, in great pain and semi-conscious, he managed to get to the hospital on time. His tester was a medical Group Captain, no less, which was rather terrifying. The gallant Group Captain explained that Co-Co was one of the early guinea-pigs to be tested on this super apparatus, which had been imported from UK all the way round the Cape. He then beckoned Co-Co through the door into the darkened room where the marvel of modern science was installed. As Co-Co groped his way in there was a tremendous crash as he hit something. The infuriated Group Captain put on the lights; scattered across the floor were the components of a night vision tester several stages beyond repair. The Group Captain sent him back to his unit with the report, 'Night Vision indeterminate but possible. Stupidity almost certain.' So Co-Co kept on flying at night and bending 'Stringbags'. To put his record straight, I have sat behind him for many a night landing on *Archer* without ever bending anything.

We left Ballykelly not for *Archer* but to Machrihanish for an updating swing of compasses and tune up of planes and equipment before re-embarking. The first evening in the Wardroom there I bumped into a chap called Cruickshank, with whom I had been at school although he was my senior, more a contemporary of my brother Sandy. I had not even known that he too was in the Fleet Air Arm. He had just become a Barracuda pilot. He went on dive-bombing practice the following morning and, once again, a Barracuda refused to pull out of its dive.

That day one of the wartime versions of a horseracing classic was run, so I had taken three tickets in the Wardroom sweep. We went up in our 'Stringbag' (not logged!) to get at a radio to listen to the commentary. To my absolute horror, because it was not the sort of thing for a visitor to do to the locals, my three tickets swept the board, turning out to be the first, second and third nag. On return to the mess, I put a notice on the board apologising for my good fortune and saying that as it was my last night at Machrihanish I would be happy to make amends to fellow officers that evening in the bar of the Ardshiel in Campbeltown. There Co-Co and I repaired at opening time and explained the situation to the landlord. As scotch was in short supply those days, we bought as many as he would allow us and set them rank upon rank on the bar to await our guests. The clock drifted past seven, half past seven and eight o'clock and no-one turned up. Slowly Co-Co and I were decimating the ranks of scotches and wondering why we seemed such pariahs. In those days most Fleet Air Arm officers would travel far and put up with quite indifferent company for an evening's free drinking. As we speculated as to the reason, the landlord joined in: 'I was surprised when you said you would be entertaining the boys down here. Tonight is the Machrihanish Station Dance and I never see them in here on those nights, they have so little other chance to meet the girls.'

If only we had known of the dance! It would have been obvious that there would be a universal preference for skirt over scotch at Machrihanish. It would seem to them that the crafty Mackenzie had offered his open hospitality on the one night when he could count on nobody wanting to accept it! So Co-Co and I set to with a little help from the landlord to try and finish the tots on the bar before closing time. 'Waste not, want not' was an important rule of life . . .

My next memory was waking, very cold, in my uniform on a hard and narrow cot. Standing over me was an enormous police sergeant. I felt like death.

'Where on earth am I?'

'Police cells, Campbeltown, drunk and disorderly.'

'What's to do now, then?'

'Get oot before I change my mind and charge ye.'

So off I went into the rain at seven in the morning and no bus or transport to Machrihanish, some seven or eight miles away. I did not get there before the Wardroom had finished serving breakfasts either. Whilst I still did not feel like food, in spite of the healthy exercise in the rain, a few cups of coffee would not have come amiss. Miserably I went round to my cabin for a bath and dry clothes. 'Come on,' said Co-Co in the next cabin. 'We take off for the ship in twenty minutes.' He had caught the last bus back the previous night, quite unable to persuade me to board it. I was putting my heart into busking for the queue for the bus, consisting mainly of Machrihanish ratings, who were tossing pennies into my cap on the pavement. I still wonder where my earnings got to. Seeing me safely led off into police custody, he had felt it fair to go on the bus. He had had it in mind to come down in the morning to see if I needed bailing out but then orders had come to return aboard *Archer*.

Shivering, I recovered my greatcoat and donned my Sidcot suit and off we went for my first embarkation into *Archer*. It was the only time I have gone aboard by crane. The ship was in Belfast, moored at a jetty at the side of Sydenham airfield, the airfield in Central Belfast which adjoined the Short and Harland aircraft factory. We were able to land, taxi to the jetty and be hoisted aboard by the ship's crane, rather as a cruiser picks up her Walrus at sea. What a peculiar ship she looked and how tiny for a carrier! But to start describing her deserves another chapter.

Chapter 24

Embarking in HMS *Archer*

COMPARED WITH *Indomitable*, HMS *Archer* was a poor thing. Standing just about as high out of the water, she was only just over half the length and had about two thirds the beam. You could see that she had been a freighter but had had all upper works amputated just below the height of the bridge. At this height, over the length of the ship, a structure exactly like Brighton Pier had been erected except that the superimposed kiosks etc. had been omitted. (see Plate 11) Abaft the bridge structure, as was, where the original after well deck had been, the underside of 'the pier' was walled in in steel sheeting down to the original gunwale. Within this was the aircraft hangar. In the bridge, as before, were the officers' quarters and mess. However, with the crews for twelve Swordfish and four Martlets, about twice as many officers had to be accommodated as the original design had allowed for. After serving in the steam turbine propelled *Indomitable*, there always seemed in *Archer* to be a permanent stink of diesel, the means of her propulsion. In those days, this seemed a very 'Merchant Navy' sort of smell.

The Navy had had some difficulty in providing trained crews for this sudden rush of mini-carriers being produced for us by the USA. At the same time, perhaps owing to ship losses, there was a fair surplus of merchant officers and seamen. Logic pointed to their transfer to the Royal Navy to crew these ships, whose hulls were after all merchantmen's. This was done by dint of the infamous 'T.124/X' Agreement with the National Union of Seamen. This was typical British compromise resulting in astounding ine-quities and all because the Government, who had the powers to draft merchant seamen into the Navy, had not the guts to do it cleanly. The underlying reason was that the merchant seaman, rank for rank, was paid just about twice what his naval equivalent got. Under T.124/X, they had to don naval uniform and come under the Naval Discipline Act, but they retained their merchant rates of pay and right to active membership of the NUS. We had the incredible sight, each time we came into the Clyde, of

11. HMS Archer *1943. The 'pier' construction supporting the flight deck shows clearly in this picture.*

the local NUS boss coming aboard for his meeting with our (very) RN Commander! Naturally, at all levels there were some non-T.124 naval men. As examples, they were required in the gunnery, torpedo and signals sides of operations. The Captain, Commander, First Lieutenant and all aviation staff were genuine Royal Navy. You thus had a community sharing all pleasures and dangers divided into two-thirds who were paid extremely well and one third who were on standard naval rates. It says much for the team spirit of wartime and the leadership of our commanders that this gross inequity did not in fact prove divisive within the ships' crews to any serious extent.

To add to the differential, our T.124 men also qualified for tanker crew's danger money. Tankers were the prime U-Boat targets in a convoy. When hit, their flaming cargoes not only illuminated the convoy but also led to terrible injuries as well as substantially reducing the chances of rescue. This was recognised, as in all good unionised circles, by significant extra wages. They qualified in Escort Carriers for several reasons: (1) When with a convoy, a carrier could be assumed to be a higher priority target than any tankers within it. (2) Besides our diesel fuel, we carried huge quantities, about the same as a Fleet carrier, of sensitive aviation petrol. Unlike Fleet carriers, whose aircraft fuel was carried in seawater-flooded tanks within the double bottom, ours was in simple tanks in the erstwhile freight holds,

12. HMS Archer *viewed from a boat on her starboard quarter. Note boom for mooring ship's boats in harbour. A boat's crew are climbing up/down. Note the 'nets' – a walkway all along the side of the flight deck, about shoulder high level to deck, and the 3.5-inch gun, our main armament! Also an Oerlikon (20 mm) pointing skywards at after end of the flight deck on the starboard side.*

relatively unprotected. It was believed that should we be hit, there was every chance that we would blow up. This belief had been much strengthened by the demise of our sister ship *Dasher* a few months before. She had inexplicably blown herself to smithereens coming down the Clyde. All that was known was that the last heard of her was by the lightkeeper at the Cumbraes, which she was passing. He heard a pipe on her Tannoy:

'There is a petrol leak on the port side. Out pipes. No more smoking until further notice.'

There were no survivors. When, a year later, *Biter* limped home from an Archangel convoy after surviving a torpedo hit, the entire Navy thought it miraculous.

I, too, got significant 'danger money', or 'flying pay', as it was called, of some five shillings a day. The Admiralty, never quite believing that flying was a standard contemporary art, still classified it as a dangerous pursuit. Even so, my T.124 officer's steward received considerably more pay than me and initially, in Merchant Navy tradition, expected a tip from his officer at the end of each voyage. I quickly explained the injustice of that.

It was a very friendly Wardroom. *Indomitable*'s had seemed informal enough, but now we had a much more 'Merchant Navy' atmosphere. A main difference was that being a much smaller ship's company, we seemed to have to work much harder at sea. In *Indomitable*, Wardroom drinking continued at the same steady rate at sea, except in emergencies, as in harbour. In *Archer*, we were almost dry at sea and paralytic in harbour. In *Indomitable*, gambling, other than bridge and backgammon, were not allowed. In *Archer*, contrary to all Royal Navy rules, one seemed to spend one's entire off-watch wakeful hours playing poker for unaffordable stakes. You could lose a month or two's pay in an evening. Fortunately it mattered little because your victor would always 'see you all right' when next ashore.

The greatest character amongst the T.124 officers was the electrical officer, a huge great ugly bear of a man from Belfast by the name of M'Neilly. He was like a godfather to young aircrew on places to go ashore, drinking much but holding it, seamanship in very rough weather, poker tuition, womanising . . . you name it. Although married and with a grown-up family, he was still apparently the most stoatlike officer aboard, and the tales of his doings whilst the crew were put up in the Barbizon-Plaza in New York whilst the Brooklyn Navy Yard prepared *Archer* for handover, were legion.

In the Yard workshops he made a duplicate key to his hotel room. This he would lend to his lady of that evening so that she could retire there whilst he finished his drinking, which took time. One evening he encountered a super girl whilst on his last nightcap, so persuaded her to come along up with him. As they entered the room there was the embarrassment that a girl was already naked in the bed. Worse, there were simultaneous cries of : 'My God, my mother!' and 'My God, my daughter!' They beat him up that night, but the tale relates that such were his charms that he continued in happy liaison with both, but separately!

Back to business. We sailed from Belfast up past Londonderry, from which emerged the fellow units of 4th Escort Group to meet us. These consisted of about a dozen ships, one or two destroyers, the rest frigates and corvettes. At this stage of the War, we had given up having virtually the same escort to a convoy from sailing to destination port on either side of the Atlantic. A minimal escort force went virtually all the way but, through the most dangerous part of the voyage, an escort group joined them to give protection when it was most needed. These were a group of ships who had worked and exercised together for considerable periods. We tended to join a convoy before it got to the dangerous gap in mid–Atlantic and stay with it until it got to the far side of the gap, and then leave to join another convoy going in the opposite direction, back again across the gap. Sometimes we would go into port to re-store in the Clyde; occasionally, but not while I was in *Archer*, into Halifax, Nova Scotia or St Johns, Newfoundland, or await the contrary convoy whilst refuelling near the middle of the gap at Hvalfjord, Iceland.

As we went up the Minches, we picked up the bits of convoy which had come up from Liverpool and out of the Clyde and the last elements who had been waiting in Loch Ewe. I had never realised what incredibly old ships were being pressed into Atlantic convoy work. This was a slow convoy for the lamest ducks, capable of no more than five knots. Day after day, we butted into big North Atlantic seas, flying anti-submarine patrols all the time that daylight gave. Occasionally there would be a little depth-charge activity as a plane or an escort vessel thought it had made a contact. Big convoys of ships, particularly small sized ships like these, have always been one of the most fascinating sights to me as they battle through rough weather in formation. The size of the sea and its apparent power contrast with the ships in orderly lines as far as the eye can see as they wallow and struggle to make progress. This was, however, a bit too much of a good thing. At under five knots, you look down over the side of the ship and the water seems not to be moving past at all. How long the journey? Two weeks? Three, perhaps? You had never believed that anyone could contemplate crossing a dangerous sea at such snail's pace. Boredom, hard work and an underlying fear of U-Boats seemed to go on and on and on.

I do not know what was in these ships travelling westwards, mostly ballast, I suspect. Some things were made in UK and wanted in USA, e.g. special aero engines (Merlin) and other specialised engineering parts. By and large they must have been 'returning empties' going westbound.

Remember, one was not only travelling at snail's pace, one was by no means going the shortest way. First, the convoy never kept a straight course, which would ease the U-Boats' problem. We steered an irregular zig-zag about the general line of advance to confuse them. The general courses to follow were also changed from convoy to convoy. You sometimes went through Denmark Strait, north of Iceland, with a New York-bound convoy. It was not unusual to take two or three weeks with a slow convoy. In fact, for this first one for me in *Archer*, we were off Halifax and leaving the convoy in just over two. M'Neilly was terrified we would go into Halifax for fuel – Nova Scotia was a dry state – but fortunately we turned and moved at a decent pace back to Hvalfjord.

This was the American naval base in Iceland, a picturesque fjord with snowy peaks around. There was a big busy anchorage and functional timber buildings ashore. One of these was the US Officers' Club, which gave us honorary membership for our stay. It seemed quite staggering after so long on wartime standards our side of the Atlantic. All the way out in the wilds like this they had WAVES (American WRNS equivalents) and civilian female volunteers to run the Club. The food was fabulous. As Co-Co and I stood at the buffet table for steaks, they put so much on our plates we thought at first that they had served us the amount to take back to our table for the rest of the Squadron party. They had enough whisky to float a Fleet, and we did our best to reduce it.

Unfortunately, Co-Co and I rather overdid it. We went and missed the last boat back to *Archer*. Fortunately, we had taken sufficient Dutch courage to have the nerve to ask the senior officer of a very snooty officer's boat from a US battleship to give us a lift, even though their mooring was in the opposite direction to *Archer*. In the interests of Allied goodwill, he agreed. (I am sure he never would have done so if *Archer* had still been American!) There was not room for us in the boat's cabin, so we stood with a few others on its deck. Suddenly, I noticed that Co-Co had not responded to a question and I looked over my shoulder to where he had been. Gone! Then I saw floating alongside a British naval officer's cap. Putting two and two together with incredible speed for one so fuddled, I roared 'Man Overboard!' One thing about the US Navy of those days was that they did have well-drilled boats' crews. As my shout ended, with a great swirl, Co-Co came to the surface and before you could say the American for Jack Robinson, he was engaged by boat hooks and dragged dripping back aboard. They even picked out his cap for him. How he did not die of cold as we roared back to *Archer* on the boat I don't know, but he was certainly much more sober. Back in *Archer*'s Wardroom, over a scotch, he confessed that he had not really fallen in in the ordinary sense, he had merely passed out in the colder air. He claimed that he had been drowning and finding it a most pleasant sensation but had suddenly felt a feeling of responsibility for Hemingway, who would be unable to get up the *Archer*'s ladder unaided, so he had kicked like hell for the surface. Hemingway, incidentally, was me. He always felt that I might be prone to un-officer-like behaviour ashore and had allocated me this alias, with which he always addressed me ashore and,

13. Swordfish being catapulted off HMS Archer, whilst anchored in the Clyde; I am observer facing camera

14. Swordfish of 819 Squadron landing on HMS Archer. The 'Batsman' can be seen, on platform over the 'nets', giving 'cut engine' signal to the pilot. Note the 'nets', and the arrestor wire system. 1943

embarrassingly at times, used it to introduce me to people not from our ship.

From Hvalfjord, we had the luck of a fast convoy home and were back in the Clyde within the week. Not much use, we felt, arriving there on a Saturday night. Crews of ships moored in the Clyde did not count in the Greenock or Gourock pubs as the *bona fide* travellers to whom they were allowed to open their doors on a Sunday. So, what on earth to do? M'Neilly had the answer. We took the mid-morning boat ashore and went down to the Dunoon ferry where we each bought a return ticket. Ticket collection was as the passengers went ashore, so if you stayed aboard you could go to and fro as often as you liked without extra payment. There was a bar on the ferry and ferry passengers must be by definition *bona fide* travellers. Old M'Neilly had brought cards with him, so we settled to whisky and poker until the late evening. I have no idea how many crossings we made.

Next we knew was that all our rocket gear was available but they had decided that we should fly down to Ballykelly to fit it on. This entailed sending us all successively off the catapult whilst *Archer* rode to her mooring. Worrying for us, but no problem as it turned out. We caused quite a local stir as no complete Squadron had ever before taken off in the Greenock reach or, for all I know, probably ever since.

Chapter 25

Operations in *Archer*

MY SERVICE IN *Archer* was brief, a matter of months rather than years. I cannot put the events in it in chronological order at this distance in time. There were many short voyages into the Atlantic interspersed with calls at several ports, most of which we visited more than once. Thus, I will relate them in terms of recollections of the ports and of events at sea with no pretence at a tale in the order in which things happened.

Londonderry was the most frequent port of call. It was nominally the home base of our 4th Escort Group. It was a grim and poverty-stricken town, but the civilians were extremely friendly. There was a rather dull Officers' Club where we could have a drink with our colleagues from the other ships in the Group. Alternatively there were rather poor pubs where one could drink with the locals, strictly only up to 9 p.m., and avoid the other officers. Of our escort vessels, I can only remember the names of a few: destroyers *Havelock* and *Vimy*, Flower Class Corvette *Pimpernel*. There were about a dozen of them and whereas we had to lie at moorings in the middle of the stream, they moored alongside each other in two groups against the quay. Thus they only needed one harbour watch party for each moored group, rather than one per ship. This caused the Admiralty to complain. They had a higher casualty rate in harbour than at sea. There was a tendency for jolly tipsy Jack to fall from the gang planks linking the sterns of the ships as he found his way home and to be swept away on the swift tide into the dark before anyone could do anything.

What always seemed very Irish about Lough Foyle at Londonderry was that the north shore of the outer lough lay in Southern Ireland, and the south shore in Northern Ireland. We always felt, as we put to sea, that the German agents common in the south had their binoculars well beamed upon us from the north shore!

This sensitivity was not well placed in logic, because when we were in Belfast we held several Wardroom parties for civilians, contrary to all normal security regulations. Our guests were mainly female and from the upper strata of Belfast and Dublin society and I often wonder whether Mata Hari's daughter or grand-daughter was inadvertently included.

One memory of Belfast was going to court. Leaving the Club one night with a fellow Observer, John Ashton, we managed to pick up the last taxi on a wet night. Whilst I directed the driver for the Sydenham Jetty, John was accosted by a tart who took his fancy. Having no coat, he cadged the loan of my Burberry as I had the taxi home. A Burberry was a useful informal item of uniform. It was plain navy blue and obscured the rank of the wearer. Thus, on an assignment such as John's it had the double usefulness of keeping out the rain and helping to obscure the identity. Street patrols were less likely to ask where you were going if they did not know how senior you might be. Thus, on this occasion, the battered old Burberry had a use for John beyond just keeping off the rain.

In the early hours, he had found his way back into town from the lady's suburban residence only to realise that he had left my mac behind. He must have been quite some navigator to find her place again, but he did so as the sun came up. She turned nasty – it could be that she was annoyed at being disturbed at this hour – and denied that there was any naval Burberry on the premises. Anyone else would have given up long before this but not John. He went to the police. As everyone knows, the RUC are very, very thorough. Statement made, off again to the site of operations, this time in a police car with, of all things, a magistrate's search warrant. Search made, Burberry returned. To John's horror, this was more the beginning of the matter than the end. In puritanical Belfast, prostitution was a major, if not too infrequent, affront to society which must be dealt with. The girl must be charged with it and incidentally with nicking the mac. So John must appear before the beak as principal prosecution witness. I had only finished laughing as he told me when I was summoned to the quarterdeck to meet a sergeant of police. Did I recognise this mackintosh? Was I aware of what had happened to it whilst in the hands of Lieutenant Ashton? You will be required in court this afternoon to identify the coat and witness that you lent it to the Lieutenant.

So both of us had to go. I was stunned by two things. First the loveliness and innocent look of the girl; it seemed impossible that she was a thieving whore. Second, the stern and enormous magistrate was a puritan from another age. It was not enough to fine the girl and admonish her. John was given a five minute homily on the disgrace for one of His Majesty's officers coming to this fair and innocent city and abetting its descent into filth.

That, you might think was enough, but then I had to be admonished. How shameful to lend one's coat so as to assist one's friend to follow a disgraceful temptation, when clearly one's duty had been to convince him of the iniquity of his ways.

It was in Northern Ireland that, for the only time in my life, I gave a woman a really good slap on the face. At the end of the previous chapter, we were off to Ballykelly to fit our rocket gear. On arrival, we found the officers' mess in a bad way. They were virtually out of spirits. We got wind the second day there that *Archer* had left her moorings for some engine trials in the Clyde. Quickly, our Commanding Officer, arranged to send Co-Co and me to her for some supposedly left-behind essential stores. We went without our air-gunner and loaded his position in the plane with all the scotch and Drambuie (which was popular then) we could persuade *Archer*'s wine steward to spare us. The grateful RAF gave a mess party on the proceeds of this trip. At its height, I happened to be standing next to 'Tannoy', a WAAF officer so-called because of her voice. As I sipped a Drambuie, mulled to a high state of flammability on a spirit lamp as was local fashion, she struck a match for a fag and jolted me. My drink slopped into my beard. Great joke, she thought, and applied the match to the beard, which flared. In my terror, I caught her a tremendous swipe across the chops. Luckily chums around beat me out very quickly and in fact I suffered no more than shock, a badly flawed beard and a horrid smell of burning which hung around for days, like smouldering carpet.

It was to Machrihanish that we repaired more often than to other places when our planes needed servicing on shore. I have one glorious memory of Co-Co distinguishing himself there. Our planes were ready for re-embarkation. We awaited *Archer* coming down the Clyde so that we could fly back on. This was to be the next day. Co-Co had found out that one of his best chums from desert days was at Abbotsinch, so on some pretext got permission to fly up there. It was a clear, fine day, so he did not need a navigator and went solo, to find a convivial lunch with his chum. Well into the evening, a very wobbly Swordfish approached Machrihanish. Without awaiting permission to land, which would not have been immediate because another plane was coming in ahead of him, he landed on one of the taxi ways (no mean feat as they were very narrow), turned off and parked. The Duty Officer turned out the Guard, whose truck was round to arrest Co-Co almost as soon as he fell out of his Swordfish. He had almost to be carried up the control tower stairs for his chat with the Duty Officer.

'Where have you come from?'

(very slurred) 'Machrihanish.'

'Don't be bloody silly, this is Machrihanish; where have you come from?'

'I told you; Machrifuckinghanish'

'I believe you are drunk. I must know where you came from.'

'I have been too busy flying to get drunk, old boy, but you'll find I'm from Machribloodyhanish, visiting with 819 Squadron.'

'819 have only had one plane up today; took off at 10.30 for Abbotsinch; Pilot Lt. Atherton-Brown.'

'That's me, old boy.'

'Then you're from Abbotsinch. You can't have been airborne all day.'

'I tell you. I'm from Machriwhatever really, but a chap has to get his lunch somewhere.'

'Why did you land on a taxi-way?'

'Late back to claim the drink my Observer owes me. Quicker to land there by my dispersal point.'

'I shall have to report you to the Commander.'

I cannot remember by what means of negotiation our Commanding Officer managed to get Co-Co off the hook. The whole thing could very easily have become a court-martial affair. Anyway, he was very much in the doghouse for some days:

'Can't think what all the fuss is about. Chap has to meet old friends sometimes and what does it matter getting a tiny bit pissed if you don't bugger up your aeroplane?'

On another occasion, it was I who got the bad end of a job ashore. All the 12 Squadron aircraft came due for compass swinging, just as a week's leave was to be given. For reasons I cannot remember, it was to be done at RAF Renfrew, now Glasgow Airport but not recognisable as such in those days. It was suggested that if one of the Observers would volunteer to do them all whilst everyone else went on leave, he and his small ground crew, similarly volunteering, could take two days' extra leave. This 'bargain' assumed that all twelve would swing in a day, a fairly tall order, and any extra time taken would come off the leave. Reckoning myself a fairly dab hand at this game, I volunteered.

There are three compass positions on each plane: pilot's and port and starboard for the Observer's position. To 'swing', the plane is lined up by hand compass held by an Observer standing twenty yards or so behind the tail, which has to be raised on a trestle to the flying attitude. This has to be done for north, north-east, east and so on all the way round the points. In the compass bases in the aircraft, there are two small adjustable magnets and, by adjustment of these, one can minimise the variation of what the compass reads from the actual heading. These variations are charted for each heading. After the first round of all the points, one adjusted to bring the variation over all points to an optimum and then repeated the round, making a chart which was mounted at each compass position for the aircrew to use in flight. As far as I can remember, a swing only passed muster if the maximum variation on any point was less than two or three degrees.

Early on the day, my erks and I set to work on our first plane. It just would not come right in spite of the RAF having given us the best of facilities, a tail trestle on castors with a brake and dead level concrete pad on which to swing the plane. At elevenses time, after three hours' work, we had been round and round and still I could not get it right. The erks were getting bolshy. My apparent incapacities were obviously going to rob them of much of their leave. Come midday, I had reached the position that I could not even get a compass to repeat its first reading on returning to a heading without any intervening adjustments. I was about to set fire to the aircraft in frustration at its roguery when a little RAF ground officer emerged from his office from which he had been watching us for some time. 'I'm only a stores officer,' he said 'But I'm interested in what you are doing, because I have never seen our chaps doing it to their kites.' (I always thought they didn't take navigation seriously!) I explained the drill and my particular frustrations with it today. ' I wonder why they sent you down here to do it. As a civilian I worked here before the War. It was an iron foundry and you are on the bit where they dumped all the slag and the scrap. It was covered over when they levelled the airfield. Surely all that iron in the ground would affect your results?' Quickly we set up another base on the grass at a good distance from the site allocated to us. By some pretty slick work, we finished the last plane by about eight o'clock that evening.

The main memories of 819 are, of course, of life at sea. The big one was the cold. Unlike the Albacores, you were in an open cockpit in a Swordfish. It was easier to communicate with the pilot, who was just the other side of a bulkhead (a stiffening structure for the fuselage frame, it was a wall across the fuselage made of ribbed sheet aluminium. A bulkhead in a ship is similarly an internal dividing wall across, or sometimes along, the hull), but I would rather be warm and remote from him! In the north, my air-gunner and I ran a drill whereby we swapped lookout from port to starboard every quarter of an hour. The starboard side gave some warmth because the engine exhaust came down that side. The weather always seemed rough in *Archer* because she pitched and rolled so much. This made landings difficult and the hard landings had a tendency to spread our undercarriages outwards and upwards, rather as though they were of the modern, retractable variety. This we countered most effectively by shackling a wire rope between the wheels like an axle. In a really rough sea, *Archer* could get quite dangerous. One day a sofa in the Wardroom, left unlashed, 'took charge'. One of the stewards got an arm broken trying to secure it. By the time it was lashed, it had broken up quite a lot of the Wardroom. In a much more serious incident, in spite of having doubled normal lashings on the planes in the hangar, a Swordfish broke loose and charged to and fro with every roll of the ship, breaking up and breaking loose other planes in its path. In a situation like that, it takes quite a lot of bravery as well as good seamanship to recapture and secure the fugitive. On the whole, though, in spite of feeling vaguely seasick all the time and nervous of deck-landings in the rough weather, I think we preferred it because it made it more or less impossible for the U-Boats to make a concerted attack on the convoys we guarded, and all the time we felt we should catch it should there be an attack.

Apart from the loss of a straggling merchantman with engine trouble one night when we were with a convoy, we were in fact not subject to the attacks we expected and feared. She was left behind whilst she fixed her engines. It would have been stupid for the convoy to wait for her. She was picked off just after she'd got going. Distress calls were received; I fear I cannot remember whether it was practicable to sent an escort vessel all the way back to look for survivors. It took time to realise that our aircraft presence in the daytime was really effective at frustrating day or night attacks. As a result of this success and of the latest development of British technology which was on the secret list until years after the War, we came off convoys in a defensive role, and went over to the attack, making sweeps at sea in order to attack and kill more U-Boats.

For a long time, it had been possible to 'direction find' long and medium wavelength signals by taking a bearing on the source by swinging the receiving aerial to the direction of maximum signal strength. To some extent this could also be done with short wave signals but it had proved quite impracticable with VHF. Thus for their transmissions to Germany or to each other, U-Boats felt safe from being pin-pointed when they used VHF.

The British found a technique for VHF direction finding. Linked receiving stations were set up in the north of Scotland and Cornwall. These were far enough apart to take simultaneous bearings of a signal source over much of the Atlantic and establish a positional fix with some precision. If, as sometimes happened, a British force was near enough to have a good chance of a kill, it would be signalled with the position. Naturally it was desirable only to signal if the fix was good and if there were forces in the locality to make a kill. Otherwise, the Germans would find out sooner than they need that we had this technically marvellous ability.

In operation, this system was quite uncanny in its accuracy. On 23 May, (I have the date from a postcard of a war artist's picture of the event. The picture, incidentally, puts the 'Stringbag' nearer to the U-Boat as its rockets went off than would have been the case), *Archer* received a signal that a U-Boat was 'talking' in a position only forty-five miles from us. Our standby Swordfish, loaded with rockets, was scrambled and found the U-Boat still on the surface 'talking' exactly in the reported position. Thus was the first rocket attack made on a U-Boat and she went down very quickly. Many of her crew got off and were subsequently picked up by one of our escorts. They reported that the rockets had gone clean through the hull, in and out the other side, and that they had never encountered so frightening a weapon. As we had yet to advance from solid steel rocket heads to explosive ones, this confirmation of prediction gave us great encouragement.

One disadvantage of *Archer* in comparison to *Indomitable* was that she had no forward aircraft lift. This meant that when quite a few planes had to land, they all had to be parked in the forward end of the Flight Deck, forward of the crash barrier which was raised each time after a plane taxied forward (after the deck party had disengaged its arrestor hook from the arrestor wire it had caught). In *Indomitable*, undue congestion was avoided by using the forward lift in this deck area for getting as many planes as possible down into the hangar as they arrived. In *Archer*, they all had to wait until the last one had landed and then be wheeled in turn back to the lift at the after end. Even with all their wings folded, it could be a tight squeeze to get them all parked in the deck area ahead of the barrier.

This was to cause one of the nastiest frights I ever had in deck landings. I was in the last but one plane to land. The deck space was so occupied that we had to be parked athwartships immediately ahead of the barrier, with our wings, of course, folded. As luck would have it, whilst we were collecting our gear from around the cockpits, the last plane came in and missed all the arrestor wires with its hook. Inevitably it went into the crash barrier and the give in that allowed it to flail its way with its steadily disintegrating propeller through the folded wing we presented to it. This got pushed right over the top of our cockpit so that it was now impossible to get out. Luckily his propeller stalled, and he came to rest with the bent remains of his propeller within inches of my gunner's and my heads. Just as relief for that release was beginning, the next panic beset us. We were cold and wet and there was a strong pong of aircraft fuel. He had fractured either our tank or his own fuel line. We were totally soaked in fuel and totally imprisoned. The gunner looked lugubriously at me: 'Got a match?' he said, as we both inwardly prayed that none of the enthusiastic rescuers, by now trying to release us, would inadvertently cause a spark. We were free within three or four minutes, but it was my first experience of hour-long minutes.

A few days later we had a nastier reminder of our battle with the elements. We were in rough weather in Denmark Strait, north of Iceland. The day before, we had seen quite a few small icebergs; our escorts were chipping ice from their decks and rigging. You will appreciate that it was cold as well as rough. Paul Weekes, coming in to land, had the bad luck that the ship's stern dropped away as she pitched some forty feet just as he was about to touch. He opened his throttle to go round again and banked away to port, but he stalled and went over the side into the drink. He managed to get out. His Observer and gunner, maybe stunned in the crash, went down with the plane which did not last long in that sea. Realising that our little escorts could not move fast in that sea, our skipper in a fine piece of seamanship went to full speed on full helm to bring us round and back to Paul in the water. In a very remarkable piece of manoeuvring skill, *Archer* came up to Paul and stopped with him on the lee side. A rope ladder was lowered and Dicky Corkhill, our Senior Observer, went down it to help Paul on to it.

Paul got on to the bottom of the ladder quite easily so, as they could not go up it side by side, Dicky made the mistake of going up first. When he got half way up, he heard Paul call 'Goodbye', and the splash as he fell back into the water. Those of us watching over the side were flabbergasted, but our seaboat, which had been lowered as an extra precaution, was not long in reaching Paul, whose Mae West kept him afloat. He was quite dead. None of us had realised that in the flying gear we had, the cold of those waters would be fatal in five minutes. He had had those five minutes before he got on the ladder and none of us had realised that he was virtually a dead man as he had so apparently cheerfully got on to the ladder. We were naturally all appalled when our Medical Officer explained it to us. What still does astonish me is how many lives the Atlantic claimed by hypothermia in peace and war before those who faced danger in it were provided with survival suits to overcome the problem. The simple physics underlying the design and some of the elementary materials which can be used must have been known since the last century. The problem seems to have been that in spite of substantial practical evidence, the world was slow to come to the realisation that men in extreme cold pass cheerfully in a flash from apparently normal alertness to being very dead. No-one seems to have realised that keeping the cold at bay was the answer, incredibly obvious as that may seem.

Whilst off Iceland we had another tragedy. This time it was due to entirely inadequate training. We were running with a gale on our stern on a bright sunny morning, when an American Flying Fortress came over and started to circle us. Using an Aldis Lamp, she made flashes but seemed incapable of passing any coherent message. This went on for some twenty minutes and created enough interest in *Archer* to have quite a few of the off-Watch people up on the Deck to see what it was all about. Suddenly the flashing stopped and from dead astern the 'Fort' came straight at us in a descending path, flaps and undercarriage lowered as though to land on us! Perhaps I need to emphasise the impossibility. A Flying Fortress would need something about five times our total length to put down. Its main wheels were so far apart that there would only be feet to spare either side of our deck. If it had got down, the weight of the machine would probably have been enough to collapse our Brighton Pier flight deck. When it was only about a couple of hundred yards away, we realised they were really meaning to attempt a landing. Never have I seen a Flight Deck cleared of personnel so quickly! At the eleventh hour and a bit, she opened her throttles and roared off, only inches from the deck; a bit of bad luck with the timing of our pitching and we should have made an expensive contact. Again she circled, flashing ineffectually. Then again she made as if to land, this time on the sea. This time she continued the attempt flying downwind, stupid at the best of times, lunatic in a full gale. Other than that, the attempt was correct for a sea ditching by our book, nose up, hanging on the engines as she neared the water waiting to cut engines and pancake in when she was almost touching. However, just as she clipped the first wavetop all throttles were opened fully and she tried to pull off. This merely led to a stall and she went in nose first.

Our escort was quickly on the spot and picked up the two survivors. They were transferred to *Archer*. It transpired that they were a crew of five engaged on their first trip of ferrying a Fort across to the UK via Iceland. They had never flown over ocean nor had had much of a briefing about it. They spotted us when they had failed to find Iceland (surely a big enough target?), when expected and when they only had forty minutes' fuel left. They did not really know morse code, but had hoped to make us understand with their Aldis that they wanted us to give them a course to steer for Hvalfjord. Then they decided their only hope was to land on us, never realising that carriers only operate modest sized planes. At the last minute, they had realised that they were too big. Why, we asked, having decided to ditch, did they do it downwind to a gale? Well, they said, they believed carriers always steered into the wind (not wondering how they could always get to where they wanted to go if this were so), so they went in the same direction. Why, we asked again, did you try to pull off just as you were ditching correctly apart from going too fast owing to being downwind? Well, said the senior survivor, I was the co-pilot. As we were coming down, it did not look right to me because we were going so fast. The captain did not agree. At the last minute I slugged him and grabbed the throttles to take her off again, but I guess she couldn't make it. Thus perished three good men entirely because they had not been trained for what they had to do, the relatively simple task of flying a Fort to Iceland and England. I do not think they believed that the whole of their predicament could have been avoided by elementary training.

Somewhere about this time I saw a call in Admiralty Fleet Orders for officers to take the long course at Whale Island to become Air Gunnery Officers. This seemed attractive. One would be a specialist in armaments, one would be more a full part of a ship's complement – in a carrier-borne Squadron there was an element of feeling partly a visiting unit on board rather than fully a part of the ship's permanent complement. One could also be at sea with a minimum of flying, of which I was getting very sick. I cannot entirely analyse why I got fed up with flying. I would like to think it was because I had always wanted to be a pilot rather than doing the maths in the back. I suspect that really it was cowardice and that, largely subconsciously, I was scared. I think this because when I was doing a lot of it daily, it did not bother me that much, but it was hell when I went back after a spell on leave or in port. My conscious feeling was, however, more one of active dislike rather than straight fear. Anyway, in spite of protests from Dicky Corkhill and our Squadron Commanding Officer, who saw me as just nicely settled into Squadron life, I volunteered to be an AGO. In the event, the aim to be part of a ship's complement rather than a Squadron's proved a miscalculation. I had failed to realise that a very large number of AGOs served in neither but were stuck in shore bases. However, by the time that became my fate, I soon had very good reasons to appreciate shore life! Co-Co was rather fed up with me going, but he loved flying and absolutely refused to come an AGO-ing with me.

My last cruise in *Archer* was fairly eventful. We were to get yet more aggressive. Keeping total radar and radio silence, we went on a sweep in the Bay of Biscay at the extreme range of the Junkers 88 Squadrons near Brest, trying to intercept U–Boats as they emerged from or returned to their French bases. In the event, we caught none, probably because we were dogged by fog for much of the time. On one occasion, I congratulated myself on finding *Archer* in the murk, having navigated away from her for some three hours, only to lose her in the fog as we circled to await landing permission. It took half an hour of 'square search' to find her again. On another occasion, I got well and truly lost for the first time. This is an unnerving thing to do at the best of times, but this was about the worst of times. A 'flu epidemic was sweeping the ship and it was hard to put aircrews together. On this occasion, my pilot did not belong to the Squadron; he was not really an operational pilot, being one of the ship's radio directors of aircraft. He had never deck-landed a plane in the dark and I had chosen to get lost at dusk! The air gunner had not flown since before the War. He had been brought back for the War as a pensioner as a ship's telegraphist. So he had few inhibitions about making his feelings known once he appreciated our position.

Due back a quarter of an hour before dark, the ship just wasn't there when I told the pilot he should be seeing her. Thus, we had to start a square search. In times of strict radio silence, the ship would prefer to lose an aircraft and crew rather than give away her presence by use of radio, so it was no good calling up and asking for a course. A square search is quite simple. You steer in what you think the most likely direction for visibility distance, then turn 90 degrees to starboard and go for twice visibility distance, then turn starboard again and go for three times visibility distance, turn again for another three times 'v', turn for four . . . etc. etc. until you run out of gas. You will see that this drill takes you in a square shaped spiral where in theory you have seen all there is to be seen inside the spiral and for visibility distance outside it. In the dusk we had the luck on the third leg of our search to see the wake of a ship and followed it, quickly coming upon a cruiser (*Nigeria*, if my memory is correct). I knew from my briefing that she was fifty miles from *Archer* and following in her course. Thus, I set course for *Archer* and some forty minutes later, such was the speed of the Swordfish, we sighted her. By this time the gunner was praying visibly for the appropriate gifts of skill or just good luck to come to the pilot's aid. I tried to look full of confidence and prayed less visibly. We came down beautifully, just like a wet cloth on a slate, as they used to say.

'You can now stop bellyaching that you have never done a night deck-landing,' I told the pilot . . . I recall being rather overcome by the welcome back aboard from all concerned. I felt that I had disgraced myself by getting lost. The atmosphere was entirely rejoicing at the lost sheep which was found again and complimenting us on not being panicked into resorting to breach of radio silence to save our own skins.

The fault was mine and the Met Officer's combined. In my time at sea, I reckoned that from the look of the sea surface I could tell the surface wind direction to a degree or two and its speed to within five knots. From the Met report before takeoff, I used to note the change of speed and direction of the winds at the heights I might be flying in comparison to the forecast wind surface speed and direction. These changes I then applied to my own estimates of surface wind as observed during the flight. This saved doing the complicated and time-wasting drill of finding the wind every half hour or so as one was meant to. I merely dropped a sea marker or smoke float every hour or so and took a back bearing on it as a check that our track was as expected from my wind estimation. If it had not done, I should find the wind by the orthodox method. This personal system had stood me in good stead through a lot of flying.

On this flight, the Met man had warned me that at about an hour and a half's flying from the ship we should meet a front; beyond this the wind at our height would be veered 45 degrees from that at the surface instead of backed by about 20 as was the case before the front. I had used this data but been idle about my back marker check and had not done that. When we got back, the Met man confessed that when he had said veered, he had actually meant backed. Going for an hour and a half calculating on a wind direction 90 degrees wrong can get you quite a long way out with a 20/25 knot wind! The ship's radar would have been able to follow us, of course, but with radar silence they had no idea of our whereabouts. They had given us up for lost minutes before our engine was heard – and one of my warmest War memories was the general pleasure at our return. I had not realised that they cared so much!

For Observers to get lost was pretty rare, but I have no idea how often it happened; all I can say is that planes disappeared and who knows whether it was engine failure or navigational error. The navigational error was unlikely to get you so far out that a well-conducted square search would not succeed, if you had the gas. We didn't talk much about getting lost but it was an ever-present secret fear. I suppose we were all skilled dead-reckoning navigators and too proud of that to speculate with each other about getting lost.

Earlier on I commented on the old 'Stringbag's' lack of pace. This had practical demonstration one day when we were on patrol and met up with a Liberator of Coastal Command. The Liberator was an American heavy bomber supplied to both the RAF and the American forces. It was not in the front rank of performance for either: not as good as British machines for night bombing, the RAF's speciality with heavies, not as well defended as the Flying Fortress, thus less useful for the American's day bombing with heavies. The RAF had fitted the bomb bays with extra fuel tanks and this gave them enormous range and a value to Coastal Command. The Liberator wanted to check on the nationality of a destroyer she had seen, one of our escorts temporarily out of forecast position, so it tried to communicate by Aldis lamp. With us going full speed and the Lib almost stalling, she was past us in a flash. Back it came, and to 'talk' it had to circle us, much as we had to circle a ship to which we were flashing.

'Buck up,' he started.

'We are bucked up,' I said.

'We've seen ships faster than you,' they said.

'Yes, but at least we are British built.'

'Perhaps that's why you have too many wings,'

'Only the same number as you have tails,' . . . and then we got down to the business in hand.

On another occasion, our speed, or lack of it, helped to save us. Having had permission to land on at the end of a patrol, I was putting away my navigation gear and the gunner checking that his ammunition drums were securely stowed. The pilot was coming down in the approach only some quarter mile from *Archer*. We were all off the alert. Suddenly the gunner screamed, 'Bandit dead aft!' There, closing at what seemed incredible speed, was a Junkers 88 fighter-bomber. The pilot merely pulled our nose up and we were enveloped in cloud as the 'bandit' rushed by beneath! Seeing *Archer*, he veered away rather than face her close range AA fire. It turned out later that he needn't have bothered. Only about two people in *Archer* saw him. He was obscured by us to many of them, one figures charitably; the probably truth was that the rest were not being very alert. We had after all thought we were just outside the Ju.88 range from France. The main point is, though, that he never got a shot in at us. Our relative speeds were such that he had not had time between seeing us and 'drawing a bead' before we had lifted into cloud above him. I was much reminded of this incident when hearing the descriptions of how our Phantoms off the Falklands almost stopped, using vertical lift, and thereby fooled the Argentinian Mirages into rushing past beneath them.

One of my last jobs in *Archer* formed part of an extraordinary coincidence. We picked up signals from the RAF's afternoon patrol in Biscay on 22 July. When outside fighter range, they had no need of radio silence, but they too must have underestimated the Ju.88 fighter version's range. This time it was a Sunderland flying boat, not a Lib-erator. Soon they reported attack by a Ju.88; then that a second Ju.88 had come in; then the almost inevitable 'Mayday'. Being a flying boat and the sea that day pretty flat, there were good chances of survivors, so all our available planes set off to search for them, about a hundred miles from us. None of us found any-thing.

On my next leave, I heard that my great friend at school, Richard Smith, had been lost in the RAF. I went to see his mother. He had been, she told me, the tail gunner in a Sunderland. His plane had been lost on a Biscay patrol, last heard of under attack by enemy air-craft. The date of this? 22 July. On our Biscay operation, we were well briefed

15. Sgt. Air Gunner Richard E.J. Smith RAFVR in 1941; my schoolfriend, lost in Biscay, 22 July 1943.

about RAF patrols in our area and I am quite clear that there was only one Sunderland that afternoon and certainly only one reporting attack. I had, albeit unknowingly, searched for Richard. We were, in all fairness, very conscientious lookouts on our patrols but with indifferent visibility, your head in a slipstream for hours at a time and navigational tasks to perform, you can always feel that perhaps you might have done a better lookout than you actually did. Since that event, I have often wondered if I would or could have been more alert and successful had I known I was looking for Richard.

At the end of the month, our Biscay sweep was done. *Archer* was to put into Plymouth and we were to take our planes subsequently to St Merryn in Cornwall to be fitted with what, for the Fleet Air Arm, was one of the less epoch-making inventions of the century.

Chapter 26

Leaving *Archer*

BEING LITTLE MORE THAN BRIGHTON PIER built on to an unremarkable merchant hull, we felt that *Archer* was perhaps going a little above her station – '*Au-dessus de sa gare*,' as Colonel Brown used to say – in entering historic Plymouth Sound. Quite to the contrary, we received a much warmer welcome than is usual in a naval port. This was because we were the first carrier to have come in, the first ship of any reasonable size for that matter, since early 1940. Major units had since then been sent to northern ports, further from the reach of the Luftwaffe. Our arrival in Plymouth signified to the town, and also to us, that at last the powers that be were beginning to feel that the Allies were getting the better of the air and sea wars. When we saw the devastation ashore from the previous air-raids which, because it was so concentrated, seemed far worse than what we had seen in Portsmouth, it was understandable that they felt that any symptom of better times coming was very welcome.

After mooring, one of our first duties was to show parties of local WRNS over the ship, as part of their education in naval matters. This allowed us to make dates for the evening and thus get into a fairly posh dance being held that night (posh meant with partners only). So we all had a pleasant evening.

Next day we sailed again and off the coast of Cornwall 819 flew off to travel to St Merryn. This was one of the larger and longer established Fleet Air Arm airfields, where life was rather more formal than in the more remote wartime-built places like Machrihanish. It behoved to behave, as Co-Co put it. And well he might have done so, because he quickly got me on the wrong side of the Commander. We had arrived before lunchtime drinks, at which I had stood my round, but it was only after my first round in the evening that the Petty Officer Steward in charge of the bar queried my chit. In ships and shore bases, it was always the same: in the Wardroom one signed the chits for drinks and paid the account at the month end or on departure.

'Sir, have you by any chance forgotten to check in on arrival? We have no Mackenzie on our Wardroom Membership list.'

I explained that my pilot had checked me in when registering himself. As Co-Co was standing there, I asked him to confirm that he had done it.

'Yes, Hemingway,' he said all too promptly.

I think I have already mentioned that Co-Co had a standing joke that so unreliable was my conduct ashore he would create the alias of Hemingway as cover for me. The joke had already grown thin for me, a paragon of good behaviour compared to him! The PO Steward looked mournfully at me; he was well used to the odd ways of naval aircrew.

'I am afraid, sir, I shall have to speak to the Commander.'

So, with it almost time for dinner, I was asked to step into the Commander's office. He opened up, 'Hemingway, I want you to know that using a false name in a mess is an offence for which you can be court-martialled, so take care in how you explain this extraordinary situation.'

What to say without landing Co-Co in the soup? I produced my identity card and convinced him that I was indeed Mackenzie. This itself was not too easy, because I had failed to get the photo on it changed when I had grown a beard, as regulations said you should. I apologised for letting Lt. Atherton-Brown check me in instead of doing it myself – that, too, was a minor offence – and explained that he was much strained by far too long a period of continuous operations and must have absent-mindedly given the wrong name. He was getting very tired and absent-minded.

The Commander, evidently becoming more sympathetic every minute, then sent for Co-Co. He had been having a worrying interim in the Wardroom, spent in overcoming worry the only way he knew how. He seemed to the Commander, I hoped, fatigued in the modern Private Eye usage of the word.

'You agree that this officer's name is Mackenzie?'

'Yes, sir.'

'Why then did you register his name as Hemingway?'

'Well, because I feel protective towards my Observer, sir. We are only going to be here for two or three days. I thought that possibly he might get into some sort of trouble and it would be better if his real name was not traceable. Whilst for the same reason I always call him Hemingway ashore, I forgot to tell him that that was how I had registered him.'

Collapse of two stout parties, the Commander and myself. Luckily in the public service there is always an incentive to get out of handling hot potatoes like court-martials if the buck can be passed elsewhere. The Commander concluded the interview:

'I am going to report this matter to your Squadron Commander and to the Commander of *Archer*, and they will take the necessary proceedings.'

When we were safely back aboard *Archer*, they contented themselves with saying:

'You bloody chumps; you'll have to be kept aboard if you can't do better than that.'

We had come to St Merryn to be fitted with the latest device for getting at U-Boats, already in use by Coastal Command of the RAF in their much bigger aircraft. This was the Leigh Light. Not the greatest breakthrough in twentieth century technology, the essence of the idea was that the plane was given an outsize generator and, fixed under the wing, a sizeable searchlight. Thus provided, a Swordfish should be able to illuminate a surfaced U-Boat and sight its rockets just as well on a pitch black night as it currently could in daylight. Maybe it had been overlooked that the very slow 'Stringbag' would thus provide an excellent target for the U-Boat's Gunners! Flying trials of Leigh Light fitted Swordfish had already been successfully conducted at the weapons trials establishment at Boscombe Down. Our Commanding Officer got his machine fitted first. Not very surprisingly, he was none too happy about how it handled with the extra generator weight and the bloody great searchlight under one wing. He then asked for it to be loaded up with full complement of rockets, flares, etc. as would taken on operations. This time he came back and refused to equip the Squadron. He had proved in flight that thus equipped, the Swordfish's stalling speed was a mere five knots below the supposed cruising speed. This was an impossibly dangerous hazard. We would all perish without any enemy encouragement to do so. It turned out that Boscombe Down's trials had been carried out without the plane being armed!

Thus, *Archer* had less time to await the return of 819 than expected, and we all arrived back aboard as she came up the Bristol Channel. As we headed up the Irish Sea, the signal from Admiralty came : 'Lieut (A) HCB Mackenzie RNVR to proceed on leave prior to reporting *Excellent* August (?) for No.7 AGO's Course.' So, as we went up the Clyde for Greenock, I packed and had my farewell snifters with my *Archer* mates and was one of the first ashore after we berthed.

It was not a long leave and I remember little of it. By now, my mother had moved home to a large and fairly modern house in St Johns Wood –

Langford House in Langford Place. It was a nice house. Its subsequent call to fame was that it became the home of Bob Monkhouse next but one after my mother's occupation. My brother Kenneth had sailed to join the 2nd Battalion Scots Guards in Egypt. As far as I could make out from the date he went from home, I had been in the Clyde in *Archer* as he had boarded his troopship there. The Battalion had already taken part in the Salerno landings in Italy, from which Kenneth had been invalided back to Egypt with some sort of sepsis (not a war wound). Ian was still a light infantryman in preparation for his WOSB. Those recommended by their units in the Army for a commission had to go through a final selection procedure called WOSB – War Office Selection Board – which involved three days' testing of intelligence, leadership, initiative etc., before they were accepted. In the Navy we used to say of the resulting product that a WOSB, just like any other Army organisation, would never be able to identify what they were looking for in only three days!

Instructions arrived at Langford Place from Whale Island (HMS *Excellent*, or the Royal Naval Gunnery School) about my joining and the kit I should require. It was like a clothes list for school. They still kept to pre-War standards of dress for Long Course gunnery officers during their working day. Ordinary officers' reefer jackets were worn but the hard collar and tie were replaced by a white flannel scarf inside the reefer. Instead of normal uniform trousers, white flannel ('cricket bags', in those days) trousers were worn tucked into naval ratings' long guns' crew webbing gaiters, over parade (Army-style hob-nailed) boots. At Eastbourne, the rowing scarf had been of plain white flannel, which was handy, and my erstwhile Corps boots were devoid of the normal Army toe-cap, so they qualified beautifully as naval parade boots. The white flannel trousers were more of a problem as my brothers and I had not played cricket at Eastbourne and had worn shorts for activities such as tennis. Luckily, my mother had kept about everything any of us had ever worn and the prep school cricket flannels, reeking of moth balls, lay at the bottom of an old trunk. The top three or four fly buttons would not do up, but this shortcoming could be hidden by the reefer. Likewise, the fact that the trousers terminated some seven inches above the ankle could be hidden by the ratings' webbing gaiters. These trousers served well for the whole five months' course. They were in fact smarter than most, owing to being a skin-tight fit on the parts of leg which showed.

As I recorded in an earlier chapter, I had been very impressed by 'Whaley' as a rating when our Observer course went there and looked forward to returning as an officer, albeit an officer *in statu pupillari*. I suppose it must have been a parallel feeling to that of a new member of staff taking up appointment at his old school. I admit too, that having got ashore for a few months, it seemed quite a pleasant change!

Chapter 27

Back to Whale Island – HMS *Excellent*

IN CHAPTER 2, I gave an idea of the layout of Whale Island, but did not give any idea of its main objectives. Its *raison d'être* was to be the primary naval gunnery school and the headquarters of the gunnery function in the Navy. 'Gunnery' meant anything to do with weapons from the smallest revolver, through the .303 rifle and bayonet, up to the 18-inch guns in the largest battleships. It included all the rangefinders and control gear which went with the heavy weapons. It also included all the simple drill and square-bashing which went with the use of hand weapons. It did not include weapons like mines and torpedoes which involved no use of an aimed gun barrel; those belonged to the Torpedo Department, whose equivalent school was HMS *Vernon*, also in Portsmouth. Curiously, in those days, electrical distribution gear in ships came under the Torpedo Department rather than the Engineering Department. The field of aircraft weapons such as bombs, depth charges and rockets also came under the Gunnery Department.

To summarise, *Excellent*'s field was everything which was thrown at or dropped upon the enemy. *Vernon*'s was more static weapons depending greatly on electrical subtleties. Curiously, the Gunnery Department was responsible for expertise in explosive demolition work. Whale Island's objective was shown in its ship's name, HMS *Excellent*. The pursuit of excellence in training, in drill and in performance may well have been the objective of all training establishments but nowhere was it more clearly apparent than at 'Whaley'.

Discipline whilst engaged on a task or drill was enormously tight and, like all good discipline, was exercised with an underlying sense of humour and more than adequate explanation as to why the discipline was required. Arms drill and squad drill had to be excellent because those taught at 'Whaley' taught these things to the rest of the Royal Navy. Incidentally, in the Navy, these activities were called 'Field Training'. Whale Island provided the naval squads and guards for Royal occasions in London. Whilst the Royal Marines and Brigade of Guards, also present on such occasions, were known to drill well, the Navy must be seen to drill better. Big guns could be dangerous toys to those firing them. In a rough sea and under heavy enemy fire, you could do yourselves a lot of damage if you did not do things correctly. You would only achieve this in adverse circumstance if in the preparatory training you had achieved excellent standards almost instinctively . . . and so on.

'Off the job' at Whaley, there was a very happy relationship between trainers (Staff) and the trained (Trainees). Staff ruled the roost at work. In the main they were gunnery officers and gunner's mates. A gunner's mate had achieved the highest rating's qualification in gunnery and was usually a Petty Officer or Chief Petty Officer in rank. However, some of Staff were lowlier ratings. On the trainee side, there was an abundance of ratings' courses but also quite a few officers', which had to take as much or more stick from rating staff during working hours as trainee ratings did. Principal of the officer courses were the 'long' Gunnery or Air Gunnery Officers' courses, which lasted some six months. All regular (ex-Dartmouth) Sub Lieutenants did a four week course after their first period at sea. The cream of the ratings' courses, perhaps, were the upperyardsmen. For a long time back, the Navy had had a system whereby about two dozen of the best young ratings in the whole Navy were given a course to become officers on an equal footing with the Dartmouth output. There were also some very seasoned groups, such as gunlayers (the next step down in gunnery quali- fication) on course for gunner's mate. On an Officers' course, you had the problem of not only passing muster with your rating instructors; you also had to achieve the standards in things like Field Training and gun drill which were set by the most experienced ratings' courses.

An Air Gunnery Officer has charge of all air weaponry matters in his ship except for air torpedoes: that is, embarking them, storing them, arming them and using them, including training the ship's company in these activities. If the ship were one of the smaller carriers, or an airfield ashore, the AGO also served as Gunnery Officer; that is he became responsible for the ship's weaponry from 'Field Training' up to what quite often was 6-inch gunnery. This was the field we had to cover in our six months. In the main, it was highly practical work but we also had to digest enough of the underlying mathematics to be able to calculate the trajectories of falling bombs and similar ballistics problems.

16. 7th AGO's Course, HMS Excellent, *March 1944. Jock Sayer on left of front row, Mike Allison in centre. In the back row Burroughs is 2nd from left, Stuart Allison between him and me on the right*

Throughout the course, I had a very pleasant cabin (bed-sitter) in a building up by the North Battery. Owing to wartime crowding, you had to be fairly senior to get a room in the Wardroom block. The latter was an elegant early Victorian block, ranged along the top of the grass bank which marked the side of the rugby/cricket field. The most impressive feature within was the Wardroom (dining room) itself. A big hall, rather like an Oxbridge college's, housed four or five long tables. I suppose some four or five hundred could be fed there. Linen, glass and silver for the weekly guest nights were of a very high quality. The table tops were of gleaming ancient oak. The floor was in wood strip and was an excellent (pardon pun) dance floor. The table silver included many naval mementoes and silver gun-carriages were provided for the passage of port down the long tables. There were two large ante-rooms where we amused ourselves, took aperitifs or coffee, and so on. There was a billiard room with three full-sized tables. The waiting staff were a mixture of naval pensioners, serving naval stewards and quite a lot of WRNS stewards. It was about as near to a good club as you could get.

There were eight of us on our course, all just back from operational service. John Clayton was the only other Observer, the rest being pilots. Jock Sayer was a main friend on the course, also Stewart Allison. Both had been in *Ark Royal* and then ashore with the Eighth Army operations. Michael Cox was very pleasant, if a bit earnest, as perhaps he had to be as Queen Mary's godson! There were two pretty nondescript dullards, John Housden and Philip Long, the latter from New Zealand. Finally, our course clot – he became almost a mascot – who could be counted upon to get almost everything wrong, Bill Burroughs. Bill was not cut out to be a pukka naval officer, nor had he any wish to be one. The very last thing he was cut out to be was a Gunnery Officer of any kind. He nevertheless went right through the course quite cheerfully in spite of enduring every punishment in the book and regularly bringing Gunner's Mates to tears, mostly of anger, sometimes of sorrowful frustration. Later on, we asked Bill why he had ever put in for such a course. He hadn't, was the answer. His Squadron Commanding Officer had 'volunteered' him because he had been breaking too many aeroplanes.

Our course officer, the staff member responsible for all our doings, was a smoothie Royal Navy pilot, Lieutenant Mike Allison. He was no relation of Stewart's, the latter being very emphatic about that. Mike knew his stuff but was of pretty low intelligence. He fancied himself as a wag and would tend to ponce and preen if there were WRNS about. Indeed there were some in the Air Gunnery School; a course had been instituted to convert WRNS armaments ratings into Armament Stores Officers. In fact, my future wife came through on one before our course finished, but we never met at that time.

One of the great joys of the course for me was that its timing covered a full rugby season and 'Whaley' had one of the better teams in Portsmouth. I managed to get a place in it as hooker, so got regular matches and, later on in the season, achieved a more or less regular place in the 'United Services, Portsmouth' team, which was very much first class rugby so far as that existed during the War. At least we got matches against the major London clubs' first sides and more than held our own. The training kept me fit and the frequency of matches for Whaley and for 'US' took enough time to keep me from other mischief!

There was enough 'homework' to do on the course to keep down the number of 'runs ashore' one could indulge in, so for the first time in the Navy I was actually able to save some money.

There were three types of shore trip for me. First, evenings with Jock

Sayer and his wife Molly. They had digs in the town and I would either sup with them or go out for a meal. Second, evenings with Stewart; we would usually go to the Queens Hotel in Southsea for a meal, sometimes with a couple of WRNS friends. Third, evenings out alone with a Wren – usually dancing in Southsea and a café meal. There was no 'steady' girl friend at this time, but there were quite a few pleasant Wrens about who likewise preferred to ring the changes, seeing safety in numbers. You have to remember that in those days only the loosest were looking for 'a lay'; most of us were satisfied with just an evening's chat with perhaps a kiss at goodnight time. My nearest thing to a 'steady' at this time was a delightful blonde called June Hedges. She had been at Lee-on-Solent, so we had many common Fleet Air Arm friends. She too had quite a few other going-out friends, but on the whole we were each the most frequent date in the other's book. I often wonder what became of her; the last time I saw her was loaded with tragedy.

Besides her looks and good companionship, one of June's great advantages was that she was a good boozer, that is, she could drink at men's pace and hold it. Too many would try the pace and just get over-tiddly. This was her undoing. I asked her over from Lee for a major dance at the Queens, so she got an overnight pass and a room at the hotel. It was to be our farewell do, as I was at the end of my course. It was miserable; she got gloomier and gloomier as the evening wore on. This was nothing to do with my imminent departure. Our relationship was not such as to make goodbyes difficult. All evening she refused to say what was bugging her. When at last the last dance was done she said she wanted to go straight to bed. Would I give her twenty minutes and then come up because she wanted to tell me her woes. I lay on the bed beside her and she cried and cried. Then it all came out. One Saturday lunchtime she had gone for a drink with an Airborne officer we both knew. They had gone on to clubs for more booze and on into the night. The Airborne were issued with benzidrene pills to keep them awake on long operations and he had fed her some of these to keep the party going. In the end he had bedded her. Now she had just found out that she was pregnant. The old, old story, but about the last thing you would expect to happen to her. A resourceful person, she was now totally without resource. Terribly fond of her parents, but sure that they could never understand. Dreading the treatment the WRNS authorities would hand out – they treated all such cases as harlots. There was no comfort I could bring. This was the last I saw of her. I had one letter later to say her parents had taken her back on sufferance, and, just to fill her cup, she had had twins. Back to Whaley . . .

Each day began at Whaley with Divisions, a parade of all the courses and staff who were on the Island for that day held in the very large Drill Shed. The courses took it in turn to provide a Guard of Honour for Divisions, which Presented Arms as the Colours were run up for the day. The parade took the form of an inspection of all ranks by the Staff, followed by 'Fall out the Roman Catholics' and morning prayers for the rest. It was a quirk of the Navy's that the RCs got these opportunities for a smoke whilst the rest, whatever they may have been other than C of E, had to pray. Divisions was the first chance of the day for the Staff to hand out minor punishments or vituperative criticism in respect of the shortcomings of trainees. On Fridays, the Divisions were special: the guard came from one of the Officers' Long Courses; the Captain attended; there was a full Royal Marine band instead of just a few 'Drummers' to blow 'Colours'. The entire establishment was present and had to march past the Captain at the end. The Band tune for the march-past was always 'Braganza', virtually the regimental march of HMS *Excellent*. There was a historical reason for this which largely escapes me. It is the regimental march of the Surreys, or it may be the Royal West Kents. They had been carried to the Peninsular War in HMS *Excellent*, a previous holder of the name which floated, and struck up such a good relationship that the regiment conferred the honour of allowing *Excellent*'s crew to march to 'Braganza'.

Many a day went by in 'Field Training'. This embraced all the items of squad and rifle drill up to the manoeuvring of a full battalion of four (in the Navy) companies. By then the Army had three companies to a battalion. It was all taught by the Gunner's Mates. I just wish I could remember a half of the witticisms they made at our expense, their extraordinary unintentional spoonerisms and their essays in vituperation. I fear only some of the milder examples remain:

'Fred Carnoe's Circus is better than you lot.' (Fred Carnoe's was the only circus referred to – none of us had ever heard of it.)

'That will lead to fucking chasoe.' (Chaos is unknown to Gunner's Mates.)

'To fix bayonets I first gives the cautionary order "The squad will fix bayonets" and the squad stays absolutely still. Then I gives the order "Fix . . ." Now, when I says fix, you don't fix; again you don't fucking move; all that happens is that the righthand marker takes two smart paces forward.

But there is one exception to that: at a funeral firing party. For why? Well, he'd fall in the bleeding great 'ole, wouldn't he?'

'When you "Rest on your arms reversed", you adopt a mourningful expression; not like THAT, Mr Burroughs – you look as though you was kipping.'

'If you lot was Firing Party for my funeral, I can see my old woman pissing off ashamed that that's as good as I was able to learn you.'

'If you come out with that chasoe at my funeral, you'll hear me 'ammering on me coffin lid and calling on his reverence to send me back home again.'

The favourite punishment for slovenly drilling was 'Round the Island'. The Gunner's Mate would take you to the Field Training Office and kit you out with loaded pack and haversack and infantryman's ration of ammunition. He would then make you slope arms and order 'Round the Island; Double March.' As you set off along the peripheral track, he would telephone all his cronies in the various instructional departments along it. You would be, for example, padding past the West Battery when a Gunner's Mate would emerge . . .

'That Officer doubling on a punishment, ABOUT TURN'.

As you got almost out of his sight on the reciprocal course, he would give you another about turn and then go back to his class. You would be lucky to have as few as three of these reverses. It was about a mile and a half round the Island, but on this basis, you could do a good five mile run. The Army, of course, never double march at the 'slope'; always the 'trail', because a sloped rifle bangs up and down on your shoulder when you trot. 'All the better!' think the Gunners' Mates! One day they overdid it and Burroughs passed out completely. He came back after a day in the Sick Bay.

Being the Guard for Friday Divisions was somehow made to feel the most important thing in the world to accomplish perfectly. One of us would be appointed Officer of the Guard and he would be provided with a sword. During wartime, officers were not required to own swords, so this was our first experience of them; another lot of drill to be learned.

Officers' swords were of the ceremonial variety. As an aside, you may also like to know that the equivalent Nelsonian weapon for ratings, the cutlass, was still around and carried in HM Ships. They were in fact used in action in the boarding and liberation of our prisoners in the German prison ship *Altmark*. They were used for boarding enemy ships or dealing with unfriendly 'natives'. A cutlass was a short, heavy sword, about 2ft 6ins long and with a two-inch wide heavy blade. *Altmark* was a freighter in German hands; she had been with one of their mid–Atlantic armed raiders as a supply vessel and was used to imprison survivors of her victims until landing them in Germany to go to the prisoner of war camps. *Altmark* took shelter deep up a Norwegian fjord and Norwegian Resistance managed to signal the presence to London. On a very dark night, with excellent seamanship, two British destroyers crept up the fjord, ran alongside and grappled to *Altmark*. They boarded her with cutlasses and a few revolvers (firearms all round would have been a potential risk to our prisoners), rescued all the British merchant seamen and brought them home.

As Officer of the Guard, you had to take complete charge of your course and ensure an impeccable turnout for the first Fall-In on the Quarterdeck. After this Fall-In, you made them fix bayonets and drew your sword, in time to give a flashy sword salute to the arriving Commander 'G' (the Commander in charge of all gunnery training; in our time this was a Commander Casement, a nephew of the Irishman of that name, hanged – or was he shot? – for treason in the First World War). He then inspected the Guard. Unfix bayonets and march off to the Drill Shed quarter of a mile away, led by the Royal Marine Band, and take position in front of the rest of the establishment, already paraded there. Fix bayonets again. Captain arrives. Present Arms and another sword salute. Order arms. Colours bugle blows 'General Salute, Present Arms'. Then relax for 'fall out RCs' and some quiet praying. Each of us did this in turn, including Burroughs, but I just don't remember his day at it, so presumably he got by.

I used to get quite a lot of enjoyment out of gun drill. We had an old 6-inch gun and a modern twin-mounted 4.5-inch HA/LA (Dual purpose, highangle or anti-aircraft, and lowangle, or anti surface targets) as our main playthings. Then there were the close-range anti-aircraft weapons such as the twin-mounted Bofors 40 mm and the older Navy favourite, the 'Pom-Pom'; this was the Vickers 2-Pounder, like a very big Vickers machine gun, which was mounted in two, four, eight or twelve gun mountings. I suppose the pleasure came from playing with beautifully engineered heavy, but easily controlled, masses, the tremendous amount of shouting, the teamwork and the pride that came with well conducted drill.

The 4.5-inch mounting was the object of one of the Service's earliest attempts at an operational simulator. Once the crew had mastered the basic gun drills, the simulator would be switched on. The mounting was on a platform which would roll and pitch like a destroyer in a big sea. Drenching water would come all over you as enemy shells landed nearby or as the imaginary ship dug into a big sea. The enemy shells and your own fire produced tremendous flashes in the pitch dark in which the exercise was conducted. The noise of all these explosions and the shrill of enemy shells coming over all came through at full volume from the amplifiers. It was the greatest game of 'Let's pretend' anyone could want, but a complete drill through it was exhausting. You had to fire off a prescribed number of shots in the time allowance as well as having a 'misfire' simulation in the middle. A misfire is what it says: the gun is fired but nothing happens. It is the most worrying thing that can happen when firing. Many a gun's crew have killed themselves because of incorrect drill when it happens. The propellant charge may be slowly cooking, having failed to take full fire. If the breech is then opened the air admitted will fire the cordite back into the mounting. Thus there is an elaborate drill which must be gone through to eliminate the various possible causes of the problem before the breech can be opened. This must be done at top speed, to minimise the time the gun is out of action.

Besides drilling on the Bofors and Pom-Poms in the West Battery, we used to go down to the shore ranges at Eastney and fire at targets. In spite of experience of firing such things in anger in *Indomitable*, these live firings at Eastney were still great fun. It was competitive, our scores on the targets being carefully counted.

Another fun thing Gunnery Officers had to learn was 'Demolition'. This was not much more than the quarryman's art, but we enjoyed the big bangs and making things jump!

I suppose the most dreaded item of the whole training was the 'Assault Course'. Not only was it very, very strenuous, it had its dangers and produced a steady casualty list amongst the courses who had to do it. I only heard of one man being killed (on the 'G' Course but one before our 'AGO' Course) but most courses sustained wounds and injuries to their odd member, mostly light, sometimes serious. It was arranged along the north shore of the Island and most of the obstacles were in the gravelly mud just above the high water mark. It consisted in the main of the high walls, climbing nets, crawling tunnels, overhead wire traverses and so on which are common to all Army assault courses, but the obstacles were all of a tough standard. What made it a killer was the going between obstacles, much of which was harbour mud. When you reached what might have been the end at the north-east corner of the island, your rifle was inspected and supposedly it had still to be spotless. You were then formed into groups of six and had to run down to the water's edge, embark in a whaler (the lucky sixth man got the tiller) and row in a fixed time to a rifle range across the creek, run up the beach and fire ten rounds at a target at 500 yards.

All the time you were harried by Gunner's Mates bawling fit to bust, so some of the injuries came through sprains and bruises from over enthusiasm. Other more serious injuries came from the more dreaded part of the trip, the 'Long Crawl' and the 'Charge'. The first was a matter of crawling as fast as you could go for some hundred yards supposedly keeping low out of the enemy's sight. On the flank was a Gunner's Mate spraying over the ground with a Bren gun sighted about two feet above ground. Raising the buttocks to get on more speed or keep out of the mud could thus result in bullet nicks in your trousers or bottom, depending on how far you had pushed your luck. For the 'Charge', you fixed bayonet and with the most blood-curdling yell you had breath left for (a mere cheep from most of us!), you charged at a line of suspended dummies and 'stuck' them. Whilst you did this, realism was added by a few Gunner's Mates tossing No.96 grenades amongst us. This was a practice grenade with a plastic body, supposedly bursting into harmless fragments. Its fuse mechanism, however, was like that of a real grenade. It contained a steel ball to restrain the firing pin until the right moment. This ball could fly anywhere and the chances of it hitting anyone were obviously remote, but this is what had got the man, mentioned a few paragraphs back, killed. 'It's just to keep you on your toes, like.'

We all, except Bill Burroughs, took it in deadly earnest. He took no notice of those screaming at him and made his own gentle pace and was soon miles behind. He finished under arrest half way. Tangled with his rifle astride the top of the highest rope climb and terrified with heights he let out a yell: 'Fuck the whole thing!' and chucked his rifle down from the top. It stuck muzzle first, about a foot into the mud. He climbed down the other side and, hands in pockets, sauntered off the course. Bill had all our respect – and in a way, that of the Staff – for his bravery in showing total indifference to the traditions of Whale Island and, in particular, to the yelling of the staff.

Thursday nights were guest nights for the Wardroom. This meant a formal dinner in black (i.e. bow) ties and all the best silver out. A good meal with good wines, culminating with the Loyal Toast and passage of the Island's excellent port. After that, the tables were cleared away and 'Strip the Willow' and Eightsome Reels ensued. Whence came the Scottish connection, I never learned. Those of us less light on our feet retired for more drinking and rough games in the anteroom. Our course invented a new one of these. We discovered that a Nelsonian signal gun on the Quarterdeck had just the same diameter bore as a billiard ball. Thus, it was possible to stand it against the bar, to take the recoil, and feed it rather like a mortar. You lit and popped in a 'Thunderflash' followed by a billiard ball. Each team had to sight on a suitable target (e.g. a wall ventilator grating) and bets would be placed on how many shots would be needed to get a hit. It was a splendid weapon, noisy and very dangerous. The game only lasted for a few guest nights; we shattered rather too many billiard balls and put flats on others; unfortunately, the Commander was a billiards enthusiast. It didn't really spoil the party for the other guests, as it was exciting for spectators to watch even if they weren't competing. There was another ante-room for the quiet crowd to use.

Habitually, if there were a Sub Lieutenants' course finishing, they got very drunk on their last guest-night and then in the dead of night played some vast prank on the establishment. It was usually aimed at interruption of the Friday Divisions, which would be their last parade at 'Whaley'. I recall one occasion when they had pushed all the Island's lorries into the middle of the parade ground, then removed and hidden their wheels. Frantic appeals for the return of the wheels on the Island's Tannoy culminated ten minutes before Fall In with 'All leave for No – Sub Lieutenants' Course is cancelled unless the transport wheels are returned at the Rush.' Give the Sub Lieutenants and the Island their due; wheels were on and the Parade clear by Fall In.

On another occasion, the Subs' last parade came and went without any such demonstration. The Staff, who were officially always very angry and punitive about the pranks, started muttering after their departure on leave, 'Well, they were a dull lot.' Days later, after a shower of rain, there appeared on the grass bank below the Wardroom in two foot high capitals: 'Fuck Whale Island and all its Bullshit' in perfect lettering, painted on to the grass in weedkiller during a pitch black night. Whaley always got the last laugh, though. Every man jack of them was summoned back from leave. They were issued with spades and barrows and made to returf the entire bank, the turf coming from the remotest corner of the Island. It took them a day and a half.

Not all our training was, of course, in the practical bullshit of drills and assault courses. There was a great deal of classroom stuff on the chemistry

– elementary level – of propellants and explosives, the ballistics of shells, rockets and bombs, the design of the various projectiles and their fusing and likewise of the German equivalents. We also had to learn all about the storage and handling regulations which went with our trade. There were some interesting outside visits too. The main one was for some ten days to St Merryn in Cornwall for our practical air firing and bombing. Stewart Allison used to cause consternation at checking in at such places. We always had to give the name and address of our next of kin. His was his father, address: The Workhouse, Warwick. He always said it as though he was larking about, but it was in fact true. His father was Warden of that venerable establishment. We also had to go to Boscombe Down to see and hear the appraisals of the newer planes and weapons which were coming forward – it was the experimental station for operational trials of new items for ourselves and the RAF. An exciting visit was to RAF Wittering, near Stamford. Years before, my mother had always stopped there, where the A1 runs alongside the airfield perimeter, to let us watch the Hawker Harts based there taking off and landing, on our way north to prep school. Now it was the trials station for evaluating enemy aircraft. From captures and reconstructed crashes, they had at least one of each type of enemy aircraft. We were there overnight and I recall that we were very shocked, returning from the camp cinema to the mess, to be accosted by WAAFs, plying trade as prostitutes. This was the only instance of this I encountered in the War with a female service, although all services had their sprinkling of enthusiastic amateurs. It would be the RAF!

The family disaster which struck whilst I was on that course came in the second week of December. My mother had a message from the Scots Guards adjutant at Birdcage Walk that my brother Kenneth had been 'seriously wounded' in Italy and had been brought to the Base Hospital in Naples.

I went up to London for a night; nothing could comfort her or prevent her fearing the worst. Maybe, in the circumstances, this was as well because it part prepared her for the War Office telegram on 23 December to say that he had died of his wounds the previous day. She telephoned me immediately and I told Mike Allison. I was amazed at the Whale Island reaction. I was told that the Captain wanted to see me. This was Captain Agnew; at Whaley one believed that if he had met God on the Quarterdeck, God would have saluted first. He wished to make personal expression of his regret and told me to feel free to take as much leave as I judged necessary

17. Example of a microphoto airletter system for the Forces: a letter from Kenneth in 1943; letters were photographed abroad, then printed at Base when received.

to help my mother through the crisis. I cannot remember how long I stayed with her, but it must have been some days.

In due course, a letter came from his Colonel at the front explaining. The battalion (2nd Scots Guards) had been called upon to assault Monte Camino, a dominating peak in the Apeninnes north-east of Naples. Kenneth's platoon was one in the lead. As they formed up they got 'stonked' by German mortars and one landing immediately ahead of him had taken several casualties and wounded him badly in the head. The country was difficult and transport mule-based. It had taken three days to hand stretcher him back to base. He never recovered full consciousness although in delirium he had several times tried to get off the stretcher to get back to his platoon. He had had an unfortunately slow death but it was not thought that he had suffered – drugs and delirium had kept him from undue pain. He was buried in the new military cemetery outside Naples. Out of sentiment for her feelings, I do not think the Colonel gave too much detail to my mother. Kenneth's friend in the battalion knew Sandy was a doctor, I think they had in fact met in London, and he wrote with greater detail to Sandy. The above puts together all we knew of Kenneth's end. Later, the adjutant in Italy sent my mother a picture of Monte Camino and the memorial erected on it by a regiment of Ghoums to the brave men of the Scots Guards who had captured this hill. After the front had rolled forward, the Ghoums – amongst the fiercest of the French colonial troops, equivalent of our Gurkhas – were sent on an exercise assault of Camino. They were so impressed by its difficulty, they spontaneously put up the memorial as an expression of their admiration.

What were my own reactions? I cannot really remember. Shock, yes, but having lost so many friends already, I suppose the shock was less acute for me than it was, for example, for my brother Ian who had not yet been off to War and who had always been closest to Kenneth.

I was able to attend two memorial services for Kenneth. The first was the family one; I suppose Sandy had made all the arrangements. I merely turned up on a day trip from Whale Island. Somewhere in the attic archives I think I still have the Service Card. Considering the difficulties of wartime travel, it was surprisingly well-attended. Besides the immediate family, his girl friend Mary Tollit, her parents and brother Mark came, quite a few Guards officers, and a wide range of my mother's friends and a few Eastbourne contemporaries.

The service was taken by Bishop Walter Carey (erstwhile Bishop of

Bloemfontein) who in his retirement was the well-loved and respected chaplain at Eastbourne. In spite of the travel problems, he and his wife Fanny had come all the way down from Ely, where he was now the Principal of the Theological College. (Towards the end of the War, between VE and VJ Day, he baptised our son Colin in Eastbourne College Chapel.) Also, F. J. Nugee, Headmaster at Eastbourne, brought his paraplegic wife all the way from Radley.

It was a cheerful service, Walter Carey saw to that – one of thanksgiving for an excellent, albeit short (twenty years) life, rather than a weepy. I can't remember the name of the church in West Hampstead – a Victorian gothic on the left hand side of Abbey Road. After the service my mother gave a lunch at a fashionable restaurant on the south side of Berkeley Square. Walter Carey saw to it that it was a cheerful lunch; he had just the right magic touch.

The other service was, I think, a good few months later when I was on leave after the 'Whaley' course. This was a general memorial service by the Scots Guards for all their losses to date. It was in the Guards Chapel in Birdcage Walk (subsequently demolished by a bomb or a V1). All I can remember was being in a real tizz with all the saluting – Guardsmen seem to salute officers passing hundreds of yards away. Even walking away after, crossing over by the Victoria Memorial to go into Constitution Hill, the Palace sentries saluted. And I only had two stripes!

At the end of the Gunnery Course, I astonished myself in the passing out examinations. Not only was I top of the course, I had achieved by a fairly easy margin more marks than had ever been recorded in a long course! In gun drill on the 4.5 action simulator described earlier, and I had had to take the class through the complicated misfire drill, I was awarded 100 per cent by no less than Commander 'G' himself. This apparently caused a furore in the Staff Wardroom anteroom. In part, I think, the true Gunners were annoyed that this should be achieved by an AGO and an RNVR man rather than a 'G' Course 'Straight Striper'. In the main, it was felt not to be in keeping with the concept of excellence. A 100 per cent mark meant nothing less than perfect. How could anyone be perfect at gun drill? There was a Staff meeting on this weighty matter of principle in the afternoon. Commander Casement stood his ground, my mark was confirmed; I was told all that by Mike Allison.

After that, I felt that I could expect a really good appointment. It was thus a bitter disappointment to be told that I was to go to Inskip, an unheard of little maintenance airfield somewhere in Lancashire, and not even as the AGO, but merely as assistant to an existing AGO already there. All the others in the course were getting AGO appointments to 'Woolworth carriers' (escort carriers) and major overseas operational airfields as principal AGO. You should never expect your deserts from the Admiralty appointments people!

Addendum to Chapter 27

Whilst the details of its working did not come into the AGO's Course syllabus, having relevance to cruisers and battleships only, we were made aware of the computer systems used for gunnery control in the more heavily gunned ships. They may be worth mentioning as a historical item of interest to computer fans. First let me say that the word 'computer' had not arisen. It probably still awaited being coined. I cannot remember what the apparatus was in fact called – it was something like 'automatic calculator'.

Deep below the bridge of a battleship, below the armour plate belt, was the TS or Transmitting Station, from which all the guns were controlled. That is to say, at each gunlayer's or trainer's position, a pointer was made to move on the elevation or training dial by TS control. Whilst the system was in operation (it was obviously susceptible to damage to the linking cables by enemy action), all the layers and trainers had to do was to wind their elevation or training handles to bring the elevation/training pointer to line up with the TS indicator pointer on their dial. Likewise, with the introduction of automatic fuse-setting, the TS directly controlled the fuse-setting machine in each turret. All the gun crew had to do was to offer up the projectile nose to the fuse setter and that screwed the timing adjustment to provide the correct delay after firing for detonation of the shell.

The calculation of all the variables involved in order to score hits is sufficiently complex to be quite a problem for the computer of today. These variables include the following :

- ballistic characteristics of the ammunition to be used, bearing in mind we have to cater for primary and secondary armaments;

- enemy course and speed, which can vary continually;

- enemy range, does vary continually;

- wind speed and direction;

- own course and speed;

- angle from horizontal of own ship's roll and pitch at instant of firing;

- weight of propellant charge to be used;

- corrections of elevation and training from spotting of last salvo.

The last-mentioned item was the feedback from observation from the ship's spotting aircraft or from observers stationed at the masthead. The basic system was to get the line right (training) first. For range, one aimed for a straddle of the target with the salvo. If the centre of a salvo fell 500 yards short of target, for instance, the order was given, 'Up 500.' The TS converted this into a change of angle of elevation. There was no automatic feedback on temperature of the gun; changes in gun range as the gun heated up were corrected by spotting corrections as far as I know.

The calculating machine, whilst driven by electric motors, was entirely mechanical. It was like two large refectory tables in sheet brass, laid out in a 'T'. All the different factors were fed in through shafts and gearing of approximately Meccano size. Most of the calculations, as you can see, were open to vectorial solution, so there were many slides, cams and protractors within forming analogues of their respective parts of the calculating process. I doubt that they were ever fast enough calculators to give ideal solutions, but broadly speaking they did a very good job. More primitive versions of them dated right back to the First World War. They were quite stupendous pieces of mechanical engineering, but I do not suppose for a minute that any example of them has been preserved in a museum. There was so much brass and bronze in them, their value as scrap must have been tempting. Also, whilst the rush into electronic computing development is in full spate, those interested in the subject have, as yet, little time for study of the history of their art. Let us hope that at least Vickers or the Admiralty have kept drawings of these marvels. Perhaps we should ask the Maritime Museum or the Imperial War Museum whether they can find one. Failing that, maybe we should suggest to Portsmouth Polytechnic or some such that they get drawings from the Admiralty or Vickers and try to make one? They really were marvellous machines.

Chapter 28

At Inskip

OTHER THAN JOINING and leaving ships at Liverpool and going through Lancashire on the LMS in the 'Royal Scot' on the way to prep school, I had never really been in that county. Thus, I rather assumed that Inskip, in the heart of the county, would be one of those places where planes had to weave their way between factory chimneys in order to be able to land. Nothing could have been more wrong. It was out in quite remote countryside, half way between Preston and Blackpool. It was a tiny establishment without any Squadrons based there. Its purpose was to serve as an auxiliary maintenance station for overhauls. The amount of armament work required there was minimal and my boss, the station AGO, and I were totally unable to understand why two of us had been appointed. He was a nice guy, pretty elderly by my reckoning, for he must have been into his mid-thirties, called Lee. He was a Lieutenant Commander. I recall his initials as C.S.E. but cannot remember his first name. Because of his venerable demeanour, we all called him 'Colonel'. I learned later that the appointments people had sent me here to 'mark time' until the quite important appointment they had in mind for me became vacant. Meanwhile, Colonel Lee was in a panic lest I had been sent to take over his job and he might be sent off to sea. For the first three and a half years of his married life, he had been away in the Mediterranean, and reckoned that he had now earned a year or so to get to know his wife and child.

It was a dull little place. All the accommodation was in freezing cold Nissen huts, and there was insufficient work to keep the Colonel and me interested. He was an easy-going bloke at the best of times but even he found the pace a bit slow! Our main recreation was to organise a target-towing aircraft to fly for us on the range off the Blackpool coast and go and blaze away at it. Alternatively, we would go and blast off rockets into the bombing range at Preesall Sands, the beach north of Fleetwood.

The only other amusement was rugger but, being a small establishment, we had a pretty low standard team. That, however, did not stop us taking the pants off Squire's Gate, the big RAF base at Blackpool, which was quite a triumph. I cannot remember any of my colleagues in this dump other than Colonel Lee, but I was only there from the end of February 1944 to about April. Three happenings during that spell come to mind which may be worthy of record.

The first was the raid on our station rum store. At the time it seemed as major an event as the Great Train Robbery was regarded some years later. All that in fact happened was that in the middle of one night a Service's three ton truck drove up to the main gate in purposeful fashion and our dozey guard admitted it. Half an hour later it drove off out. Next morning, when the 'Jaunty', or Master at Arms, went to draw the day's rum ration, the store was found to be empty. Seventy-five gallons of Navy rum gone! This could be diluted twice to bring it down to the normal pub strength, so it was quite a haul. The civilian police were still investigating when I went off to my next appointment.

The second involved a major boob perpetrated by the Colonel and me on the great 'Salute the Sailor' parade in Preston. This was a parade and march through the town as part of a week devoted to raising funds for Army charities in which the other two services participated. Inskip produced the naval element and as the AGOs, Colonel and I had to drill them and lead them on the parade. We were a bit bolshy about it. Why should we have to go to all this trouble for purely Army charities?

Anyway, the Navy being the senior service, our contingent had to lead the march past and the parade through the town. This meant Colonel Lee alone led the march, followed a few paces behind by me on my own, then all our ratings. I have in fact got a quite good photograph of the occasion (Plate 18). The police had briefed Colonel Lee on the quite complicated route the parade was to take through the town. He had no need to tell it to me as all I had to do was follow him. To our horror, the Army band on duty played us past in the march-past to the Royal Marines' march 'A Life on the Ocean Wave'. The Navy march past always to 'Hearts of Oak' and the band-master should have known it. As soon as we were past the saluting base, Colonel Lee fell out, incensed enough to go and give the bandmaster a roasting. Bandmasters who have to play past a series of contingents in a parade over a mile long are not all that well-positioned to receive a blasting from a tetchy Lieutenant Commander. It thus took the Colonel more than a little time to convey his full feelings.

Meanwhile, yours truly led these thousands of men he knew not where,

18. 'Salute the Sailor Parade', Preston 1943, just before 'Colonel' Lee, marching ahead of me, fell out to speak to the Bandmaster.

in a town entirely strange to him. A policeman ran up to me to say that I should have turned left two streets ago. I explained that I had followed the route which seemed to have the most people lining the route. Ah yes, he said, but the street I was on was our return route. So I took the next left, quite empty and at the bottom end it was hemmed in with service transport parked awaiting the job of returning the various units to their bases. There was not room for the parade to get through marching in their formations in threes. Thus, as we emerged into the well crowded route proper, all our chaps were running about trying to regain formation. It was more like Wat Tyler's rising than a military parade. Thank goodness Colonel Lee caught us up at that point and kept us along the paths of righteousness thereafter.

The last event remembered was a disgrace entirely my own. I went in an Albacore to fire the rear gun at a towed drogue on the range off Blackpool. By 'range' all that is meant is a strip of sea parallel to the coast, marked on the charts as an area excluded to boats and shipping. As Blackpool was not far away, the rule was that you could only fire from the shore side of the target, so that your shots were directed out to sea. On the day in question it was misty, so that you could not see the coast as usual. I did quite a few runs and, ammunition exhausted, returned to Inskip. On arrival, I was told to report to the Commander. He had just been phoned by the Mayor of Blackpool, no less, to say that the sea front had been under fire from an Albacore. How did I explain it? I said that I had followed the usual drill, so it could not have been me. Unfortunately, no-one else had been firing that morning. Rounds had been picked up at the front, clearly identified as British . 303. In the fun of the chase, on one of the runs I must have thought we were going north when a look at the compass would have shown the opposite, so I had fired from the seaward side of the target. Luckily there had been no damage, the bullets had been spent at that range, so the Commander chose to regard it as rather a joke. To a new and rather conscientious AGO, it was a pretty ultimate disgrace!

Luckily my sojourn at this very dull little station soon ended, with a signal appointing me to be AGO at Donibristle, an appointment reckoned to be a Lieutenant Commander's, Donibristle ranking as second only to Lee-on-Solent in importance of the Fleet Air Arm bases. Whilst I had hoped to go to sea, I was very bucked to be given such a posting as a quite junior Lieutenant.

Chapter 29

At Donibristle

I WILL DWELL RATHER ON DONIBRISTLE, for reasons which are, or will become, apparent; it had more influence on my life than any other period of my naval service!

It was the first naval establishment I had been to which could be reached by a train stopping at a station right at the 'front door'; the LNER's Donibristle Station, on the Edinburgh, Aberdour, Kirkcaldy, Dundee line, was the opposite side of the road from the Naval Air Station's main gate. Stepping off the night train from Kings Cross at Waverley, one had time to take a good breakfast at the North British Hotel in Edinburgh before catching the train on to Donibristle. For the first trip at least, this was an interesting railway jaunt, if only a short one, because it took one across the Forth Bridge. At that time, it was one of the world's most remarkable railway bridges. It would not surprise me if it is still so regarded today. At that time, as you crossed you could see several of the larger Fleet units such as battleships or aircraft carriers at moorings off Rosyth dockyard as interesting additions to an already spectacular view from the bridge.

The base enjoyed three alternative designations at that time. It had the customary ship's name, HMS *Merlin*. It was RNAS Donibristle (Royal Naval Air Station) and it was also RNARY Donibristle (Royal Naval Aircraft Repair Yard). It served three purposes. The main one was to be the centre for major maintenance, repair or rebuild of long-served or damaged planes coming off ships arriving at Scapa Flow, the Clyde or Rosyth and from all the Scottish naval shore stations who could not handle the job themselves, most being equipped for routine maintenance only. Next it operated as a normal naval air station but with only one resident non-operational communications Squadron, performing communications roles. It was used by the Squadrons from carriers visiting the Forth for such purposes as shore maintenance tasks done by themselves, compass swinging, etc. Third, it was the 'seat' of the Admiral commanding all Northern naval aviation affairs, and his staff. His title was FONAS (North) – Flag Officer,

Naval Air Stations, North. It was a pretty big outfit as Fleet Air Arm bases went.

It lay between the aforementioned railway and road, which formed its northern boundary, and the shore of the Firth of Forth, half way between Inverkeithing and Aberdour. It was laid out in what had been the pleasant parkland of Donibristle House, seat of one of the older Scottish peerages. The single runway lay east/west, parallel to the road and was about half way from the road to the shore. It marked the southern end of the more or less level ground between it and the road. To the south of it, the ground shelved fairly steeply down to the shore of the Firth. From it on a clear day, you could see Edinburgh and Leith across the water. Between it and the northern fence lay the station's main installations. The main gate and parade ground just inside gave on to a southerly running road, towards the runway, making a slight climb up a knoll. Near the top, a left fork took you to the station's administrative offices on the left and the officers' quarters on the top of the knoll on the right. Before the fork, on the right hand side of the parade, the petty officers' mess and then the ratings' quarters stretched out westwards along the northern fence. Taking the right hand fork, past the station flagstaff, one had on the right the Captain's house, and then the FONAS offices. From here the road ran down a slope to a large array of hangars and engineering shops to the right and hard standing for parking aircraft on the left. Thence, the road became the aircraft perimeter track past the western end of the runway, round to the Control Tower on the south side and down to the various installations on the slopes down to the sea shore. Amongst these were several which came under the Air Gunnery department, the gun-butts where aircraft could test fire their guns, the clay-pigeon range, the ammunition and bomb stores. In the last we kept a fully representative range of the FAA's bombs and ammunition and rockets in stock. At any time, we had to be capable of re-arming any visiting operational Squadron.

Perhaps the only other feature of Donibristle which pilots would insist should be mentioned was that there was a considerable hill half a mile to the west of the runway. This was some hurdle to clear if taking off into the prevailing wind and nasty to have to drop down over when the wind was in the east and you were coming in to land. All in all, though, it was a happy and comfortable station. The railway made evenings out to Edinburgh quite feasible for those (rarities) with money and there was a good village pub only three miles' walk away in Aberdour.

There was a sizeable WRNS population at the station and they were, in the main, accommodated in Fordell Castle in its big estate the opposite (northern) side of the road and railway. Their officers, however, had their mess within the station, just beyond the Wardroom.

The Captain in charge of us all was a very rare species, a Captain in the RNVR. It was most unusual to have RNVR officers of such elevated rank because the vast majority of us had only come in from the start of the War and there had not been time to climb that high. He had been in the London RNVR for many pre-War years with HMS *President* on the Embankment. He was, in civvy street, a senior executive of the paint firm Jenson and Nicholson, which his family largely owned. He was a pleasant old bachelor, generally much respected by us all. I had only one thing against him. This was his refusal to recommend to Admiralty that I be made a Lieutenant Commander. This I was entitled to as all previous AGOs at Donibristle were of that rank. All it needed was his recommendation. He refused because he felt I was too young. He was deaf to the argument that if so, I must be too immature for appointment to the job. The main problem to him was that an old chum from *President*, Charles Massey, was at Donibristle as Transport Officer. His rank of Lieutenant was more than enough for that job and between them they were not going to see me overtake Charles. It made a lot of difference. Half as much pay again and twice the War-end gratuity. Careerwise, it was important to me too because at this time, I had applied to be taken on for the Regular Navy after the War. By this time Allied armies were advancing across France and Belgium, while the Russians were careering westwards. The Japanese would obviously take a very long time, but at least their advance had been stopped.

The station Commander was Commander 'Cod' Cooper. I cannot really remember how he came to get that nickname, possibly his initials, possibly because of his bulgy eyes. He was a nice avuncular old thing, although quite a stickler for having things done to true naval standards. I had known him in Trinidad, where he had been on the staff. He became a ready source of wisdom and advice on such things as applying to be taken on post-War, asking for Nicholson's recommendation for my two and a half stripes, and so on. He had been a great chum and admirer of my predecessor, Mike Clifford.

They had been serving together in the Mediterranean when Mike had had to force land and be interned in Algeria by the Vichy French. He was vitriolic about them; they had starved and beaten him, and the Algerian troops guarding him had stolen all the personal things he had with him, such as his watch. They had handed him over to the Italians when we invaded Algeria. They had passed him on to the Germans. He said that the Ities and Krauts were gentlemen in comparison. He had not taken too long to escape from the Germans. Unfortunately, Mike died within a year of my taking over, supposedly from the effects of the way the French had fed, or starved, him.

I had several days with Mike taking over from him. During this period he was asked by Cod to use demolition charges to blow out some large oak stumps which had been felled to level some ground to the south of the runway. I went along too. I was quietly appalled at the weight of explosive my senior was using for the minor task of getting them out of the ground. The objective was to do no more than lift them free so that they would be easy to cut up. Cod was given the fun of pressing the plunger for the first one. With a great roar one and a half tons of oak stump sailed into the air, over the roof of the Wardroom, which it would have demolished if landing on it, and on to the hill the other side of the runway. Luckily it landed on some waste ground.

'That's clever,' says Cod, 'How did you manage that, Mike?'

'Just a matter of calculating the charge weight right,' says Mike. 'Too little and I might have dropped it on the Wardroom or left it in the ground; too much and I could have dropped it on the road.'

He knew that I knew that he had not the least idea what he was doing and had the grace to thank me for my silence later. Weeks after Mike had gone, a similar task needed doing, so it was my baby. Cod came along as a keen spectator. I got it right. With a loud thump, the stump heaved itself off its roots and sat up on the surface. Cod commented, 'Very dull, compared with one of Mike's.'

Next in seniority after Cod was 'Black' Pugh, the Commander (Flying). He was nicknamed Black, I suppose, because he was very dark, a diminutive Welshman, and totally humourless. The funniest thing he ever did was not his fault. Like all Fleet Air Arm aircrew, he had to get in a minimum number of flying hours per month in order to continue to draw the extra 'Flying Pay'. This meant that once a month, on a day when the weather was nice, he would venture up for a few hours in any Swordfish or Albacore which was going spare. He always taxied out to the runway with great care and trepidation and would then sit on the end of the runway revving his engine and endlessly testing the magnetos until trebly assured that he would not be taking undue risk in getting airborne. If the word had got round in time that he was venturing forth, it usually drew quite a crowd of spectators. Came one day, he safely achieved the end of the runway. Brakes full on, he sat at full throttle for a minute or so. Then he released brakes and again gave the old Stringbag full throttle. The engine came off in one piece, the propeller screwing up into scrap on the runway. He sat mournfully in the cockpit as his Swordfish contemptuously peed petrol on to the breakaway engine. Luckily it did not catch fire. The spectators forgot themselves far enough to break into raucous applause.

Another great character on the station, a senior pilot in the communications Squadron, was Lt. Commander Chris Draper. He has already been commented on in Chapter 4 as a result of my first encountering him in Trinidad.

The next Lieutenant Commander of importance to me was Anthony Dixon. He was a smoothy of the first order. He was the Staff Air Gunnery Officer on the staff of FONAS (North), whom I have already mentioned as flying his flag at Donibristle. Tony Dixon knew so little about his job and was so lacking in grey matter, it is impossible to see how he had got to where he did. It must have been a matter of the right friend in high places; this I came to believe more firmly later when he secured adoption as a parliamentary candidate. Actually he had married the daughter of the sitting MP, and in those days in the Shires, being Tory MP was a family job! He habitually referred to me all the technical gunnery questions which came his way for a private answer. Thus, without thanks, I had more than half his job to do besides my own. You will see in a later chapter the form his thanks eventually took, an attempt to get me court-martialled and cashiered from the Navy.

On the WRNS side, there were some quite jolly types, even if amongst the officers at the time of my arrival there was nothing in the way of startling looks. In Charge was 1st Officer (equivalent of Commander) Rombulow-Pearce. She had great ability and charm and most successfully gave the appearance of being a hard-drinking old battleaxe. She seemed to put away gallons of pink gin and gin-and-tonic without turning a hair. Later, when my wife Frances and I were in her confidence, we learned that the Wardroom Wren stewards were under secret orders to make up 'dummies' for her with no gin in! She was a great and cheerful leader of her women. Only a few of us knew she had nothing to be cheerful about. She had already lost her husband and two sons at sea, and her last son was at sea. I have no idea whether he survived, as we lost touch when we left Donibristle.

The next WRNS officer, amongst the characters when I arrived was Minnie. I cannot remember her surname. As far as I recall, she was the only woman there in charge of one of the station's departments. Hers was of some importance, the Parachute Department. They had to service and periodically re-pack all the parachutes. She was the ugliest woman for miles around, a skinny Jewess with enormously bandy legs (probably as a result of rickets) and outsize hooter, sallow complexion and spots. She was cheerful and full of fun, unaware or totally uncaring of her lack of looks, and a very good friend to all the nicer people. When things were quiet in the daytime it was always sense to go round to 'Parachutes' for a cuppa with Minnie, a guinea's worth a minute.

Next to the Armoury (my department) was the station Accounts Department, presided over by a dull and humourless Paymaster Commander RNR, an Edinburgher who in peacetime was accountant to Jenners, the major Princes Street department store. We spread a rumour that he was responsible for some disgusting graffiti appearing in the heads we shared with his department. At least it came back to him, for the whole heads were beautifully repainted throughout. Offsetting his coldness, his department was redeemed by his assistant, a 3rd Officer WRNS Alison Casement. She was a cousin of the aforementioned Commander 'G' at Whaley. Nothing spectacular to look at, other than being plump, she was full of fun and a ball of fire at parties. She hid it well, but I later learned from Frances that Alison had 'quite a thing' for me!

Now to my staff in the Armoury. It was a mixed staff of artificers, air mechanics, seamen and civilians. Some of the air mechanics and civilians were female, but it was predominantly a male team. Senior under me was Lieutenant Summerfield, in the role of Gunner. Gunners were the result of promotion of Gunner's Mates to Warrant Officer rank. An operational ship would have two Gunners, one a general help in the Gunnery Department, and one to run the armament stores, magazines, storekeeping records, etc. for the Gunnery Officer. I had a 'Gunner' in the latter role; it just so happened that his great seniority before retirement had carried him up to the rank of Sub-Lieutenant. Before the War it was usual to move a man up a rank on retirement, so he had become a full Lieutenant. He had then been called back to the colours in his dotage, for shore jobs during the War. He was the most appalling old muddler. He was a widower with advanced signs of dementia senilis but, much worse than that, a cocker spaniel called Judy which had to come to the office too. This somnulent beast not only suffered from dementia senilis of the canine variety, it emitted the most ghastly and concentrated aroma. This was supposedly caused by 'a slight canker of the ear'. Cause did not matter; the effect was that of combining the athlete's foot of a battalion with very old Camembert cheese and the pong of an overfull tropical mortuary whose ventilation had failed.

I also had a Warrant Artificer, James Henderson. He was a nice guy and very helpful to his very green departmental officer. Very quiet and conscientious, very proper. He was married but his wife did not lodge locally. There was some sort of estrangement which was perhaps the root of his sad demeanour. I shamelessly used his patience to get answers, when required, from Summerfield rather than go and ask myself. I just could not stand the business of endlessly clarifying the question and then awaiting the shuffle through the files and papers and several palpably wild answers before one got what one wanted. All the while one would be holding back the retching occasioned by the putrefying Judy beneath his desk. James had a strong sense of duty and, most probably, a totally deficient sense of smell.

In charge of the disciplinary side (like an Army Sergeant-Major) I had an excellent PO Air Mechanic, Petty Officer Charnley. A great big fellow, he had a huge sense of humour and was much respected by both his seniors and his juniors. In civvy street, he had been a butcher's boy; his father was a butcher somewhere in the Midlands. He is not to be confused with a dreadful old creep of a PO Air Mechanic also on my books, Petty Officer Chandler. He was a non-commissioned version of old Summerfield, a pensioner brought back for the War with hardly any skills which were usable but, thankfully, without a senile dog. He was a devious liar and totally unsuitable for supervising Air Mechanics, which is what he was meant to be doing. Wartime manpower shortages forced a situation whereby establishment numbers would tend to be made up with such people in shore bases. Chandler did not know one end of a Browning gun from the other or a practice bomb from a real one. He had been a civilian since just after the First World War. He was drafted into the Fleet Air Arm because his previous service had been in the old Royal Naval Air Service, in which he had been a balloon handler. It was as relevant as drafting a longbowman from Agincourt into the Royal Artillery.

We used Chandler to go in charge of trucks sent out to collect vital stores from the more distant depots which supplied us, such as the one in Stirling. His trips became longer and longer in duration. For example, the round trip to Stirling should have taken about four hours, allowing for delays at the depot. He tended to be away for it for the whole of the day. We discovered from ratings going with him that he had developed the habit of calling at houses on the way, claiming to be a stranded sailor on a journey who had not had food or drink for ages, and getting invited in for cups of tea, or things a bit stronger and, when in real luck, maybe a meal. He could not even see that for a well-fed naval man to cadge food or drink off heavily-rationed civilians was an outrage. Even in uniform, he managed to look like a half-starved Scrooge. He slobbered as he spoke; he had copious drips about his nose even in summer time. I became very fond of my team at Donibristle, but you have perhaps deduced that this never extended to Chandler.

Amongst the Armourers (or Ordnance Artificers, as they were officially designated) an endearing character was Puckey. He was, as his name might imply, a typical cheeky cockney. After short service in the RN he had secured a job in Woolwich Arsenal until being called back to the Andrew for the War. He was a great specialist in 'Rabbits' and was continually being hauled before me by James Henderson for their perpetration.

Rabbits were unauthorised manufactures from service materials in service time using service workshop facilities. They were usually made as gifts for friends and relations: they took such forms as table lighters made out of, say, a 20 mm cartridge mounted on the nose plug of a 250 lb bomb or perhaps a paper rack made from a row of bullets screwed on end on a suitable backing plate. His excuse was that he had never had his mates' opportunities for such diversions at the Arsenal, so felt that it was only fair to make up for lost time. Apparently, at said Arsenal, his job was a turner's, but his lathe was not a handy size for rabbits. He turned 16-inch naval guns; his lathe was about forty feet long and turned things of around three feet to five feet diameter. He would set his cut at the start of a shift, get into his seat on the tool-saddle and maybe get most of the way along the gun barrel in the course of a shift:

'Dead dull, sir, it were.'

When we were getting married, Puckey came up with a quite shameful array of obvious rabbits, most beautifully made, as wedding presents.

'My best wishes to you both and fair dos if you do want to run me in for them.'

A contrast was Rutherford, another Ordnance Artificer, a quiet Scot. He made up in conscientiousness and hard work, together with the occasional philosophical remark, for all Puckey's ebullience. He gave us a marvellous 'suspect rabbit' for our wedding, a wooden egg-box. These were useful things because whenever a flight went up to the Orkneys, if you had a box, you could get the pilot to fill it for you. Eggs in the fresh state were great rarities, even to the shore-based Navy. This was a tactful present, which we still have; being made of wood, it could in no way proclaim itself a rabbit! Knowing Rutherford, however, it probably wasn't. He was a trained choral singer with a beautiful tenor voice, which greatly improved the singing at our wedding.

Of the civilians, three stand out in the memory. First Mr Aitken. It was generally unheard of for a blue-collar worker to qualify for a 'Mister' at work, but he was always Mr Aitken. To me he seemed about ninety, but I now suppose he was in his later sixties. He was in fact a master-craftsman gunsmith from one of those very high class sporting gun and rifle shops in Princes Street. Silently, in a workshop full of servicemen, he would work away all day, turning out work which made the OAs stand back in awe. The Naval Ordnance Artificer is no mean craftsman either. Very occasionally we had had to make a new part which needed 'blueing', making that black surface common on gun exteriors. There was a laid down naval procedure for blueing, but, said Mr Aitken,

'That'll nae last a man's lifetime.'

So he would do his own secret system. No-one was ever allowed to watch; even his Edinburgh employers and their apprentices working under Aitken were never let into the secret. For the several hours he took to work his magic, the shop or the corner where he worked had to be cleared of all personnel. The result was a lustrous blue-black. The boys tried the results out too; parts he had done were painted with salt water and then left in the rain; still the lustrous blue-black and not a speck of rust.

Then there was Lily. She ran our gunstores, as a civilian storekeeper. She was very much a local Fife girl; seemed quite old to me but was probably then in her mid-thirties. At first her thick Fife accent bordered on the unintelligible. She was scraggy and ugly as sin. She had a bad cast in one eye. She could fly into terrible tempers if anyone seemed to trespass upon the good order of her store. In the slum cottage in Hillhead, the local village where she lived, she maintained a bastard girl. (Much speculation amongst the lads on how dark a night and how lunatic a man had caused it to be sired.) Even so, I think we all loved Lily. I wish I could remember her surname.

The other civilian I will mention was also a Fifer and villager of Hillhead,

Bob Crawford. He was a great big man, probably in his fifties, white haired, with a moustache and face very like Bairnsfather's cartoon character, Tommy Atkins. Officially he was our labourer; mostly he cleaned and drove our transport. This consisted of two Triumph motorbikes, another with side-car, an Austin pickup (a lorry-backed version of the Austin saloon car of immediate pre-War era) and the Mercury truck. The last was a miniature low-loading truck of the type used inside large factories for distributing stores. The driver sat on an open platform at the front, so it was not the world's most comfortable drive in the open air in a Scottish winter. We used it to take serviced gun sets out to aircraft at dispersal sites for instal-lation there, or ammunition for test firing and similar chores around the airfield. I can see Bob still, puce face, flat cap pulled well down, filthy muffler scarf and donkey jacket, careering back to the Armoury and pulling up with a skid stop. That truck was his Mercedes at Le Mans or Bentley at Brooklands. It was not clear what he imagined, but he must have been someone like Sir Malcolm Campbell once he took the wheel of the Mercury.

On our staff, we had a rather horrid young seaman called Simpson to help out with unskilled work and he too enjoyed the Mercury. Nothing was more calculated to send Bob off beserk in a true Fifer's temper than to send Simpson away on an errand on the Mercury. Bob seemed in a permanent state of semi or total intoxication or deep hangover. Asked how he spent his evenings, the answer was a peculiar gutteral noise like 'Keuits,' pro-nounced mono-syllabically. This revealed his abiding passion, a local game played mostly in the back yards of pubs with plenty of natural lubrication for the participants. Related to quoits, it was a matter of hurling rings down the pitch, attempting to encircle a stout wooden peg at the far end. It was no game for ladies and little boys. The pitch was long and the quoits were big steel rings, obtained I expect, from ship's cable fittings in the dockyard at Rosyth or from the Inverkeithing breaker's yard. It was a game for the strong and skilful who had limitless capacity for sinking strong scotch ale and fluency in the vituperative end of Fifeshire dialect. His great contempt for all the English, until my wife, whom he adored as an exception, turned up, always showed through the respect which he outwardly showed his seniors.

In picking out characters for mention, I must not forget Mrs Wilson. She was really Writer Wilson WRNS. It was quite improper to use handles like Mrs within the Service although, curiously, it was both proper and customary to refer to a Gunner as Mister So and So. She was a well-trained secretary in peacetime. A plain girl but with gorgeous red hair, she was a really good secretary. Not only was she my mainstay; behind the scenes she spoon-fed Charnley with the administration of his personnel records so that that aspect of our department was always in perfect order. Mrs Wilson spoiled me in a way. As the only secretary I had ever had, I had no idea how unusually good she was; I was a very long time in post-War industry before I found her equal. She was a calm person too; sitting at my right hand taking notes, she was totally unperturbed by the two Irvin episodes in my office.

Irvin was another ordinary seaman on our staff for odd jobs. A small, wiry man, he was from the remotest Highlands and, at the best of times, highly strung. One day, Charnley had to put him on my Defaulters parade because he had abused and threatened to thump one of our Petty Officers who had pulled him up for some minor offence. Having heard both sides of the story, I started to lecture him on the errors of his ways before putting him on the Commander's Report, which I was bound to do in view of the gravity of the offence. I was suddenly confronted with an extraordinary phenomenon. Never before nor since have I seen human hair bristle as Irvin's did. Maybe the coiffures of today's young men will make such manifestations more visible. The length of sailor's hair in those days, particularly on the back of the neck, where bristling is most apparent, would – you would think – make it impossible to see. He clenched his teeth and dribbled down his chin as though rabid. Then he flung himself across the desk to attack me. Charnley jumped him with excellent timing, got a half Nelson on him and held him still while I pronounced 'Commander's Report'. Irvin relaxed, accepted his punishment and that was that. Charnley warned me that he was a strange (the word in those days would have been queer, without its modern connotations) guy and that I would probably have similar trouble when we came before the Commander. I warned Cod Cooper before the case came before him, but there was no trouble, and a week or two's CB (Confined Barracks) was handed out. Charnley and I had decided not to bring up the misbehaviour in my office which we thought was due more to being 'fey' than an intent to do wrong. That seemed to be the end of it.

What was so good about Charnley was that he did not leave it at that but inquired into the background. Seemingly, Irvin was spending all the hours that God and the RN gave him spare in a tremendous strength building regime. He came from an impoverished family in a remote area where there was a lot of in-breeding and the 'highly strung' were common-place. Very probably he was not all there mentally; certainly his phenomenal strength for such a small man was increasing weekly. A month later, one of our Petty Officers (POs) caught Irvin away from his work, doing more physical exercises, and started to tick him off. One punch from Irvin laid this fellow, twice his size, flat for five minutes. So, back he came before me.

For striking his senior, Irvin knew as well as I did that I had no option but to put him again before the Commander. This time, I knew not to indulge in avuncular homilies before ruling. Even so, before I could say 'Command . . .' the bristling happened and Irvin flung himself towards me. In his state he was really frightening. I got up from my chair (but of course Mrs Wilson sat imperturbable!) to receive the attack. Charnley got him first from behind and they crashed to the floor. Charnley was no fool and had privily got three of his toughest mates to stand outside the door with instructions to come in if they heard a commotion. They came in and grabbed Irvin by the arms and got him to his feet. All the time he kept crashing his head against the wall screaming, 'I want to die; I want to die.' Charnley got up, one ear half-severed where Irvin had bitten him in the fracas. I had to ring the Guardroom for a party with a straitjacket. It took all of them to get Irvin secured. He really did have fantastic strength. He now needed luck and not a little help if he were to avoid court-martial. Charnley and I agreed that we wanted to supply the help. The chap was not bad – he really did need help. In the circumstances, the Guardroom had no option but to put him in cells pending Commander's defaulters. He was perfectly calm and lucid when I went in for a chat with him in the cells. It all came out. No hope of a future at home where, as 'fey', he was the outcast of the tiny community. He liked the Navy because there was always enough to eat but there was the trouble of a discipline he could not at times endure. This only bothered him if the Navy interrupted his training for the career he intended after the War. Once he had seen a circus which had had a strong man act. The strong man had been a great big man. The idea grew in Irvin's mind that the act would be twice as good if all the same things were done by a small man of equal strength. Irvin was training to be just that man.

We were lucky to have a Commander like Cod, whom I sought out in the Wardroom and told all about it. It was amazing to me how great was Cod's quiet grip on what went on. He seemed to know half of what I had to say already. On his advice, I asked the PMO (Principal Medical Officer) to go and see Irvin before his case came up. We had a nice old (I suppose now he was all of forty!) PMO who was sympathetic. He gave Cod his view before Irvin came before him. On the day Cod heard the briefest statements of 'evidence' and stated that it was a court-martial offence unless there were mitigating circumstances and then pronounced 'Remanded for Medical Report'. Again Irvin went out of control but sufficient regulating staff were around to prevent damage to Cod.

The PMO got him off to a mental hospital with honourable discharge from the Navy. I thought this a good outcome. Unfortunately we have heard more since about mental institutions and I often wonder what became of Irvin. Cod said:

'You keep some odd types down in that Armoury of yours, Hector, don't you? For God's sake, don't let them get at firearms!'

The last person I will mention, because he became a thorn in my flesh, was the Torpedo Officer, Wilkinson. He was a Lieutenant Commander RNR. He was miles older than me, an ex-Merchant Navy Officer who had been in the RNR pre-War and had done a short course on torpedoes, but was mainly in shore jobs because of his electrical knowledge. At Donibristle, he had a much smaller department than mine. He seemed always to re-sent that, as Gunnery Officer, I took such things as parades rather than him and that, for example, his department had to come to us for bomb storage space for the few torpedo heads carried at Donibristle. As an old friend of Captain Nicholson's and pulling his rank as hard as he could, he continually sniped at me and my department. He was large and coarse, conceited, friendless other than Nicholson, opinionated and endlessly parading his half-knowledge as fact. We had a few nasties in the Wardroom but he took the prize for the most heartily disliked. 'Who on earth had the idea of making that cunt an officer?' commented Cod.

This chapter seems to have led itself into being a chapter of personalia. Maybe we should move towards happenings at Donibristle.

Chapter 30

Frances Appears

I SUPPOSE I HAD ARRIVED at Donibristle in April 1944. At the end of Mike Clifford's handover of the department to me a week later, we had both to discuss its state with Nicholson and Cooper before Mike left. The main point which emerged was that old Summerfield was somewhat past being able to hold down his pretty important job. For once, the powers that be took fairly prompt action.

By the end of May, Admiralty signalled that we would get what was a brand new animal in the Navy, a WRNS 'Gunner'. The male Gunner for looking after armament stores was a man who had successfully come through a career at all rating levels of gunnery practice and had very wide knowledge of all aspects of weapons usage as well of the explosives and how to store them. By this stage of the War, there was a great shortage of such experience. For the Fleet Air Arm shore bases, therefore, they decided to give WRNS armaments ratings (mostly Ordnance Mechanics) a specialist course at Whale Island to fit them to undertake the Armament Storekeeping aspects of Gunner appointments in order to release Gunners for sea service. They were not just any female Ordnance Mechanic. Besides being good at that trade, they had to be people recommended for promotion to officer rank. In the case of WRNS 'Gunners', they would be full Third Officers. There was no Warrant Officer rank in that service. Our female Gunner would come to under-prop Summerfield.

On the evening of 'D' Day, when all we were interested in was news from Normandy, Rombulow-Pearce rolled into my office to introduce the newly arrived Gunner. She was tall and willowy, gorgeous auburn hair and with looks in a league miles from the Donibristle WRNS officer norm. Terribly smart, all brand new uniform, I suppose, terribly 'Pusser' (i.e. formal – lots of 'Yes sir, no sir' and businesslike). Next morning she reported for work and I put her into Summerfield's hands to be introduced around the Department. In advance, we had prepared a desk for her in Summerfield's office. This was no kindness, of course, in view of the pong

19. OM F.E. Purkis WRNS, a corker, 1943.

of rotting Judy. 3rd Officer Purkis, the new arrival, even kindly patted Judy without batting an eyelid. Stern stuff! Later James Henderson came into my office. 'I reckon we've got a corker there,' he said.

Fairly quickly we got to know her less formally in 'out of hours' contacts. There were the station dances in the NAAFI canteen. I took her for walks. James Henderson started to teach her golf.

There were occasional parties or guest-nights in the Wardroom, WRNS officers' mess and at Fordell Castle. Then there was the standard evening out consisting of a walk down to the Star, the pub in Aberdour which kept open to all hours of the night. Occasionally, one took the train into Edinburgh for a film or (rarely) a lobster dinner at the Café de Paris. This involved more exercise; the late train back did not stop at Donibristle, so one had to dismount at Inverkeithing and walk the last five miles.

The Star was 'Home from Home' for most of Donibristle. It was where one could have a drink with one's petty officers and ratings as well as officer friends. Hosted by Mr and Mrs Scott, excellent publicans, the big draw was their daughter Iris who was a helper in the bar. Very young and ravishingly pretty, she was the untouchable (Mrs Scott saw to that) toast of Donibristle. Quite a few villagers of Aberdour came there as well, including Mr Anderson, the village bobby. After his duty hours, he would don a tweed jacket instead of his uniform one and drink with us until midnight or later. The official legal closing time was 9.30 p.m. About every three months the Fife Constabulary would raid the Star and we never understood why they did not lose their licence. Maybe, rightly, the Beaks reckoned the Star as a necessary part of the War effort, because of what it meant to Donibristle. When a raid happened, it was always accompanied by 'Mr' Anderson, now Constable Anderson in full uniform. With his colleagues he would go round the bar collecting names and addresses of those with whom he had been boozing until past midnight the night before and never did anyone bat an eyelid or give him away. He would then be back for a late sip the next night. All understood his differentiation between duty and pleasure.

As we got to know Frances better, we learned that, as an outfit, the Fleet Air Arm did not stand very high in her estimation. Here at Donibristle we were undeniably far from the War. Before becoming an officer she had been in Combined Operations as an Ordnance Mechanic servicing the guns of invasion barges. As she had travelled up to Donibristle, she had seen the sky covered with the fleets of bombers, transports for Airborne and gliders indicating that D-Day had arrived. We were having a very soft time compared with her erstwhile colleagues. I may say that we all felt out of it too. In the early days after D-Day, we were all desperate for news as the somewhat literally cliff-hanger battles for Normandy took place.

Just as we had got used to Frances, she left us again. She was suddenly whipped off to the military hospital at Bridge of Earn for a hernia operation. I was hopping mad one day to find that James had taken one of the Armoury motorbikes and gone up to visit her. Never had I imagined that they allowed visitors, least of all male officers to visit female ones. I realised that I was jealous and I took my first opportunity of going up to the hospital in greater style, using the Armoury pick-up. She was not long away; I cannot remember her even being given convalescent leave. After her return I was able to take her out in the evenings more often. I had an advantage over my rival James – he was already married. Of course, I was also senior to him, but that was not, I think, an item to cut much ice with her. Anyway, I was soon left with a clear run because James suddenly got a new posting to a ship in the Far East.

Around this time Frances distinguished herself in her job to no mean tune. In the course of getting the records in order from Summerfield's chaos, she found that some 120 Browning machine guns and a dozen or two Hispano 20 mm cannon were apparently entirely missing. Evidence was not immediately clear whether it was a gross book-keeping error or whether perhaps the guns had been stolen (IRA? Enemy agents?). Frances thought it was probably the former, but it was difficult to emphasise because that reflected on her boss, Summerfield. Because of the serious implications of the matter, however, we had to report the loss through the Captain to the Admiralty.

All hell was let loose and two senior Gunners were sent up by the Admiral commanding Air Stations at Lee-on-Solent to investigate. Luckily one was Mr Humphreys, who had been one of Frances' instructors at Whaley. I knew his colleague, Mr Griffiths, well. For days we had Summerfield in a tizz, opening files and scattering papers. Judy was calmer. She acquired a taste for carbon paper and happily settled beneath Summerfield's desk to chew the fairly plenteous supply which was snowing down from above. Her purple slavering jaws added to the pong, and did nothing to add to her popularity with the visiting Gunners. I feared she was not helping her master escape the inevitable recommendation as to his future.

The Gunners, Humphreys and Griffiths, not only recommended that Summerfield be retired but that in view of her proven competence, Frances be appointed the sole Armament Storekeeping Officer at Donibristle. As her Course had been the first experiment with WRNS officers for this purpose, caution had led authority not to appoint any of them immediately as sole 'Gunner' at any station. They had all started as assistants to an existing traditional Gunner. Thus, by this move, endorsed by Nicholson and me, Frances became the Royal Navy's first female Gunner and at one of the biggest air stations. Not too long after, she made further naval history by becoming the first Gunner to marry her Gunnery Officer! By sheer bad luck, it was only after she had left that they decided the importance of the post deserved the rank of Second Officer.

Around this time, on a walk one Sunday afternoon in Fordell Park, I 'popped the question' and (much relief) got accepted. I gathered later that it had been rather unexpected. Apparently Alison Casement had been making much about signs that I reciprocated her feelings and Frances had rather expected that I should be trying my luck in that direction. So we became engaged and announced the fact to our many friends on and around the station. The first major surprise was the reaction down at the Star. Mr and Mrs Scott first asked us whether we would like to use their own sitting room whenever we were at the Star, if we wanted peace on our own. We were both invited to have drinks on the house, something unheard of in a Fife pub! I had to kiss Mrs Scott and Iris. Thus I became the first from Donibristle to embrace – at least with parental knowledge – the delectable Iris.

Telephoning the news to my mother, I got a chilly reception. She was still in the first thrill of my elder brother's announcing his engagement to someone known to the family for some time – the proper way to do things.

In spite of that, and a reception of her news with little greater warmth in the Purkis home, Frances and I decided to take the first opportunity to introduce each other to the respective families. We had no long (week or so) leave in the offing, so decided it could be done on our next weekend leave.

This meant rushing for the Edinburgh train as as soon as we got off work on a Friday evening, which would just leave time to snatch a meal at Waverley Station – I expect it was little more than a pork pie at the station buffet – before getting the night train to Kings Cross. We had come to call these pork pies 'Waverley Pie' on cinema evenings in Edinburgh; there was just time to buy them before the train back across the Forth and we ate them on the train. In those days there were no sleeper berths for junior officers like us. You counted yourself jolly lucky if you got seats and indeed that night we had luck. Even so, it was no great comfort. So crowded were the trains that four a side was the custom even in our first class compart-ments. Because of the headrests for three a side, this made them rather less comfortable than the third class (as it was called in those days).

We arrived exhausted at Kings Cross at about eight o'clock on the Saturday morning. To 'perk up' before meeting my mother, we went into the Great Northern Hotel and, after a good wash and brush-up, had the excellent breakfast still provided there at this stage of the War. So we arrived at Langford House at about half past nine. 'Wherever have you been? We've been saving breakfast for you for hours!' was the greeting. What must have been Granny's and Mrs Davis' bacon ration and egg savings for weeks had already been cooked for us. I coped manfully with a second breakfast. Frances, with the additional trauma of the not very warm first encounter just could not face it. First black mark! Conversation was all the time directed towards the excitement of Sandy and Jean's impending marriage. If one tried to turn towards ours, it was dismissed.

'I'm quite sure there's no question of you getting married for quite some time yet, you've hardly met each other. Sandy and Jean have known each other for over five years.'

It was explained that we had to go on that afternoon to Swanage to meet Frances' family, but agreed that we would be back by Sunday evening in time for a drinks party arranged for us to meet some of the family friends. After a sticky morning and lunch, it was some relief to get off on our own to Waterloo for the Bournemouth train. We had to wait at Bournemouth for an hour or so for the train on to Wareham. There we changed in what seemed the dead of night on to the 'Swanage Flier', the little two-coach puffer down to Swanage. There Frances' sister Nancy greeted us and for the first time that weekend we felt we had some warm and welcoming relations. Nancy gave us a huge (for wartime) dinner and so off to bed. She was proprietress of the Wolfeton Hotel in Swanage in those days.

About mid-day on the Sunday, it was our turn to go to the station to meet the train. Mr and Mrs Purkis were coming down from Wimborne to meet us for a family lunch at the Wolfeton. At the station, we encountered the (to me seemingly) charming Uncle Charlie, who sponged on Nancy, living in the annexe to the Wolfeton. Also with the parents was Frances' younger sister Elizabeth who still lived with them, being in the Land Army on a farm not far from them. We formed up to march in pairs back to the hotel. I was with Uncle Charlie. From astern I heard 'OL' at the top of her penetrating voice (OL – old lady – was the Purkis girls' nickname for their mother):

'I don't know why he wants to walk with that dreadful old man.'

But the die seemed cast. I did not see how I could drop the old geezer and form up somewhere else in the family. So we all sat down in the office, a little tense, for aperitifs. Frances' father, conscious of his responsibilities on such an occasion, led off gently:

'And what were you doing before the War, Hector?'

Before I could begin an answer, OL cut in:

'Don't be so silly, Leonard, you can see he is too young to have done anything before the War.'

Recognising the hush this had caused, she felt obliged to lead off, using her own subject:

'Do you play a musical instrument, Hector?'

I confessed to not having progressed beyond the gramophone. This was classed as not funny. Nancy, eager to relieve the tension, offered me another gin. Accepted pronto.

'My goodness, what an amount young people drink these days,' comments OL. And so to lunch . . .

After lunch we all caught the train for Wareham and Bournemouth, dropping the parents and Elizabeth at Brockenhurst, and proceeding on to London, by this time totally exhausted. We arrived in time for the Langford Place drinks party. At least Sandy was there and he was nice to both of us. The rest were old fogie friends of Granny's. The most remembered were the Dewar-Druries (thereafter called by us the Dreary-Druries), very long-standing friends from Brighton days. The old D-D quickly manoeuvred me into a corner. 'Surely, my boy, you are not going to go ahead with this lunacy?' Asked what he meant, he explained the intended marriage. Tired and perhaps a little bit pissed, I pitched into him. He had barely met Frances, so by what effrontery was he calling it lunacy? Well, he had heard much from my mother and to go ahead would cause her grave upset. So, she put you up to this, I challenged. No, he said, he had felt it his duty to do so, having heard how she felt. Then, I said, you have no right to come to a party supposedly to celebrate our engagement if your motive is to finish it. They were the only friends of Granny's who failed to give us a wedding present.

After a snatched meal, we went down to Kings Cross for the 10.15 night train back to Edinburgh. This time no seats: all taken by American officers. They had the money to bribe the porters to put Reserved tickets on all the seats before we could get on to the train. As we waited for the train to come in, we had our first experience of a V–1 or 'doodle-bug'. These were the robot plane/bombs the Germans launched against London after D-Day. By then Londoners knew all about them. Their basic rule was that there was nothing to fear whilst the engine kept going. That meant it was going further on. If you heard it stop, that meant you were possibly in the area where it would explode. We knew nothing of that. The sirens had gone but we stood our ground on the platform, still hoping for a seat. Then we heard the quaint puttering noise of the doodle-bug and the A/A fire directed at it. Then it stopped. That did not seem significant until one realised that in a flash one had become alone in standing on the station; everyone had taken cover at the rush. I contemplated crawling under the tank engine which had pulled a train into the other platform, in the silly way one does at such moments but it was far too late. A massive explosion down the street announced that it had not landed on us. As quickly as the station had emptied of people, it was full again.

Arthur's Seat on a gloomy morning is a gladsome sight, if Edinburgh is your destination and you have stood for nine or ten hours in the corridor. It was more of a joy to hear the American comment from within the compartment: 'Say, that must be Ben Nevis.' 'Who's he, a Jewish tailor?' Thence the train to DoniB; straight to Monday's work. What a weekend!

Thereafter, work continued normally and apart from evenings when I had duties such as 'Officer of the Day' or Frances an equivalent WRNS duty, we had the evenings and weekends to enjoy together. There was not of course a lot one could do in those parts. Neither of us could invite the other to our quarters or mess for a drink, meal or just chat when we did not feel like going 'ashore' and spending money. The main options were just to walk – less practicable of an evening as the winter approached – or go to the Star in Aberdour, the occasional film in Dunfermline or the rarer big splash of an evening in Edinburgh. The Departmental transport was subject to strict journey logs being kept and therefore virtually unavailable for 'jollies' unless one got the Commander's permission, which could not be sought too often. Thus you were much confined to where the railway could take you (Inverkeithing or Edinburgh) or the very limited local buses (Aberdour, Dunfermline or Inverkeithing). More often than not, there was no bus back from Aberdour or Inverkeithing so there was a long walk home.

One of our favourite ways of spending Sunday afternoons was to hold shooting matches against each other. We controlled both weapons and their ammunition, so it was easy to draw rifles, tommy guns, revolvers and shotguns and go on to the range for an 'all weapons competition' against each other. With everything except the shotgun on clay pigeons, Frances won consistently although I was rated as an above average shot, so these little competitions became all too predictable as to outcome.

We managed to get a weekend leave to go to Sandy's wedding to Jean Haslegrave as I was his best man. That was a slightly happier encounter with the Mackenzie family than the first, although you will appreciate that that is not saying much. My mother was still adamant that we should wait until we had known each other a great deal longer before we should begin to contemplate matrimony. It was Frances' first encounter with Aunty Peggy (Lady Ramsden), with whom she got on famously. The Ramsdens lived fairly close to Painthorpe, the Haslegrave home, and were even longer standing friends of the Haslegraves than of the Mackenzies. It had in fact been through the Ramsdens that Sandy and Jean had first met. Frances and Peggy had a pleasant tiddly time mixing up the wine cup until it tasted just right. To my recollection, that was our only escape from Donibristle until our own wedding came up.

In mid-December came the Admiralty's hammer blow with the signal: 'Lt. HCB Mackenzie to proceed on embarkation leave January 13th 1945 prior to taking appointment of AGO to MONAB No . . .: joining details to be promulgated.' MONABs were a new concept for the Pacific War; it was assumed this would be a war involving the invasion, one by one, of the vast string of islands across the Pacific which the Japs had occupied. A

MONAB was a mobile naval air base, all the personnel and equipment for an operational air-strip on a desert island would be embarked in transport ships. After capture of an island, we would nip in and set up a defended airfield from which Squadrons could operate. It was the worst of all worlds, frighteningly operational without the joys of sea life with the Navy. It was obviously a Pacific appointment and in those days no-one posted there in the Navy expected to be back before the Japanese War was over and it really looked like lasting for years and years.

With this bleak outlook, Frances bravely thought it would be better to get married before I went and (very selfishly, I suppose) I agreed. Thus, with only my embarkation leave for a honeymoon, we must marry in January and not waste precious leave time going to England for the wedding. So we fixed to get the station Padre to marry us in Aberdour Episcopalean Church. Only Frances' youngest sister Elizabeth was able to get there from the Purkis side. She had never travelled so far and it was a journey of much angst for her. She arrived starving, having been too nervous to seek food in transit. For the Mackenzies, Granny made the trip in spite of her reservations about the marriage, Ian came as best man and Jean came. Sandy, now in the RAMC, had been sent to India at the end of their honeymoon. (His daughter Anna was about a year old before he got back and saw her for the first time.) Granny accepted the *fait accompli* pretty philosophically at the time and was embarrassingly generous with presents.

She came up the night before and stayed that night and the one after at the North British Hotel in Edinburgh. Jean and Ian, as well as Elizabeth, came up the morning of the wedding. On the wedding eve, old Rombulow-Pearce insisted on dining Granny, Frances and me in her quarters. We anticipated a terrifying evening, but, such was the old girl's tact and charm as a hostess, it all went off very easily.

We never got any decent photographs of the wedding. I had asked for the services of an excellent peacetime press photographer who was an NCO in the Photographic Section. No, said the section officer, for an occasion of this importance, he must do it all himself. His efforts were more useless than any amateur's could have been. The station treated it as a big event; it was rare for two officers at the same establishment to get married on that station and this was the first time in all naval history that a Gunnery Officer had married his 'Gunner'. It is the custom in ships and shore bases that when a member of the ship's company is getting married, a ribboned laurel wreath is flown from the masthead. In our case, two of them were flown side by side.

The Saturday morning of the day was an ordinary working morning, so I did not get away from the Armoury until about midday. Quick change into my best uniform and buckle on the borrowed sword and a dash to the church with Ian. He had arrived at the main gate resplendent in his Scots Guards cap and caused quite a stir.

'What a pretty hat,' said Puckey.

My only clear memories of the service were Rutherford's singing and my embarrassment when I got the tip of my sword scabbard stuck in the church's central heating grating in the floor. Granny reported to me after her shame at the large hole in my shoe sole, presented for all to see as we knelt.

The wedding reception was kindly provided by the WRNS officers in their mess and very good it was. They also conjured up a magnificent tiered cake of peacetime quality. They had saved ingredients and arranged for some to be flown down from Orkney. Frances' sister Nancy had sent the icing sugar and marzipan as a wedding present from Swanage.

The only problem was that we were only allowed officer and civilian friends in this mess, so could not include our excellent petty officers. Many had made presents; nearly all had been specially nice to Frances since she had joined the department. They truly took her into their hearts. This was evident from the frequency with which, illegally, they gave her 'sippers' and occasionally 'gulpers'. Sippers is when you give a friend a swig at your daily rum tot as a mark of respect or thanks. Gulpers is when you take this to the extreme of handing over all, or the best part of, the issue. The POs quite understood that the customs of the service prevented their attendance at the official reception, so they mounted an unofficial one in their mess to run concurrently, which bride, groom and best man also had to go to. Quite a riot. They were determined to get us all pissed before we could escape. Frances and I got away in just reasonable order, leaving Ian 'to the wolves'. Puckey nicked his 'pretty hat' and would not let him have it back until he had had another for the road, and another, and another . . .

He was in a sorry state but bravely acting sober as he turned up for the 'going away', after which he had to escort his mother and one sister-in-law back for the night in Edinburgh and his other sister-in-law on to the train back to Wimborne. The bride, of course, had had to be married in uniform and officially we had to go on honeymoon in uniform, so there was no changing. The Captain, who had given Frances away in the absence of her parents, had authorised a station car to take us as far as Carlisle, well on our way to Keswick, where we had chosen to go. The choice for honeymooning sites was limited. Keswick was not too far away and we believed there was a good chance of being snowed up there, thereby getting one or two extra days without getting into trouble.

At Carlisle we went for a snack at the station hotel before catching the Keswick train. In those days there was a branch line from Penrith to Keswick. There I found I that I had set forth without any money. In the rush to change before the ceremony, I had left my wallet in my working uniform! Luckily, as old Captain Nicholson had escorted Frances down to church he had apologised for not having got her a present, so had slipped her a five pound note (quite generous for those days). This proved enough to keep us going for the first two days, when my wallet arrived through the post. It is interesting to recall that in spite of their loss of manpower to the forces, the Post Office maintained an inland service very nearly as good as the pre-War service. One would have been surprised, for example, if a letter posted in the afternoon in London did not arrive first post the next morning at Donibristle. All for one and a half pence, or o.6 of new pence.

The day of departure from Keswick brought snow but unfortunately not enough to stop our afternoon bus for Carlisle getting out on time. We were infuriated to read in the next day's press that Keswick had been cut off a matter of hours later.

It was cold, snowing and miserable when we got off the train in the late evening at Inverkeithing to seek a taxi or bus to Aberdour where we had a room booked at Mrs Leslie's boarding house. The minutes were indeed now running out towards my departure to the Far East. Frances would have to stay on, of course, in her post as 'Gunner' at Donibristle. Very late we got to Mrs Leslie's, too late for her to feed us. She did make a cup of tea to fortify us for the very cold bedroom. There was, she said, a message for me, sent down from Donibristle. We could not get more depressed, so opened that night what we expected to be the details of my marching orders.

Compliments of Captain Nicholson; following signal received from Admiralty yesterday: 'Further to No . . . ref: appointment Lt. HCB Mackenzie to MONAB stop. This appointment now cancelled, repeat cancelled, Stop. Mackenzie to continue in present appointment at Donibristle until further orders.'

20. Happier days at Kirkcaldy, July 1945

No-one could have gone to bed famished, weary and in near sub-zero temperature as happily as we did. But as I drifted off to sleep an awful thought occurred to me. I would have to phone Granny with the glad tidings. Would she really believe that I had had a posting which had been cancelled, or think the whole thing had been a ruse to get round her objections and hurry on our wedding? Frankly, I never felt sure I had the answer to that one in all the years after the event.

When she said goodbye as we left the wedding, she was not expecting to see me again for quite some time and, after Kenneth, was probably fearing to some extent the worst. So, when I did phone the good news, I think relief that I would be shore-based at home for some time longer overcame any suspicions she may have had, so far as her reaction went. She was also in a pretty euphoric state because the news had just come through that she was going to be a Granny (Jean was in the club) and also that Sandy had arrived safely in India. So, after all, all seemed well.

Thus, we took up life again at Donibristle much as it had been before, so far as daytime activity was concerned. Out of hours, it was very different. We assumed the formal 'Living Ashore' status married personnel were allowed, so no longer had the wearisome business of walking back to Fordell or Donibristle, as the case may be, after an evening in the Star. At the Star, we continued to be allowed to use the Scott's own sitting room whenever we wanted to be quiet on our own. The only horror was Mrs Leslie's, but more of that in the next chapter.

Chapter 31

Donibristle Life

A T THIS DISTANCE, it is quite difficult to remember even how the daily routine went. It was something like this. 'Call the Hands' would be blown over the Tannoy at around 6.30 or 6.45; breakfast would be dished up in the various messes and the Wardroom at around 7.30. Considering that it was wartime, this was a pretty substantial meal for officers and men alike. Once a week I was Officer of the Day, so had to walk the ratings' mess decks at each meal, officially to see if there were any complaints. Thus I was familiar with their fare. Always porridge, sometimes cornflakes as an extra option, bacon or banger (sausage) with canned tomato or baked beans, scrambled dried egg. The last, cooked in bulk, was an acquired taste, mostly disgusting. Kept hot it congealed to a crumbly pale yellow mass (rather like the curds at the beginning of cheesemaking to look at), floating in the water which had drained from it. It tasted like the cardboard cartons in which it had been supplied. Every blue moon there might be a real egg, glorified by the euphemism 'fresh egg'.

At 8.00 'Fall In' would blow. The entire station would fall in by Divisions (Departments) in front of the flagstaff. At the last minute, the Captain would turn up, but sometimes Cod Cooper stood in for him, and, to the accompaniment to 'Colours' on the bugle, the White Ensign would be broken out to watch over our day. 'Fall out the Roman Catholics' and 'Off Caps' followed, with a couple of mumbled prayers from the Padre. 'On Caps', remuster the RCs, Divisions double march to their places of work. Our lot would double down to the Armoury where, usually, Petty Officer Charnley would read off the allocations of work for the morning, which could take our chaps and chapesses all over the airfield. Thus, work proper started at around 8.30. Around 11.00 the Tannoy would go again. 'Stand Easy'. 'Hands to place spit-kids'. At workshops and offices tea was served from trolleys or self-brewed by the connoisseurs. Spit-kid was Nelsonian for ash-trays; he had no fags so had to chew tobacco and spit. Then work on until 'Hands to Secure' at about 12.30. Quarter of an hour later, 'Up

Spirits'. This was undoubtedly one of the day's high points, so far as morale was concerned, but the pipe actually meant to get fell in on the Quarterdeck for the daily issue of spirits – the rum ration. Then at 1.00 'Cooks to the Galley'. Lunch for the ratings would be a stew with spuds and greens or roots (usually turnips), followed by a suet pudding with jam or treacle, or (less popular) stewed dried fruit or rhubarb and custard. In the Wardroom, we started with a soup, had a roast or something such as liver or a chop and then a rather less rough and ready sort of pudding before cheese and biscuits. The difference may seem unfair, but we had to pay for our meals, the ratings got theirs free. If they preferred and had the cash, they had also the option of going to the NAAFI canteen, where they could buy such things as bacon and egg or chop and chips, or that favourite, fish and chips. It was, though, much more an option they took up at the evening meal.

At around 2.00 p.m. 'Fall In' again, this time outside the departmental place of work. Needless to say, at each fall in the roll was called; there was little opportunity for skyving. Another 'Stand Easy' at 3.45 p.m. and at about 6 p.m. 'Hands Dismiss'. Those in the Duty part of Duty Watch would have to get their evening meal quickly after this because before 7.00 p.m. they would be reporting for their duties, such as Guard duty at the gates, manning the anti-aircraft guns (there were still the occasional enemy aircraft alerts) and other station requirements. They would then be on duty all night, as would also the officers given rota duties, but this is not to say that on a normal night they would miss more than a few hours' sleep.

The rest of the station could take a more leisurely approach. Ratings did not have to rush for their 'Tea' in the messdecks and, if staying aboard, would probably go after that to the NAAFI for a pint and a game of darts or 'shovers'. One or two nights a week, a film would be shown in the NAAFI and there was a dance there at least once a week. For these items, in the big hall of the NAAFI, officers were allowed to attend. The dances were very much just station affairs, devoid of outside civilians. However, there were enough WRNS on the station for there to be a reasonable balance of the sexes at the dances. It was all to the traditional style of the time – 'Tum to Tum' – to the music of the amateur self-selected band of the station. Much beer was consumed and there was much groping outside in the murkier corners of the station. One of the better celebrated examples of the latter was when Captain Nicholson returned from a dinner ashore. As he drove into the garage at his house, what should he see but Lt. Commander

Barrington screwing a Wren against the back of his garage. Being the diplomat he was, he did dip his headlights but this barely reduced his illumination of the scene. 'Barrington,' he said later, over a whisky in the wardroom, 'I want it clearly understood that the garage is for me to park my car in, not for you to park your organ.'

For the officer, the day had embellishments over and above the above. At lunchtime, the bar was naturally open, so a few stimulants could be put away before eating. As Donibristle, with its resident communications Squadron, was the sort of crossroads in the air-ferrying game which Heathrow is today for international civilian flying, one frequently met old pals in transit at lunchtime or of an evening. The result was a tendency to over-indulge in the joy of reunion, so that one could return to afternoon duty a little 'tired' as *Private Eye* would say. As examples, Prangle Pike, Colonel Brown and Stuart Allison were all my guests at various lunches and thus helped to give Frances the impression, after her sober WRNS officer's mess lunches, that I was a drunk in need of reformation. How good of her to devote her life to that! Being Officer of the Day was a repeating bore. Really it involved getting around doing for the Commander the things within his field of responsibility which he did not have time to pursue thoroughly. Additional to the rounds of messdecks at meals, already described, one did rounds of all the ratings' huts to ensure adequate standards of cleanliness. One took the preliminary stages of the morning Colours Parade. One was responsible for a round of the ratings' quarters before lights out to ensure that all was peace and that no-one was so drunk as to be a risk to himself or his messmates. One was responsible for the evening changing of the guard and for the conduct of the overnight guard. On the four or five days a week when there was no Commanders' Requestmen and Report, the Officer of the Day had to take a similar session. This meant dealing with all the cases he judged to be within his powers and deferring the others to the next Commander's Report. First the parade took the cases of requestment, usually requests for compassionate leave because of family disasters (death or illness at home, or being bombed out, being the most common) or for promotion when the qualifications had been obtained. Then came the offenders: mainly those involved in minor disciplinary breaches such as returning drunk from shore leave, but they sometimes involved more serious things like thieving or striking a senior officer. You got to know your men but it was always a horrid job to have to dish out pretty heavy punishment for minor transgressions on one hand or to have to probe deeply into the private affairs of requestmen in order to judge the validity of their requests for leave. There were plenty of men very capable of 'pulling the wool' and one had to avoid having the entire Navy away on compassionate leave in wartime!

On Saturdays, the routine was varied by the fact that there was morning work only for all except those on Duty Watch who were on all day. After 'Up Spirits', the rest were free. On Sundays, the morning parade was smarter – everyone in best uniform – full mattins following 'Fall Out RCs', held in the canteen if, as was usual, the weather was inclement. After that, all except the duty part of Duty Watch were free to go ashore. Frances and I usually walked, if we were not having one of our shooting competitions. We tended to walk in the Fordell grounds or along the seashore from Aberdour, but one day, as we looked over the railway bridge, inspiration struck. The communal sitting room for lodgers at Mrs Leslie's was very cold. Only a quarter of a scuttle of coal was provided per day. If the lodgers stoked a bit more than her measley rate, it merely meant that the supply ran out in early evening. Looking over the bridge, we could see lovely lumps of coal which had fallen from the locomotive tenders to lie on the track. We dashed back to Mrs Leslie's and picked up our hand luggage bags. There were no trains on Sundays, so we could safely walk the tracks, filling our bags with coal as we went. There was no profit for our effort with the wily Mrs. Leslie. By the second time she came back to stoke that evening we had a real man sized fire going and the room was getting tolerably warm.

'I see ye have yere own coal,' says she and promptly picks up her scuttle and carts it off!

It was all very well for her; she lived in her warm kitchen and slept in the double bed compartment behind the kitchen range, which was common for Scottish houses of that date. Also, in the bed she had for comfort her No 1 lodger, Mr Ross, a ghastly old creep who had taken over the 'Mrs Leslie warmer' duties when Mr Leslie was called to higher things some years previously. Though what could be higher than that compartment!

I do not recall much in the way of sporting activities at Donibristle. We played a few rugger matches against local teams. Compared with rugger from *Indomitable* or Whale Island, though, it was pretty poor stuff. On one occasion, the Sports Officer persuaded me to box in his local competition. If he could get some officers to box, he thought, it should be easier to drum up rating competitors. In those days, officially, officers were only meant to box against fellow officers. Two days before the event, he confessed that he could not find me an officer opponent. Would I mind boxing a warrant officer, especially if he were quite a bit lighter than me? I said OK, so long as the man was not a good boxer. I had not boxed since school, where I had in fact won the heavyweight title, in spite of my lack of inches. He promised that.

Come the night, I was introduced to my opponent in the canteen changing room. He seemed rather young for a seaman warrant officer, but quite a tidy bit smaller than me. As we changed, I was a bit apprehensive to see how well muscled he was – I had by then got quite unfit and soft. When he donned a PTI's (Physical Training Instructor) vest, I began to realise that Butcher, our well-named Sports Officer, had perhaps put me in a trap. PTIs do not achieve Warrant Officers' rank unless they are a bit special. Come the first round, it took no time for me to realise that I had never been in a ring with anyone so fast; he scored points off me all the time. My only encouragement was the realisation that his punches were not hard enough to be likely to knock me out, whereas when I did land one of mine he was visibly, if only instantaneously, stopped. I could not hope to win on points but, given a bit of luck, I might get a knock-out. Such are the thoughts that optimism is made of. He ran further ahead of me on points in the second round but again I was encouraged by the few thumps I landed on him to still prolong the belief that I could deal the mortal blow in the last round and recover my dignity. My sight had been a bit troubled at the end of the second by a small split he had opened above my left eye. To my annoyance, the referee called the doctor to look at this cut in the interval and he said I was unfit to continue, so I never got my chance to land the knock-out. Looking back on it, I doubt that I ever would have done, but I was angry with the quack. I remarked to the opponent afterwards that he seemed to know a bit about boxing. Oh aye, he said, he had been amateur champion of Scotland at his weight before the War! After that I went to meet my fiancée as she then was.

'Fancy being beaten up by a little chap like that,' said she contemptuously.

My only other sporting effort whilst there was a row in the officers' whaler in the Rosyth Fleet Regatta. The whaler is a funny boat, nice to sail, but rigged for some strange reason known only to Nelson, for rowing by three oars on the port side and only two on the other. To be on the two-oared side was thus quite hard work and I was one of the unlucky two. The course was a mile and a quarter long and we were fools enough to get into the finals, which meant three races in the afternoon. I just cannot remember whether we won or came second. I think we narrowly won. Anyway, I have never been so tired. The whaler is a fullblown seaboat; our times for the course were much the same as were achieved in shell fours at Eastbourne, albeit round a lot of steep curves. Anyway, it felt good to be in a shore-based crew and to beat those from the ships in harbour.

Ships visiting Rosyth tended to provide a fairly constant stream of old friends to visit. It was generally accepted that those in ships with duty free drink in the Wardroom were better set up to entertain than those of us ashore. For them, a pub sized double gin cost 2*d*., rather less than 1p. In our Wardroom, it cost around 8*d*. so friends afloat took pity on those ashore. *Biter*, a sister ship of *Archer*, was in Rosyth for a long time. She was there for repairs, having made history by being hit by a torpedo on a Murmansk convoy and not actually blowing up. I knew her AGO well, but I cannot now remember his name. It was on a joint visit to her, when he was transiting through Donibristle, that Richard Meakin gave me his demonstration of how a bottle of duty free Johnnie Walker would slip into his aluminium leg and thus through the customs, which we always had to clear coming ashore. Richard, you will remember, was my first pilot in *Indomitable*.

Biter was in for so long that most of her crew had been transferred to other duties. She was thus available and used as a barrack ship for the Russian crews who came to Rosyth to take over the battleship *Royal Sovereign* and four old submarines which the Navy presented to Russia. What a well-named ship to give to the Communists! They were an extraordinary mob, although they did not surprise our friends who had been at Archangel. The discipline was quite mad; they even went through the dangers of saluting officers between decks. It was very difficult to get used to returning salutes when so unexpected below and they absolutely crashed to attention to salute like guardsmen, even if you were passing at the opposite end of the hangar. Officers and men, watched by their mates in the OGPU (or was it KGB by then?) avoided any social contact with the few remaining British sharing the ship with them, which was most peculiar in a relatively small ship. Their officers drank at such a rate, preferring scotch, that an arrangement had to be made that no Russian officer could have more than two scotches in an evening. Supplies were not unlimited to ships in harbour and scotch was short. They could and did have as much as they wanted of any other drinks. I remember one junior officer going up to the bar. 'Big glass,' he said. When that was there: 'Three gin, now two vodka, now four cognac, now a spoon.' He carefully stirred the mixture and then scoffed the lot. 'Again,' he said. After three goes at this potion, he went off to his cabin and returned with an ancient windup gramophone and sat listening to some rather marvellous Red Army Choir records. Then back to the cabin with the phonograph and up to the bar for one more of his long mixes. Again, the fourth went straight down the hatch. Then off he went to dine in the Wardroom, sober as a judge. After dinner, one more of his little drinkies and off to bed.

Discipline came hard in wartime Russia, maybe in peacetime too. They had to be told to desist from thrashing their sailors for minor offences whilst in British ships. It is said that when the British Commander of *Royal Sovereign* took his Russian opposite number through our daily and weekly routines for running the ship, the first Russian question when he had finished was, 'On which day, Commander, do you carry out the weekly executions?'

This may not be as apocryphal as it sounds. I know from first hand of an incident at Archangel. When a British convoy arrived, having fought through all the way with considerable losses, it was important to unload and get off home as quickly as possible without too many more losses from German air-raids on the port. With only a few berths, ships had to wait their turn at moorings. Those unloading had mainly to use their own derricks. It was also in the Russian interest to turn them round fast; the port would not be bombed for so long and cargo losses from raids would be reduced.

When the first ship of the convoy my informant was in had berthed, Russian sentries were placed at the bottom of the gangways. At this ship, the sentries would let no-one off, so they could not get a crewman onto the wharf to guide the donkeymen on the derricks, so off-loading could not begin. Before long a Russian Colonel turned up and cursed the British Captain for not getting on with unloading. He was told the reason. 'Bloody fool,' he said, 'He is going beyond his orders.' He went to the bottom of the gangway, drew his revolver and shot the sentry; unloading then began quite smartly.

We were amazed to find them much more like automatic animals than pre-War anti-Soviet propaganda ever led us to believe, and we had by then had a few years' propaganda in favour of our gallant ally.

One of the more momentous ship visits was when *Archer* came in to Rosyth. Hearing that I had got engaged, they insisted that Frances be brought aboard for dinner. They were determined to get her drunk. I was kept busy one end of the ante-room whilst she was chatted up and lubricated at the other. It was a great credit to her stamina that she walked ashore quite steadily, although I do not think she remembered doing it! Apart from a fine reputation gained with *Archer* and the devil of a hangover, she also came away with a rather sore ear. M'Neilly had been far from sober at the end and, taking his leave of Frances on the quarterdeck, his baser instincts had rather taken over. She was lucky to be dragged away from him before he had chewed the ear right off!

Perhaps the saddest visit to a ship in Rosyth was the one to the *Indefatigable*. She was the newest Fleet carrier of the time, even bigger than *Indomitable*, having two full length hangar decks. Our host was 'Colonel' Lee, my erstwhile boss at Inskip, newly appointed to her as AGO. This was her last call in UK before sailing to the Pacific to join the Allied (mainly American) Fleet, then in close and fairly continuous combat with the Japanese. From the start of the War, he had hardly seen his wife, and had not met his first child until he came ashore for the few months he did have at Inskip in 1943/4. Now, with a second child on the way, he was off for the very indefinite future. He was sick to the teeth and could not hide his feelings. It made us appreciate our luck as mere newly weds still to be together on shore. I never heard what became of him. Whilst *Indefatigable* did come home at the end of the War, she had sustained her share of Kamikaze hits and accumulated some casualties.

It was not just luck that we were continuing to serve together on the same station, whereas it was normal naval practice to post one or the other if husband and wife were on the same establishment. Nicholson had had to report our 'respective' weddings but he put one of us down as being HMS *Merlin* and the other as RNARY *Donibristle*, hoping that as a result we would escape the official eye. He seemed to have been successful.

The worst happening in the department in our time was caused by the dreadful Torpedo Officer, Wilkinson, whom I have already mentioned. He came into my office one morning like the cat who had swallowed the cream. 'I have just put your Leading Air Mechanic Wade and Air Mechanic Watson on Commander's Report. I found them smoking beside No.5 Bomb Store.' I sent for the men to get at the truth. Both were such reliable men that they must know that smoking around bomb stores was one of the most heinous crimes in the book. They explained that when Stand Easy came, they went outside the store, which they had been sweeping, and sat on the bank about twenty yards from it and smoked. They did not reckon that from the smoking viewpoint No.5 counted as a bomb store, because all it had in it was unfused practice bombs. As these are inert, they certainly had a point in logic. When they came before Cod Cooper, I did not raise this point on their behalf, knowing that the seriousness of the charge left Cod no choice but to send them on to the Captain's Report. Primed before that, Wilkinson would have cooked up all sorts of arguments to put up against it.

When I did raise it in front of Nicholson, Wilkinson weighed in as quick as a flash that a bomb store was always a bomb store whatever it had in it. The rule must be rigidly upheld because ratings could not be expected to differentiate between explosive and non-explosive filled bombs. I commented that these two men should know perfectly well by their training what a practice bomb was filled with. Quick as a flash, Nicholson asked Wade what they did contain. 'Titanium tetrachloride, sir,' he said, 'This is an inert chemical which is harmless.' The Captain asked how the filling worked, if inert. I explained that the detonator, when exploded in fused bombs, had enough power always to burst the bomb body. In air, the chemical evaporates very rapidly, making an inert and non-toxic white cloud. Wilkinson, by now way out of his depth, argued that anything which evaporated rapidly must *per se* be either a fire or an explosive risk. The Captain, of course, did not know which of his 'technical experts' to believe. He took the easy way out.

'I consider that a bomb store is a bomb store even when empty and thus you have breached regulations of court-martial gravity. I accept that you felt that the store was safe and will thus deal with you summarily and not send you to court-martial unless you request it. Seven days cells; first three on hard lying.'

There was a sort of logic about naval prisons and confinement to cells. Life at sea for a rating in a small ship or submarine in bad weather was extremely arduous. In wartime, the discomforts of it, cold, often wet through, rarely any hot food, long Watches, threat of danger, could go on for very long periods. For that matter, it was little better for their officers. Punishment, it was felt, must be even more hard to bear. Otherwise the men would have an incentive to offend so as to get the relative comfort of a sentence to a shore prison or cells in a shore base. As their Divisional Officer, I was the only one allowed to visit Wade and Watson in their cells, other than the Padre. I had never been around such places and I was appalled. It was the middle of a Fifeshire winter. Each was in solitary confinement in an unheated cell with room only for the 'bed', a two foot wide space the length of the bed and a bucket for 'natural functions'. The bed was planks nine inches off the deck, with a 6-inch by 3-inch by 12-inch block of wood for a pillow. The only clothes they were allowed were vest and pants and the cotton duck uniform ratings wore for work in the tropics. At night they were also given one blanket. Whilst on 'hard lying', their sole rations for the day were one quart of cold water and a quarter of a small loaf of bread. I think one of the more awful things about it was that the average rating in for the War only had never been told what he could expect if he got 'cells'. I am absolutely sure the worst for these two, other than perhaps the cold, was the terrible shock that the Navy could actually treat people like this. They were two very good ratings who both knew and knew that I knew that any offence they had committed was a nit-picking technical one. They could not help seeing that I was virtually reduced to tears; maybe my sympathy was some help, but it could do nothing for their physical comfort.

I went to the Wardroom for a drink and there met Wilkinson. I asked him if he had ever seen men enduring hard lying and he admitted that he had not, but, he blustered, out of his long naval connection he knew quite well what would be involved. How, I asked, could he be so pleased with himself for engineering two excellent ratings into this plight for a purely technical offence. 'You're too soft,' he said, 'If you go on like this, we shall never get your division obeying regulations like the rest of us do.' Cod Cooper overheard and came over as Wilkinson moved off. 'This sort of thing happens from time to time in the Navy, Hector, do not take it too much to heart.' He explained the Navy's reason for making the punishment tough. 'But you mustn't blame the Andrew for a case like this. Most times the officers who bring the charges know enough about the rigours of punishment only to charge when they see real fault. Likewise, the officers who dish out the sentences. Here you have the accident that both those involved were wartime amateurs who had no idea what they were actually doing.' That night, I later discovered, Wade and Watson were accidentally issued with two blankets each. I am sure Cod organised that although in no way was he empowered to do so.

Things got better after the hard lying. They were re-issued with serge uniforms and jumpers, got a palliasse to sleep on with a proper pillow and had ordinary issue meals. I expressed sympathy to them both when they returned to duty but by then they were quite philosophical about it. Wade, who had suffered the more because he had inevitably also lost his Killick, said, 'It's almost enough to make you give up smoking, isn't it, sir?'

One of our great days was a royal visit. This was by Princess Marina, the recently widowed Duchess of Kent. The Duke had been lost when in transit in an RAF aircraft. It was perhaps more of an occasion for Frances than me, in that Princess Marina was an honorary Commandant of the WRNS and was visiting to see what our WRNS were up to. Frances paraded all our girls for her and then, with me in the background, took her all round our armoury workshops. All I recall were her staggeringly good looks and my surprise at the very foreign accent with which she spoke. She had married into our royals from the Greek royal family.

I had never ventured into such high society and remember a great nervousness lest I commit some awful breach of protocol. We were still in the days of expecting our royalty to be very straight-laced, as had been the case right up to the War. The King and Queen had done a lot to break this down, particularly on 'walk-abouts', visits to bombed cities and visits to the Forces. Even Queen Mary, rumour had it, had got quite informal and had even gone so far on occasion as to give servicemen a hitch in her Daimler. Marina was certainly very relaxed on her visit.

I suppose the most formal occasions I had attended at Donibristle in the earlier days there were one or two balls at the C-in-C Rosyth's residence. I think it was Alison Casement, who had many naval connections in high places, who had taken me along as escort. It was a huge stately home with a terrace overlooking the Firth and was a marvellous site for a formal ball, rather like the hunt ball of one of the more fashionable hunts, I would imagine. There was much Dashing White Sergeant, Stripping the Willow, Eightsomes etc. I was very glad to have had a refresher in such arts relatively recently; the Commander at Whale Island used to insist on us having such dance nights on Guest Night about every other month.

Besides our own station dances, we used to get around to others in the district. The most officer-dominated one was at the Combined Operations Headquarters at Pitreevie, nearby. It was officer-dominated purely because as a staff HQ there was a high officer/other rank ratio. I remember bringing Frances back from there after one dance when I had had quite a tankful. Still in the camp, I rounded one corner in our armoury pick-up a bit tightly, in all senses. The bit where the pick-up lorry back stuck out caught the corner of a Nissen hut. I put my foot down and neatly peeled off most of the outer skin of the hut. In spite of the noise, I managed to get out of the

Main Gates and well away before the residents got after me. There was another dreadful night when, making unauthorised use of the pick-up, I was taking Frances back to Fordell, before we were married. Somehow we ran out of road in the drive and stuck in the ditch. She had to hoof it back to be in in time. I took half the night extracting the vehicle. Do bear in mind though that night driving was no piece of cake: vehicles had hardly any lights; you had to know where you were going and drive more by memory than vision, if you wanted to make any pace. But it was better to be cold sober.

One of my activities was akin to an undertaker's job. In wartime, there was no messing about taking corpses of servicemen back to their home areas for burial. Basically, they were 'put under' in the nearest cemetery to where they had pegged out. They did have, however, a full Service funeral parade from their own Service. Around the Edinburgh area were many small airfields where from time to time a naval aircrew would come adrift. A frequent site for coming unstuck was Drem, on the south shore of the Firth of Forth. It was in use for experimental proof of a new form of airfield lighting, which became known as Drem Lighting, whereby pilots could be guided in supposed safety with a minimal amount of illumination to attract enemies. Each of these funerals had to have a funeral firing party to be a Guard of Honour and fire the customary three volleys over the grave.

Starting by preparation for a Donibristle funeral, Charnley and I drilled and drilled our party until we achieved a perfection rarely seen beyond Whale Island. Our volleys (twelve hands behind Lee-Enfield rifles) cracked off as one shot. We came to be in demand for all the naval funerals in the district. It came to be quite a good outing for the lads, rather like going to a football match. We were never acquainted with the deceased, so were in no way very emotionally involved. On the way back from Drem, for example, we had two pubs fixed as ports of call for the bus or lorry. Two because that was better than one; it meant also that the two men who had drawn unlucky and had had to stay and guard the rifles at the first stop got their tankful at the second. It became quite a competitive business to get into the party, so we never lacked volunteers for the rehearsal drills or enthusiasm on parade. It came a bit expensive for me, towards whom everyone of the twelve (and Charnley and the drummer taken along to blow the Last Post) looked for the first round.

Married life starts as bliss even in wartime and so did ours. This did not stop us noticing that with Mrs Leslie's meanness and the lack of comforts in her house, she was doing her unconscious damnedest to de-bliss our situation. A slight bone of contention arose on our first working day staying with her. She asked what time we would be back from Doni-B for her 'tea' and explained that she always provided a nice 'Finney' for her lodgers at 'tea'. Flabbergasting my wife, because neither of us really had the nerve to stand up to this formidable woman, who was perfectly capable of throwing us out into the snow, I announced that I was not able to eat Finney. My loathing of it since prep school days was such that I would venture Victoria Cross deeds to avoid it. Thereafter daily my dear wife would be served her Finney on return from work, whilst for me the changes were rung with such delights as bacon and egg, liver, kidneys, meat pies and so on.

With that and the incident of our railway coal, we devoted all the free hours which God gave to the impossible task of finding somewhere better to live. Eventually we succeeded; a Mrs Lochtie, widow of a local forester for some twelve years, decided to take us in. Hers was no peacetime summer boarding house. We had our own bedroom and the use of her bathroom and kitchen. We were to cater for ourselves, retrieving our ration books from Mrs Leslie, who had kept them. With a friendly butcher in the village, we did quite well. He had haggis, for example, which was free of rationing cards and he told us sassenachs how it should be cooked. We grew quite fond of it. At least Frances did not have to face her daily Finney any more.

So that we would not interfere with her arrangements, we asked Mrs Lochtie early on when she would be likely to be wanting the bathroom. The answer was that she had no use for it. Since her husband had died, she had felt 'no able' to take a bath. Never did a man's decease have such catastrophic effect on the widow, except perhaps in the case of sutti in India. We were later to discover that hair-washing and cutting, foot washing and most forms of personal hygiene had all been brought to an abrupt end by Mr Lochtie's departure. It was perhaps just as well for her by no means intense social life that she dwelt on the lee side of the village in respect of the prevailing wind.

Perhaps it was lucky that we only had wintertime experience of cohabitation with her. So far as I can remember, so long as you took a deep breath before traversing the room in which she stayed day and night, the pong was not too stifling. It could be that long exposure to the atmosphere of Judy had reduced our olefactory sensitivities. I think our main problem there was with the bed, presumably the original Lochtie matrimonial couch. On arrival, we had been introduced to it as the greatest treat in store, a real feather bed. I would imagine that it had been made from the carefully gathered feathers of a contemporary pterodactyl, which had been working themselves into inextricable lumps for ever after. If it had been bliss for a forester, that could only have been because prior to it he had only slept on oak chips.

Whilst we were there, I got what seemed a marvellous offer. Based on the Donibristle station was a unit which operated very independently of it. They were almost a law unto themselves, called the 'Salvage Unit'. Equipped like a mountain rescue squad, but also with several 'Queen Marys' (the long articulated lorries with a well in the deck for transporting aircraft), their job was to go off anywhere in the wilds of Scotland and recover the remains of any Fleet Air Arm aircraft which might have crashed. Similarly, they went down to the docks and fetched back for salvage the remains of any deck-landing crashes the aircraft carriers brought home. The unit was commanded by an enterprising Lieutenant Commander called Hind. In the course of two years based at Donibristle, he had managed to build a super timber bungalow with all 'mod cons' down on the foreshore of Donibristle estate. Suddenly he got a posting to Australia and offered to sell me his bungalow, fully furnished. The price was dirt cheap; although it would stretch my means to the limit, it seemed an opportunity not to be missed. I was on the brink of buying when Cod Cooper, that wise old bird, sidled up to me in the Wardroom bar. 'Don't touch it,' he said, 'I can't tell you why now, but you'll hear in a week or two. To touch that place is to play with fire.'

In the course of the next few weeks, it all came out. The bungalow was the biggest 'rabbit' of all time! All the super teak cladding and mahogany planked flooring, the lights, heating, cookers and so on had been stolen from Rosyth dockyard. The whole thing had been put together by Salvage Unit labour; Hind had not even made any arrangement with the naval authorities, wartime tenants, or the estate owners to have the site. His method for getting the large amounts of material had been simple. All his men were in on the act. Whenever they had to send a 'Queen Mary' to the dockyard for a crash from a carrier, they first called at the Chippy's shop and loaded timber in the well of the truck (the chief Chippy was in on the act too), before loading the crash on top. When they got to the dockyard gates for the police check, they claimed that the plane had secret equipment on it and they were not allowed to remove the covering tarpaulins. Time after time they had got away with it. I believe he was court martialled after being returned from Australia, but the outcome was unknown to me.

Frances and I had one narrow escape at the dockyard gates. Lunching one day in *Biter*, our friends had loaded us up with duty-free cigarettes. We put these under the tip-up passenger seat in the front of the pick-up. At the gates the policeman asked whether we could give a man standing there in civilian clothing a lift to Inverkeithing Station. This meant Frances getting into the back, trying to keep the cigarettes out of sight as she tipped the seat to do so. Drawing up at the station, we explained to the civilian the near catastrophe he had inadvertently caused. He asked how many cigarettes we had, so we told him.

'Well you are in luck,' he said. 'I do not want to hear any more. I am in civilian clothes because I am going on leave but I am a Water Guard Officer in the Customs. If it weren't for the fact that I want to catch my train, I would do my duty and run you both in for this. Thanks for the lift – and good luck!'

Our first idea on getting married was to have a child before I got an overseas appointment. One was continually meeting the seemingly great tragedy of wartime, the fathers who never met their own children until they were a year or two old. We were terribly disappointed, I remember, when only a few days after our ten day honeymoon, the evidence arrived that we had yet 'to ring the bell'. It did not take much longer and so Frances had to report to her WRNS authorities that she was in the Club. Neither of us had anticipated the extent to which the news would be frowned upon.

Mothers-to-be could not stay on long into pregnancy as girls at work can today. What it amounted to was that as soon as it was getting impractical to wear the uniform, you were out. You did not get normal demobilisation privileges, such as a civilian clothes ration, terminal gratuity, service medals etc. You were just told you were out, almost as though you had been dismissed the Service by Court Martial. Married WRNS were justifiably very upset by this treatment, which was exactly the same as that for those entering the Club without the benefit of wedlock. In days when public services tried to protect the morality of their girls and to stand by former standards of morality, it seemed grossly unfair to treat both cases the same. It must also be remembered that in practice, a married woman had virtually no control at all of whether or not she was pregnant, beyond the Navy's traditional resort to the 'rusty knitting needle'.

Around this same time, the War had been going well enough at sea for Atlantic shipping losses to be well enough contained for petrol stocks to be rising. The first concession was to allow a petrol ration for going to work from home for armed forces personnel and civilians in very essential activities, if they could prove difficulty of doing the journey by public transport. If you were allowed the ration, then you were allowed to register the car. Granny, bless her, agreed to lend me her lovely Lanchester, laid up on chocks since the civilian petrol ration finished in about 1940. She got a garage to get it to Kings Cross, whence it was despatched to Inverkeithing. This immediately allowed us to hunt for a home more distant to the area crowded out by the Donibristle base. We found a flat in Kirkcaldy up the coast on a similar basis to Mrs Lochtie's. This time the owner was much younger, the grass widow of a man away at the War. On the whole, it was fairly comfortable, though Kirkcaldy was a dreary little industrial town. It was a matter of swapping one pong for another; Kirkcaldy's industry was linoleum. In that pre-plastic age, lino was made by combining ground cork with linseed oil and other mixers and rolling it out on a hessian backing, on which it was stoved to dry it. The whole town and all its working inhabitants stank of rank linseed.

Once she was out of the service, the days must have been dull for Frances and the Armoury was not the same without her. I had a new WRNS officer as 'Gunner', one Jean Beer, a pretty unornamental stout party of the 'jolly hockeysticks' variety. She was real dimwit, but she got Frances and me angry on one of her sharper moves. Having made the point that, like Frances, she was the only WRNS officer doing the full Gunner's job, rather than just assisting a male one, and all the others were Third Officers, she got it agreed that she should be a Second Officer. Why did we not think of that for Frances?

We did not have the use of the Lanchester for very long. With the War moving towards its end more and more obviously, civilian petrol rations would be re-instituted before long and Granny would want her car. Now that Frances was quitting the WRNS, I could commute from our Kirkcaldy nest by motorbike. So when our leave came up in the first week of May, we decided to take the car and much of our luggage back to the south. What a journey it was! As we emerged from Edinburgh, along through Portobello, the Lanchester boiled. Assuming that we must have set off short of water, we filled up the radiator and carried on. Another ten miles and we were boiling again. Eventually at a garage we learned that we needed a new water pump but at that stage of the War, no-one stocked waterpumps for Lanchesters, which had not been made for five years. It was a roaring hot day, 8 May, and stopping every half hour to find water was a major bore. At some spots, for example a garage, one could also pick up on the news (car radios had yet to be invented) on that fateful day, but after years of no petrol ration, you could probably count all the garages on the length of the Great North Road which were still open on the fingers of a hand and a half. Late that night, we arrived at Langford House. By then we had had Lanchesters in general and were swearing at this one in particular, which upset the proud owner, who was prompted to ask what we had been doing to the lovely thing to get it into such a state. Thus we missed out completely on the national celebrations of VE Day.

Frances, of course, must have had a dull time during this period, once she was out of the WRNS. Neither of us can remember how she spent the day but other than buying wool and knitting for the little one to be, one cannot think of any diversions which Kirkcaldy could have had to offer. We were counting our days. With the War over in Europe, the next appointment for me must be expected soon and now the odds were heavily stacked on a Pacific appointment. They were already transferring RAF aircrew who would not be priority cases for demobilisation into training for the Fleet Air Arm.

After leave, back to the grind of routine at Donibristle. One funny had happened in the interim. Captain Nicholson had suddenly been picked by the Admiralty to go across to Bergen to take the German surrender there. He was only there three days, but this bachelor in his late fifties returned with a Norwegian bride in her twenties whom he had never met before. She must have fallen for him in the euphoria of the German surrender. When she was later found to be more partial than most ladies to a 'cut off the joint', it was perhaps less surprising. The next Christmas, the Nicholsons went to stay in his friend Charles Massey's (the Transport Officer) home. The party broke up on Christmas Eve when Joy Massey, entering the drawing room, found that the new Mrs Nicholson had got the sixteen-year old Massey son into a legover situation on the sofa.

The new bride was something of an embarrassment to us later on. Our first child, Colin, arrived when I was at Whale Island, so we arranged the christening by Bishop Carey in the Eastbourne College Chapel. Nicholson had insisted on being a godfather, so they came along as well as half the College staff and all Granny's friends. At the meal after in the Grand, Mrs Nicholson kept on loudly to me the whole time about how lucky Frances was to have a husband who could make babies happen. Could she borrow me to show Bernard how to do it properly?

Thus, when August brought the signal, we could not believe our luck. I was to be a Staff Instructor at Whale Island as the Course Officer to an Air Gunnery Officers' Long Course.

Addendum to Chapter 31

Whilst in the later stages of my time at Donibristle, a new routine was begun which may be of interest to the social historian. To my mind it certainly reflects great credit on the width of thinking of a Government which was so intensely involved with the prosecution of the later stages of the War in Europe, plans for the relief of a starving Europe and for helping the occupied European nations emerge from a political vacuum. Not least, they were also having to plan the shift of military resources on a vast scale from the European to the eastern hemisphere.

It is well known that at around this time the famous Beveridge Report was commissioned, indicative of ability to think also about post-War domestic improvement. Also, though, they had identified a need to be getting the population at large, so much of which was in the armed forces, to start thinking again about domestic politics. For five years the nation had been led by a coalition of the three main political parties, who had worked together in such harmony that public discussion in party political terms had become a more or less forgotten habit, art or diversion, according to how you view it.

For the armed forces, it thus became decreed that officers should weekly, whenever circumstances permitted, gather groups of their men and women together for discussion groups on such matters as the social, economic and political changes desired for the post-War era. Officers were briefed that they must try to be politically neutral, seeing their role to chair the sessions by way of keeping the ball rolling and trying to provoke discussion of the various different party attitudes. The aim was perhaps to put us all in the position, when a post-War election came, where we had given the issues a little more mental attention than the vague memory of the last pre-War election, for which many of us had been too young to vote anyway (twenty-one years old).

When I had joined up in 1940, I was pretty unpolitical, but I suppose you would describe my position in today's terms, in so far as I took a position, as right on the right of Labour or probably at the wettest end of the Tories. Stupidly, I had imagined that this middle-of-the-road position was that held by the majority of my fellows.

Thus the discussions were an eye-opener to me. Every man Jack was so rabidly socialist that balanced discussion was nigh impossible. It was not so much that all, even though in most cases only as children, had been through the Great Depression; much of it was idealism to see a new system arise from the War whereby the collaboration of the classes and the sharing of hardship would continue, perhaps more so, than had been the case in the War. It was not just a desire to nationalise everything in sight. Profit itself was an eminently dirty word and a sinful sort of incentive. It was no surprise to have a bunch with this viewpoint. It was staggering to find it universal, held perhaps most intensely by Charnley, for example, son of the entrepreneur butcher. The parents' system had failed, the nation needed a brand new start.

Looking back, I am even more astonished that, after this lesson, I was still surprised when an election which came up, earlier than we had expected, in a few months, brought Labour into power in a landslide. I suppose that I, like so much of the rest of the world, would never have believed that the nation would ditch Churchill in the hour of victory. It was, after all, a more unlikely happening than ditching Thatcher immediately after the Falklands campaign.

Chapter 32

Yet Again, Back to Whale Island

W E HAD, of course, nowhere to live together in the Portsmouth area, so I had to start at 'Whaley' living 'aboard' and leave poor Frances to the tender mercies of her not at all fond mother-in-law. At Langford Place, she spent her time being sent on shopping errands and being regaled with tales of the virtues of her sister-in-law Jean, who by this time was very pregnant with Ann. Mrs Davis was a source of sympathy and one who had studied to a fine art the practice of philosophical patience in the face of the sometimes bitter tongue which Granny could wag. Frances was a quick, if not too willing, learner from this example.

At the Air Gunnery School, things had changed a bit for the better. Lt. Commander Stokes had disappeared from command, replaced by Mike Lemon, a nice enough fellow. He was not the conceited exhibitionist that Stokes had been and unlike Stokes he did not make continuous passes at Ruth Biddle, the rather yummy girl (3rd Officer) in charge of the WRNS under training. She was a 'Nice Girl' type and we all had resented Stokes' efforts to make her otherwise. Unfortunately, from my viewpoint, the second in command was Anthony Dixon, erstwhile Staff AGO to FONAS at Donibristle. How he had got here with his ignorance of the subject matter, no-one could begin to guess. He was now starting to give voice to parliamentary pretensions, hoping to land the candidature for the Tories at Brigg in Lincolnshire, where up to then his father-in-law had been the geriatric sitting member. With this end in mind Anthony had developed a Churchillian lisp and intonation of speech!

As a member joining the Island Staff, my first interview was with the Captain, Captain Agnew. He turned out to be very pleasant and said with obvious sincerity how much he welcomed having another RNVR officer on the Staff. His next posting was the very important one, in command of *Vanguard*, the very last and most super battleship the British ever built. She was completed too late to see any action, but he did take the King and Queen in her for their first post-War tour of South Africa.

My course were a nice bunch of lads. All were pilots, in contrast to my being an Observer. All were RN regulars, in contrast to my being RNVR. I suppose that by that stage of the War, Admiralty were already thinking of reserving the long and expensive courses for those who would be staying in for a career. Apparently a couple of them complained to Lemon the first day that it did not seem right to have an RNVR Course Officer. He soon put them right, pointing out that RNVRs of my seniority by then had had at least as much naval training and experience as any regular and that in fact no regular had as yet got as many marks on the course as I had done! After that it was forgotten.

It was in many ways less enjoyable than being on a course. Less carefree; all the time you were on your best behaviour and I had never had too much of that. One more or less had to spend more time in the Staff ante-room at the Wardroom than in the general one, used by those on courses, to keep up with what was going on with the running of the place. I spent the evenings urgently looking for somewhere for us to live ashore. Here I was lucky. A fellow Staff Officer was posted away and I went after the flat he rented and secured it.

This was the top floor of a lovely Georgian house in the village of Westbourne, just north of Emsworth. My elder brother Sandy was then serving as MO to a West African infantry battalion in Burma. His wife Jean did not drive in those days and generously offered us the loan of his pre-War Morris which would serve well for daily commuting to Whaley. The lower parts of the house were occupied by the landlord, a venerable retired Admiral and his wife. You would think that an Admiral would live pretty comfortably on his pension but this one seemed to be almost on the poverty line. Whilst he had a beautiful house, nicely furnished, he was always grubbing around for the last penny he could find. One of his money-making enterprises amused us. This was keeping ducks in the garden. On the garden side, they were securely fenced in but this had not been achieved so well along the stream which bordered the garden. Each evening he would round up the ducks and as often as not there would be several failing to answer their names at roll call. Anyone around would then be prevailed upon to join a search along the stream to find the defaulters. They would then be sentenced to so many days confinement to the coop but they were worse than ratings at the assimilation of discipline.

Less fun were his apple sales. He would knock on the flat door and then, as one doling out largesse, announce, ' I have selected some garden apples for you.' You were virtually obliged to take them unseen and then he would demand a price quite outrageous in comparison to the shops. By the time he had gone and you could look them over, the special selection was revealed as the most bruised, moulding and worm-eaten collection of windfalls you could find in a day's march. If we said, having learned the lesson, that we were all right for apples today, thank you, he would be furious. Enough was enough and what with a two-mile walk to the shops for a very pregnant Frances, followed by climbing the two storeys of the house each time, and trying to avoid the apple pedlar, we searched for other premises.

Luckily we found a complete house to let furnished, our first real independent home, Broadhaven, Westbourne Road, Emsworth. It was a four-bedroom house with a sizeable garden. One bedroom was locked up, supposedly containing private possessions of the landlord's. He was a sinister looking little man reminding us of Crippen, who had lived nearby. When we learned later that he was now with his fourth wife, we wondered whether he had Crippen's habits and whether every hump in the garden was a departed wife. There were two such where the Jerusalem artichokes grew particularly well. When Frances' younger sister Elizabeth came to stay, she was terrified one night, swearing that the place was haunted. Much noise had emanated from the locked room.

We were very happy there, though, and we had a particularly good neighbour across the road, Mrs Wood, who let us put the Morris 8 in her garage. She was a very game old widow living all on her own in astonishing untidiness and pong. No mean huntress, though. One day, we watched in awe as she rampaged up and down her garden with a clothes prop wielded as by a Bengal Lancer, with which she eventually did to death her quarry, a very large and agile rat.

All the time, we felt our days were numbered. The Course was progressing and at its end I could hardly expect anything else but a Far East posting after such a long sojourn in UK. Even so, it was nice to live at Broadhaven and feel at least settled until Colin, our first child, should make his appearance. For reasons I know not, his prenatal name was Angus. The situation did one thing. It made me think that a permanent naval career was no longer attractive for a married man and father-to-be. I withdrew my application to be taken into the RN at the War's end. I wonder how wise this was? How could I have guessed that the peacetime Navy which followed took their wives with them nearly everywhere and felt unusually hard done by on the rare occasions they were at sea for three weeks! I suspect that I suffered far more separation from my family in my commercial career than I would have done in the RN!

Then the general election was sprung upon us. Off went Anthony Dixon to fight the Tory corner in Brigg. His in-laws had held the seat with large majorities for so many generations that we felt that we had seen the last of him at Whaley. Little did we realise the speed at which the good burghers of Brigg could recognise a twit in double quick time. He was back amongst us having lost both the seat and his Churchillian modes of speech before we could learn how to spell Clement Atlee.

His absence on 'campaign leave', as all serving men who were Parliamentary candidates got, was the indirect cause of my getting into trouble. He had set two of the papers for my Course's mid-course examination. In one of them two of the questions were ambiguous beyond belief. Also he had instructed, 'You should attempt seven questions, three only from the first part of the paper, the other four selected from the second part.' In the second part of his paper, he had only set four questions!

Whilst my boys struggled with this, Mike Lemon was away, so the invigilator had neither him nor Dixon to refer to. Thus she came to me. The first ambiguous question started, 'State the series number of the Admiralty Fleet Order covering the loading of 500 lb GP bombs to the MkIII bomb rack.' It continued with something like, ' If the loading crew have omitted to fit one of the fuse activating links, how can the pilot manage to activate that fuse?' I set them an entirely new question. I did the same in respect of the other ambiguous one. I also made up a new question for the second part of the paper so that, as presumably the examiner had intended, the candidates did have a choice.

For my own protection, I wrote a full report to Lemon and the absent Dixon on what I had done and why. For example, on the question quoted above I said: 'I submit that there is no purpose in AGOs trying to memorise the actual series numbers of particular AFOs, when they are well indexed and it is certainly not mentioned in the curriculum that they should. The second part of the question is meaningless, because in no way can the pilot actuate the bomb fuse if no link has been inserted.'

When Lemon returned, he seemed happily to accept the action I had taken. He laughed and said that maybe Tony had had serious parliamentary matters in his mind when setting the paper. He thought that perhaps I had been a bit generous in the extra time I had allowed them to cover time lost whilst I set the new questions.

When Dixon got back, the tone quickly changed. I still never found out what strings Dixon could pull to get so much influence. Lemon sent for me again. Dixon regarded my action as one of open insubordination to a superior, calculated to bring him into disrespect with the Staff and Course members. This was a court-martial accusation, so to avoid that, I must be ready with a full justification of my action.

I thought that my defence would be easy enough but little did I know the workings of that creep's mind. Of course it mattered little if they did not know the AFO number. It carried hardly any marks if they did. The purpose was to have something they were unlikely to remember so that those who got rattled easily would get rattled. I had missed the whole point of the rest of the question. The good pilot should go round his bomb load and inspect it. Then he would see the missing link and have it rectified. Then he could activate it. I pointed out that it was not usually practicable for the pilot to do this. At night on a darkened Flight Deck, the most likely time to be bombed up, it would be impossible. Yes, said Dixon, but that is the only way he would get the fuse activated and therefore the correct answer to a reasonable question. Argument about the rest of the paper was on the same level. It waged to and fro over several weeks and it was really only the Hiroshima bomb which saved me!

Towards the end of October, we grew increasingly anxious as to when Colin was going to put in an appearance as he added day after day to his overdue score. Granny had come to stay to help with the home over the birth period and we were beginning to wonder if it would ever happen. On 2 November, we took the mother-to-be on a trip in the car. First to Bognor Regis for a large dose of ice cream, which had been the pregnancy passion (it would be as it was hard to find!) and then down the very bumpy road to Selsey Bill for a walk on the beach. The ice cream, followed by bumps in the Morris 8, worked like a charm. On the evening of the 3rd, Frances was settled into labour at St Mary's Hospital, Portsmouth, where I had taken her earlier in the day. In the early hours of the 4th Colin arrived. St Mary's was pretty modern for its day, so the babies were stowed in a ward (sounds like hammocks!) separated from their mothers, in contrast to the previous tradition of babies being on the ward with their mothers. The fathers of new arrivals had to queue at the doorway of the babies' ward and a nurse would bring the progeny to the doorway to meet its Dad. Ahead of me was a Colour Sergeant of the Royal Marines; his nipper had been born with an unusual amount of hair. Fond Daddy gazed long at his firstborn.

'Didn't you say it was a boy?' he asked the nurse; she confirmed it. 'Get its hair cut,' he ordered, about turned and marched away. Colin was the most marvellous, good looking thing I had ever seen, but looking back at the early photos, I fear that in reality, he must have been a rather ugly, over-cooked little object!

The Whale Island Wardroom had been shocked to its foundations by the General Election results. They pulled themselves together manfully as the weeks after rolled by and life in fact seemed little changed, apart from the fact that the rather drab Atlee had replaced Churchill at the Potsdam Conference. At least the worst fear was not realised: it had been rumoured – doubtless started by a humorist in our midst, because there were one or two – that Dr Edith Summerskill was going to be appointed First Lady of the Admiralty in the new administration.

Before Colin was born, after Divisions one morning, I was in the Staff Room getting my papers together for a lecture. Often there was time to listen to the 9 a.m. news headlines, if one were slightly slack about punctual starting. World shattering news (literally!): a new device, the best-kept secret of the War, had been dropped on Hiroshima. There had been some pre-warning to evacuate the city which seemed not to have been heeded. Destruction enormous. Immediate suggestion to the Japanese Government that as they had no answer to such weapons, they should save life and surrender.

Not knowing the true horror of the weapon, we were absolutely thrilled. Even if we had known, I doubt that we would have been that much less pleased. Remember, to us the Japanese at War were animals – the way they had treated prisoners, the philosophy behind Kamikaze, the treachery by which they began their war, their pre-War behaviour in China and Korea. They were still very, very powerful and, whilst confidence was growing that we should eventually beat them, it looked as though beating them would be a long-drawn out attrition of invading island after island up the Pacific and then eventually Japan, which all believed to be a much harder nut to crack than invading Europe had been. A sudden end to it all was the greatest miracle God could bring us, although I grant you that the deed itself was not one in which God would want to claim any part.

As you know, the Japs would not surrender, so after a day or two, again after pre-warning, Nagasaki was given the same treatment. That brought the end.

Almost immediately, the Government put into action plans for the demobilisation of those in the Forces for 'hostilities only'. This was to be a phased plan over a year or two, so that not too many people were dumped on to the labour market at once and at the difficult time whilst industry was converting back from swords to ploughshare production. Basically, everyone was given points in accordance with their length of service, weighted a bit for the degree of operational nature of it and service overseas. The months during which the various points scores would be released were announced fairly well in advance. Some additional priorities were also granted on compassionate grounds and for *bona fide* students who had broken off courses and could show that their institution had immediate vacancy to take them back. Released prisoners of war got virtually immediate release.

My points indicated that I could be released by the end of January 1946. It suddenly dawned upon me that whilst I had acquired a wife and son, I had not really stopped for a minute to think about a career. It seemed best to turn to the original schoolboy idea of being an engineer. To do so, perhaps it would be best to get a qualification? I did not know and had no-one to ask, but, as luck would have it, it turned out to be the correct appreciation.

All academic institutions were legally bound to give places as early as possible to those accepted before they had gone off to the War, just as all civilian businesses had to have back employees who had gone to War. So I wrote to Caius reminding them of my entrance attempt in 1939. They reminded me that they had taken such a dim view of my scholarship effort that they had only offered me a place to read Engineering on condition that I pass the qualifying examination, which was usually waived for deserving failed scholars. The same still held. The qualifying examination would be held in May and, subject to passing, I could come up in October.

Now I did sorely regret my playing about at that 1939 scholarship exam! Determined to go into the Forces, I had regarded the trip to Cambridge as just a good holiday from school, and I would down pen and walk out after two hours of a three-hour paper if the pubs were open. Now, how could one recall the necessary maths for the qualifier after six years of mental corrosion? Fleet Air Arm navigation made no deeper call on one's mathematical ability than School Certificate level geometry and vector analysis. Luckily, I thought, I found that the Navy were running educational courses at Warrington for those about to be demobbed and they did maths. So I applied for both the course and my discharge papers.

Lemon sent for me. How could I let down my course of officers by trying to get out before they were through? I should remember that as RNs, their careers were at stake. Indeed I did. I judged that the effect on their careers of having a mid-term change of Course Officer much less catastrophic than the effect on mine should I miss my place at Cambridge. Then, of course, Dixon saw his chance of revenge as our debate about his examination setting had not been concluded. Lemon warned me, though I could see his heart was not in it, that if Dixon won his argument, I should be court-martialled. I would in no way be allowed out before the case had been held. I was on tenterhooks. Eventually he sent for me again. He had had a long conversation with Captain Agnew. Luckily the case had not yet 'got off the Island' (i.e. had not been reported to the Commander-in-Chief Portsmouth's offices), so was still within his jurisdiction. He thought there was slim chance of the charge against me standing up in court and mainly he felt that the Service should not behave in such a vindictive way to one who had served for six years, when taking action could spoil my chance of Cambridge whether found guilty or not. If I would make personal apology to Dixon, that would end the matter and he would tell Dixon that.

So, in Lemon's presence, I had to apologise gracefully to Dixon. He accepted the apology gushingly handsomely and besought me to see that there had been nothing personal in his actions. He had merely been pursuing what he had thought to be his duty.

So came the great day for my demobilisation. Funnily enough, both the Whale Island authorities and myself fell into the same error of believing that I had to be demobbed before I went on the Warrington mathematics course. First, I had to hand in all gear officially on loan. At Whale Island they were totally unfamiliar with Fleet Air Arm flying kit, which was all officially on loan. The Stores Petty Officer asked me whether I would mind taking it away with me, rather than have the trouble of finding out what to do with it. Gladly, he wrote out the chit which allowed me to call the kit my own. It consisted of a flying helmet, given subsequently to Freddy Bryan-Brown for motor-cycling, goggles, Sidcot suit liner, an overall of quilted artificial silk, a Sidcot suit (traditional RAF style flying suit), leather gauntlets and real silk lining gloves (excellent later for bicycling through the 1946/7 winter from home to the Cambridge Engineering Labs), fur lined flying boots (which lasted for many a winter of peacetime), and naval binoculars (still much in use).

Then off to the Demob Depot for Portsmouth Forces. This was a huge warehouse where the people leaving all three services in the area were issued with His Majesty's first kit-up for civil life. We were given civilian clothing coupons for three months and (for men; we never found out what the women got; as Frances had left in the 'disgrace' of pregnancy, she was not offered either clothes or ration coupons):

1 hat, choice of trilby or bowler
2 vests, wool, thick
2 pants, wool, thick
2 shirts, cotton, choice of collar-attached or separate
2 pairs socks, wool (just like service ones but brown)
1 pair shoes, choice of brown or black
1 suit, thick but obviously cheap, tweed
1 overcoat, choice of single or double-breasted

At the input end you were measured and issued with what were thought appropriate sizes of all the above except the last two. For these you were advanced to the 'tailoring' section, with a great call as to which section of it you should be directed. I was infuriated that the call in my case was 'short portlies'. Thus I got a suit where two of me could have lived in the trousers which, in the end, I gave to Freddy Bryan-Brown when up at Cambridge.

After a farewell evening with my course boys, I was for all intents and purposes a civilian. We packed up at Broadhaven into the Morris, which left Colin's carry-cot (he within) jammed against the roof, and returned to Langford Place.

Fairly quickly, I had to abandon family again and set forth, once more in uniform, for my course in Warrington. It was an extremely gloomy Nissen-hutted camp, with the most depressing Wardroom I had ever seen. There were very few officers who had volunteered for courses there, so the place was less than half full. When the old Commander in charge there suggested that we on courses joined the roster for Officer of the Day duties, we nearly had a riot! We all pleaded that we had come for serious study and needed all our evenings for studies. He ticked me off, very justifiably, for wearing non-regulation shoes. For the course I had donned my demob issue, a rather tasty pair of blacks in Norwegian design. Who cared?

The first morning, I discovered from my mathematics teacher that the syllabus at the top of their curriculum was about the level of School Certificate (GCSE these days). I pointed out that I needed revision in things such as integral calculus, imaginary numbers etc. and it was quickly apparent that there was no-one on the staff who had ever heard of them. At lunch time, therefore, I formed up to the Commander and asked whether a tutor could be found. Impossible, he said. OK, said I, then I might as well push off. No, no, he says, you've come on this course and you'll bloody well stay here until it ends and you won't get your Demob before then. To his great dismay, I pointed out that I was already demobbed. So he could not stop me going and off I dashed to Langford Place.

Luckily I found a maths coach from a press advertisement, who turned out to be an ace. His full-time job was lecturing at Imperial College. I was his cash on the side. He was a rabid communist, although not averse to cash on the side, but a brilliant maths coach. Thanks to his tuition, I passed the qualifier at Cambridge so well that they offered me the 'fast course' whereby I could do the Tripos Hons degree syllabus in two years instead of three, like the scholars did. Whilst they then had to do another year's residence and study before being granted a degree, by means of an ordinance passed towards the end of the War, I could graduate after two years. The ordinance said that three years of service in the Forces was to be regarded as equivalent to one year's residence in the University. Thus my friend from Imperial advanced my career by one full year.

Anyway, that was it. It only remained for me to swap my uniform jacket for a slide rule with a colleague at Cambridge who wanted to cut a dash at the Cruising Club in a reefer and I became a fully-fledged civilian.

Chapter 33

Epilogue

IN ASKING ME TO DO THIS MEMOIR, a main emphasis requested by my daughter was to show how one felt about events as they unfolded. This is why I have dwelt so much on how I felt about the whole thing once it was over. One had to remember that whilst serving in a War one quickly develops the habit of living entirely from day to day. One had reactions to events on a short-term basis, which I have tried to indicate when I can recall them. One did not indulge in the deep long-term think about the meanings of it all, which would perhaps be the sort of thinking one would remember forty years on. Likewise, in the trauma of trying to jump quickly on to a career bandwagon immediately afterwards, one's thoughts were directed entirely on the problematic future and not to reviewing the merits and demerits of one's past experience.

Thus, quite honestly, it is only at the end of this particular exercise that I have ever started to put together how I have thought about it all. That is not to say that what is put together is only thought which occurs today. It is today's collation of thoughts and underlying feelings during the last forty years.

One could start with the questions: What did it cost me and my contemporaries? What were the gains we got from it? After that, if one can hazard answers, maybe some deep philosophical and entirely unoriginal thoughts may occur.

Costs

Let me first indicate the loss of contemporaries. I would think I am a pretty average British example. We were not decimated as a generation like that of the previous War, but:

I lost a brother, whose career promised well;
I lost my main friend at school, who was perhaps closer than my brothers;

300

In the Maths Sixth (form) at school, we were all pretty good friends; there were seven of us, three of whom were lost. Five of the rugby XV in which I played were lost;

Three very good friends in the Fleet Air Arm were lost and dozens of very valued colleagues

I was at a school of 300 boys, with 60 per year coming in, that means I had 540 contemporaries at school, of whom 73 were lost, about 14%.

Just in death, then, it was a high cost. I suspect that its effect on those who lived through it was in fact less than the mental agonies of long family separations; living in real hardship for long periods; being a prisoner of war, particularly of the Japanese. I was lucky to escape these worst aspects. But we all had a share of long, long periods with little knowledge of what was going on in the world. When we got back home, would it, and particularly those in it, still be there? The out-of-touchness with our families, three to six months' wait for the reply to one's last letter. The terrible waste of bombing attacks on civilian targets, not just loss of life and limb. Loss of well-remembered townscapes for all time; worst perhaps of all, the millions of maimed with a whole life to live with their disabilities.

Counting personal losses against the above, I was far from being at the least lucky end of the spectrum. With perhaps a selfishness which should be forgotten, I believed, and still do, that one of the greatest losses we all suffered who went to war was that the six most valuable years of life for education were devoted to learning a trade quite useless to anyone not making the armed forces his career.

This showed up for at least the first half of my post-War career. All the time one had to strive to catch up on the germane experience of those of one's age who had not gone to War. At the beginning of a career, the man with six more years' experience of the industry or trade has a great advantage. They could all tell you what bad luck they had had to be in a reserved occupation and what a terrible life they had had as wartime civilians. At the same time, one knew from one's service colleagues that it had not been the least bit difficult for anyone who really wanted to go to get out of his reserved occupation and into uniform. The main exceptions were the young doctors, the Bevin Boys (those directed into the mines) and the medically unfit. Most of all, we were jealous of those in reserved small businesses who made big businesses on the back of the War. One contrasts my father-in-law who abandoned his farms because he felt he must get to the 1914–18 War. I suppose it was plain jealousy, but it was annoying as a junior in GKN on about £500 a year to have to do business with some of the small engineering firms in Birmingham where my contact would be of my own age but relatively experienced Assistant Managing Director of what the War had allowed his father and him to create under the 'reserved occupation' label!

Personal costs were nothing alongside what the nation lost corporately. In money terms, we started the War still up to our eyes in debt to the USA for what we had bought when fighting the first three years of the First World War before they came in. This was repeated in 1940 and UK was forced by the US Government to sell all British assets in USA on most disadvantageous terms. We had great big firms there, for example Courtaulds; these had to be sold to the US Government at the prices they nominated. The US Government then sold them on the open market at a profit of 400 per cent or so. The supposedly generous Lease/Lend arrangements, whereby War supplies continued to flow after we were bled white, helped us through the War but left more assets to be returned at the end. We emerged from the War broke, and have never recovered. As one of the main victors, we were at the back of the queue for USA's post-War aid, which concentrated on getting the vanquished Germans and Japanese back on their feet and after that on the countries which had been occupied. This seemed fair at the time because our industries had only been a bit damaged, not smashed. The longer term outcome was, though, that others installed brand new capital equipment whilst we paupers carried on with our outdated machinery.

There is some truth in saying that this is to cry over spilled milk. It has been galling for us as a nation to watch the losers forge ahead from their defeat, whilst we borrowed money from all and sundry to finance our socialism. I fear that at the heart of the matter it was not so much money. Our six-year effort left us as mentally and morally exhausted as our erstwhile enemies. With little moral fibre left, we tended to sit back on the idea that as we had won, the world now owed us a living. The vanquished, having nothing, realised quickly that whilst material aid was useful, what was really needed was back-breaking effort to secure recovery, pulling themselves up by their bootstraps. From all of that, perhaps we learn that in the modern world, if you are in a non-nuclear world war, it will pay in the long run to lose it.

Gains

Obviously, most of what one learned about guns, bombs, ships and planes was wasted education. Equally, I do not believe one could have a better education for life than the Navy provided. It taught the values of discipline, for example, and the uselessness of discipline if imposed without a purpose or by bullies; its necessity in a large society; that it can be fun when imposed not only for a purpose but with humour and sensitivity; how in a disciplined society self-discipline evolves, reducing the need for imposition from above. One came to appreciate the corporate *esprit de corps* which comes from pride in conforming to a discipline which is accepted by all.

One was thrown together with all brackets of society from all parts of the land, indeed from parts of many lands. This taught a different form of snobbism. One valued one's fellow humans for their qualities rather than the juxtaposition of their social background to one's own. One made friends within all brackets. These things are easier to experience in today's more egalitarian society than they would have been then without service experience. After the education in the British Empire I had had at school, one had the chance to learn of other nations and – quite a surprise it was – to learn from colleagues from the Empire that the British were not automatically loved by their overseas dominions and colonies. The Afrikaner positively mistrusted and disliked us. 'Down Under' they thought us rather soft wingers. White Rhodesians and Kenyans felt that UK took much from them and gave too little back; even in the touchingly loyal Caribbean, they felt that they had had all too little support from UK and a deal of bad management. All of them seemed to think that the British had so rigged the terms of trade, as indeed they had, that they had to make do with inferior British products, such as motor cars and trucks, instead of European or American. You may be surprised, but it was an eye-opener to me that anyone could think British products were not best. In short, one learned quite fast how incredibly complacent we British were at the time.

One learned a little of the world. Everything in the USA was not as super as one had appreciated from Hollywood films. In fact, colour discrimination in the southern states was quite shocking. South Africa was almost as bad in this respect, but whilst they had a colour bar there was widespread affection for their blacks, in contrast to the almost universal antipathy in the deep South. One learned in Kenya and in India the suspicion of the local whites over missionary efforts, whereas one had thought they were universally supported.

All these may seem small things; there were many more, but I pick a few examples. It was a great opportunity to learn more of the truth about the contemporary world.

The Navy taught humour in a big way, in so far as this quality is teachable. No-one and nothing was too holy to be laughed at. The tighter the circumstance, the more the jokes about it arose. It was substantially based on self-mockery and laughing with people, not at them.

It provided ample exposure to various kinds of fear. I do not say it taught one to cope with it, who can? I suppose it had provided an adequate background of drill discipline so that one could carry on duties in spite of it. There was the sudden panic fear, seeing the bombs come away from the Junkers 87s diving on you and awaiting the impact. The longer drawn out fear when trying to get out of a dreadful situation – lost, or engine failed, flying far from one's ship. The almost permanent fear for weeks on end, living in a ship in U–Boat waters which all believed would blow up if touched by a torpedo.

One had experience over quite long periods of the closest comradeship which can be found – one of life's most enjoyable experiences. I am sure that it can be found in the Army and Air Force and indeed in civilian life but I warrant that the level of it will not surpass that in a happy ship in wartime.

What gains came to the nation? The world's most socially snobbish nation learned how to work together in harmony and without barriers. Maybe it has backslid quite a bit since. We took pride in being the one nation in all the world which had no significant black market, in spite of rationing being as tight as anywhere. Yes, we all might occasionally buy a few eggs off a farmer friend. Yes, there was a tiny minority who found ways to fiddle and profit by so doing habitually, but there was never a general black market where those with the money could, or would, get what they wanted.

The nation learned to suffer loss (for example, one's home or business in an air raid) stoically, although I fear we have praised ourselves overmuch on this; I believe we suffered little in this respect compared with the Germans.

Perhaps the greatest thing we gained was a national resolution that we would never return to the non-caring sort of society we had been before it began. And I do not believe that even 'Thatcherism' has brought us near to that.

The Balance

We set out in no jingoistic mood, more one of quiet moral compulsion to stop Hitler. We achieved that. In logic, we should have taken the opportunity to finish the equally evil Soviet regime which had allied itself to Hitler at the beginning. We never started on that one. On the contrary, under Roosevelt's soft leadership, we gave whole countries that were not ours to give to the Soviets. Strictly speaking, we set out to save the Poles from being shared between Hitler and Stalin. We finished by giving all Poland to Stalin. Our success was to save a lot of Jews from Hitler and to liberate those parts of western Europe lost to him after it had all begun. Not on balance a staggering success.

In the Far East, I think we did better. I believe we killed, at least for decades to come, the expansionist ambitions of old Imperial Japan. It was of an evil and unsubtle form, straight unprovoked military conquest. The War taught most of the Far East nations of what the Japanese were capable, and suspicion will maintain vigilance for years to come.

We hear much of the horror of Hiroshima and Nagasaki and I think it should be put in a fairer perspective. The nature of science is such that if the Allies had not developed the bomb, someone else would and it was known that the Germans were trying.

The points I would emphasise are:

1) Science knew the weapon could be developed and would be very terrible. Inevitably, therefore, someone was going to do it. Better us than unknown others (Germans? Russians? Japanese?). Whilst we were at war, surely we must make every effort to be the first.

2) The first to have it must surely win the War once the weapon's power was demonstrated.

3) Beating Japan looked like being a long drawn out campaign taking years and hundreds of thousands – more probably millions – of lives, if it were left to conventional warfare.

4) Having developed the weapon first, its war-finishing potential and the fact that we really did have it had to be demonstrated to become credible.

5) The Japanese were warned to evacuate Hiroshima because the demonstration was about to happen. The Allies cannot be blamed too far if the warning went unheeded. Same again at Nagasaki, even though the Japanese had seen at Hiroshima what the bomb could do.

6) The casualties in both towns, immediate short-term and long-term, were appalling. The Japanese themselves were partially to blame for not

evacuating. The total casualties were probably chicken feed in comparison to what would have arisen had we had to fight Japan to a standstill by conventional means.

7) I really believe that getting there first, we stopped Stalin from eating up Europe.

I think our generation was absolutely right to go to war to stop the German evil and then the Japanese. In parallel circumstances, we should have done the same as one by one Hungary, Czechoslovakia, East Germany and Poland, not to mention Afghanistan, were raped. The nuclear threat, however, makes it so impractical that the moral obligation vanishes because the token effort would be no more than world suicide. I think the 1914–18 and 1939–45 Wars taught us that even with conventional war, it may be morally right to turn to it to stop an evil, but the suffering which then has to be endured, the evils which get committed in the heat of battle, can come preciously close to a balancing evil.

Never have major powers been deterred from pursuit of a strong self interest by pure talk from others or such resorts as economic sanctions. It is only the ability to threaten retaliation of those remonstrating against forceful pursuit of interests which can be effective. The UK, without threatening war, used to get a big ear around the world when we had a Navy which could blow the rest of the world's navies combined out of the water. So, unfortunately, we must have military power if our moral message is to be heard or our way of life to be preserved.

Now that we spend all we can in the laudable fields of helping our disadvantaged, we shall never afford the dominant military power to be independent in resisting major aggression. Fair enough; by that we have improved our moral stature but reduced our ability to contribute to world morality. All we can do is ally ourselves to the power who most nearly conforms to our ethics and live under its shelter. So that we are not totally dominated by this major partner, we still have to maintain a military contribution to the alliance which looks significant – one which the ally would welcome in time of threat. This also allows us to take our own line in more minor matters (e.g. Greek v Turk in Cyprus, or the Argentinians in the Falklands).

To sum it all up, the experience of the War leaves me convinced that we must maintain some little military capability if we are to have any moral influence. At the same time, we can only use it judiciously to counter threat. We can never again take a major initiative. Without doubt, the War was on balance a national disaster in material terms; we would probably now be sitting pretty economically if we had gone along with the Germans. Whether we could ever again have held up our heads is another matter. For all of us who took part, it was something of a disaster but most of us went in with our eyes open and a belief that it was the right thing to do. Only a madman puts his head on the block for jingoism. It was not all personal disaster; it taught certain of life's verities more intensely than any other circumstance can. What comradeship can really mean and how easily it can transcend social and national barriers. Mostly what a marvellous animal homo sapiens is in his reserves of endurance and sheer courage. The biggest examples which come to mind come from the enemy. The men who fought the *Bismarck* to her death; the bomber pilots I watched keeping perfect formation as they dived on *Indomitable*, through all the flak our convoy could throw. From our side, the Airbornes at Arnhem, the seamen battling in the Atlantic winter.

Thank God it did end eventually.